OFFENDER ASSESSMENT AND EVALUATION
The Presentence Investigation Report

Todd R. Clear

Val B. Clear

William D. Burrell

 anderson publishing co.
2035 reading road
cincinnati, ohio 45202
(513) 421-4142

OFFENDER ASSESSMENT AND EVALUATION
The Presentence Investigation Report

Clear, Todd R.
    Offender assessment.

    1. Presentence investigation reports--United States.
I. Clear, Val. II. Burrell, William D. III. Title.
KF9685.C54 1989   345.73'0772   87-1429
ISBN 0-87084-138-6   347.305772

Kelly Humble *Managing Editor*

To parents and their children,
especially Leo and Molly Burrell.

Acknowledgments

The authors acknowledge the assistance they received in preparing this manuscript. Able clerical work was provided by Sandra Wright and Touraine Coleman; we thank them. The careful editorial assistance of Rose Johnson was extremely helpful. The special tolerance and support of Mickey and Susan Braswell and that of Kelly Humble were greatly appreciated from the beginning of the project.

Contents

Introduction

When John Franklin woke up on Labor Day, 1986, he was still a little hungover from the previous night's drinking. Even so, he was in a good mood because he and some friends were planning to spend a lazy day in a local state park, drinking beer and watching girls. He felt he needed a day off because life had been hard the last few months. A little over a year ago, he had been arrested for burglary, and his court date was nearing. The public defender assigned to him had been non-existent for most of those months, but just recently called to say the prosecutor was resisting the offer to plead guilty in exchange for a probation sentence. Franklin was upset about this; he didn't want to go to prison.

Until the burglary arrest, things had been looking up for him. His job as a janitor was bearable, and he finally had enough money to buy the motorcycle he always wanted. He thought to himself, "If only I can beat this burglary charge." He had no idea this day would change his life.

That night, as he sat alone in a jail cell, his head was spinning. He was in real trouble now. The events since the morning had seemed like an emotional roller coaster. Sitting in the park had been fun until they ran out of beer. Then there was the thrill of breaking into the house, followed by a spree of stops at liquor stores. It was all terrific, until the police pulled him over. Now, here he sat in jail, in the worst trouble he had ever known.

The next ten months were to pass like decades. Infrequent meetings with his public defender followed by court appearances, then return to jail. His earlier hopes for a plea bargain were gone, and now he simply sat, waiting for the system to work its way around to his case. In time, a date was set for his trial, and this set into motion a series of conversations between his attorney, Art Wohlford, and Mr. Jarvis, the prosecutor handling the case. Finally, they agreed to an indeterminate prison term of two to five years, with two of those years suspended. With credit for jail time and good time, Franklin would be eligible for parole in less than a year. Franklin was not happy with the deal, but he realized it could have been worse.

Is this an appropriate sentence? How do you know? What criteria do you use in answering this question? Is it fair that this important decision, the punishment society imposes for a crime, should be determined by two attorneys in a negotiation process? If not, what safeguards ought to apply? What considerations, other than the crime and the attorney's heavy workload, ought to influence the ultimate penalty the offender will serve?

This book is about these questions, because it is the primary function of the presentence investigation report (PSIR) to assist the judge in determining

1

an appropriate sentence. What the attorneys have agreed to is only one consideration. The judge must take into account a variety of factors in arriving at the ultimate sentence.

If you were the judge about to sentence John Franklin, what would you want to know about the case in order to make your decision? Would it be important to know Franklin's prior criminal record? Why? Would you want to understand Franklin's current situation, his physical and emotional health, the likely impact of incarceration on him? Why? Would you want an idea of the options available to you in sentencing Franklin? Would you want to know how offenders similar to Franklin have been sentenced in the past? Why?

The PSIR can provide just about any information, but first there must be some determination of which information is important. That is how the PSIR gets its name: it is a report to the judge of the results of an investigation. During the investigation, the correctional worker (usually a probation officer) collects information from the offender, the offender's family, the victim and other parties. Where appropriate, this information is verified through other sources. The often massive amount of information that results from this investigatory process is then sorted and written into a report complete with documentation. This report serves as the court's central decision making tool.

This investigation/reporting process is simple to describe, but in reality it is quite complex. Often the investigator encounters resistance, unclear leads, ambiguous information and even misinformation. It takes a level of skill and experience to translate the amalgam of data into a straightforward report. Moreover, some controversy surrounds the report itself, especially in terms of the contents of the report and its recommendations.

This book is concerned with the skills involved in the production of a PSIR, and it is also concerned with the issues, controversies and complexities of its uses. The authors represent several perspectives on the investigation function; one is a corrections worker who writes investigations; one a corrections administrator who uses them; and one a corrections educator/researcher who studies them. We have combined these backgrounds to help the reader develop a more complete understanding of the investigation/reporting function in corrections.

Technically, a presentence investigation report (PSIR) may be defined as a narrative summary of an offender's criminal and non-criminal history, used to aid a judge in determining the most appropriate decision as to the offender's sentence for a crime. However, investigating offenders is one of the most common activities in corrections, and it occurs at many stages other than that of sentencing. The kinds of investigations conducted in corrections range in variety from pre-release investigations to parole revocation reports.

Figure I-1
Flow of Common Correctional Decision-Point
Which Require Investigations*

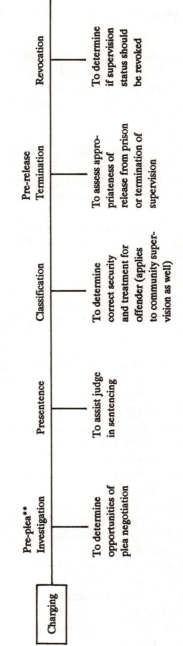

Charging

Pre-plea**
Investigation

To determine
opportunities of
plea negotiation

Presentence

To assist judge
in sentencing

Classification

To determine
correct security
and treatment for
offender (applies
to community super-
vision as well)

Pre-release
Termination

To assess appro-
priateness of
release from prison
or termination of
supervision

Revocation

To determine
if supervision
status should
be revoked

* Steps do not always occur in order listed in figure.
** Not practiced in all jurisdictions.

Some of the common types of investigations are described below (see also Figure I-1).

Pre-trial release report. Usually prepared by a probation officer, this report provides information about an accused person's ties to the community, such as family, home and job. A judge uses this report in deciding whether to release the defendant prior to trial, to set an amount of bail or to release the defendant on recognizance.

Prison classification report. Often prepared by a committee of prison staff, this report describes the convicted offender's security needs at the time of admission to the prison. The report is used to place the offender in a job assignment, a treatment program and a security level while in prison.

The parole report plan. A prisoner's counselor will usually prepare this report, which describes the plans for the offender's work and living situation, should parole be granted. The parole board considers this report in its decision as to the offender's parole date.

The revocation investigation. Prepared by a probation or parole officer, this report summarizes the offender's overall adjustment to community supervision as well as the nature of the specific misbehavior that has provoked a revocation hearing. The report is used by a hearing officer (frequently, a judge) to decide if the offender should be removed from the community and sent to prison.

Thus, at virtually every critical decision point affecting an offender's status, corrections professionals are required to prepare a report that is used in making the decision. Each correctional investigation is designed to advise a decision maker of the offender's criminal behavior, the options available to the decision maker for disposal of the offender, and the risks to society and the offender for each option.

The prototype correctional investigation is the presentence investigation report. The information contained in the PSIR summarizes the nature of the offense, the offender's risk, the sentencing options available to the judge, and often makes a recommendation as to the appropriate deposition. Normally, the PSIR is the most comprehensive investigative report completed in the criminal justice system, and it is the cornerstone of the information corrections relies on in processing offenders.

For this reason, this book focuses on the PSIR as the best illustration of the investigative/reporting function in corrections. There is no aspect of any correctional investigation/report that does not have a direct analog in the

PSIR. Moreover, the PSIR frequently serves as background information to the preparation of the other investigative reports in corrections, and it is used by corrections staff as they prepare reports for decisions made later in the system. While we will sometimes allude to these other decision points throughout this book, our primary focus is on the PSIR, with three main objectives:

To inform the reader of the function of the PSIR as a tool for sentencing decisions.

To assist the reader in developing investigatory skills for judicial and correctional decision making.

To acquaint the reader with the broader importance of the PSIR at points other than sentencing.

To reflect these objectives, the book is divided into three parts. Part I is a critical assessment of the function of the PSIR. In this section, we review studies of the presentence and of correctional decisionmaking. Part II is a presentation of the content of the PSIR. This includes a description of the kinds of information contained in the report, and a guide as to how to gather that information. Part III is a description of the broader applicability of the PSIR to the corrections process. We also consider current trends in the investigation/report process in this section.

Throughout the book, we have provided illustrations, exercises and discussion topics to help the student assimilate the material covered. It is hoped that these exercises will help the material come alive for the students, as it is fascinating and exciting to the authors.

Incidentally, for those who are interested, a sample PSIR for John Franklin is provided in Appendix A.

Part I

The Function of the Presentence Investigation Report

Chapter 1
Overview of the PSIR

When John Franklin walks before Judge Thurston to receive his sentence, Judge Thurston will certainly consider the crime Franklin has committed as he pronounces sentence. No matter what else, the sentencing decision is an opportunity for the court to make a public statement of the reprehensibleness of Franklin's conduct. In addition to the crime, Judge Thurston may consider a whole host of factors in selecting a sentence for John Franklin. It is the function of the presentence investigation report to inform the judge of those factors, from which he will derive the sentence.

As the probation officer, Mack Ray, develops the PSIR on Franklin, he will be faced with a series of decisions: What information should be included? What facts emphasized? What conclusions drawn? Unfortunately, there are no uniform answers to these questions. In the case of Franklin, as Ray has found generally to be true, a good deal of judgement must be exercised, both in investigating the case and writing the report. Because Ray has worked closely with Thurston, he has a good idea of what the judge is most interested in knowing, but the final report will ultimately reflect the thinking of Mack Ray.

As might be expected, the PSIR process is not uncontroversial. Whether Mack Ray's beliefs about Franklin ought to be a part of Franklin's ultimate punishment could be (and has been) openly debated. In this chapter we present the major function of the PSIR, and we critically review its use in the courts. Our conclusion is that the PSIR is a necessary part of the court's process, but it is attended by several issues which must be considered by any person involved in the PSIR process.

Despite the variation in approaches to developing the PSIR, some types of information are always included. There is always a description of the offense. After all, the offense is the reason corrections is involved in the offender's life, and the seriousness of the crime must be considered in any decision about the offender. There is always a summary of the various options open to the decisionmaker. Depending on the nature of the decision, these options often vary from institutionalization in a secure facility, such as a jail or prison, to release into the community under the supervision of the corrections worker, such as a probation or parole officer. Finally, there is an assessment of the potential (or likely) consequences of each option for the offender and society.

The consequences for the offender can be severe, because the decision to incarcerate an offender subjects that person to the considerable hardships of the prison and results in loss of several civil rights. The consequences of the various options for society are also potentially severe, considering the risk of future crimes an offender may represent. While there is pressure on the PSIR writer to consider the community's safety in developing the report, it is equally important to remember how expensive it is to incarcerate people, especially including the social costs incurred by a nation in which much value is placed on human liberty.

The PSIR is designed to advise a judge of the offender's criminal behavior, the options available to the decision maker for disposal of the offender, and the risks to society and the offender for whichever option the judge might wish to choose. It is a momentous document, for the decisions it advises balance significant considerations of legal rights, human liberty and community values, among them community safety.

Discretion in Sentencing

Discretion exists when a decisionmaker is allowed to use judgement in arriving at a decision. When there is no latitude in making a decision, the decision maker lacks discretion. In the latter situation, the ultimate decision is tied directly to factors for which there is no leeway in interpretation or application. These factors are often referred to as decision rules. An example of a decision rule is a grading system in which a person must score 95 points or higher on a test in order to receive an "A" on an exam. This would be a single stage (or single factor) decision rule. Elaborate arrangements of decision rules (sometimes formed into "decision trees") can be created to take into account a variety of factors considered important and still leave no discretion to the decisionmaker. Figure 1-1 is an illustration of a simple decision tree for sentencing an offender. In this illustration, any case will result in a decision simply by following the branches on the "tree."

By contrast, discretion occurs when decisions have insufficient "rules" to fully determine all situations that may occur. The latitude given to the decision maker depends upon the situation. For instance, the law may require that all felony repeaters receive prison terms, but other offenders may be sentenced to probation at the judge's discretion. Most judicial decisions have at least some rules that constrain certain decisions, but allow the judge latitude when these rules do not apply.

Figure 1-1: Illustration of Sentencing Decision Tree

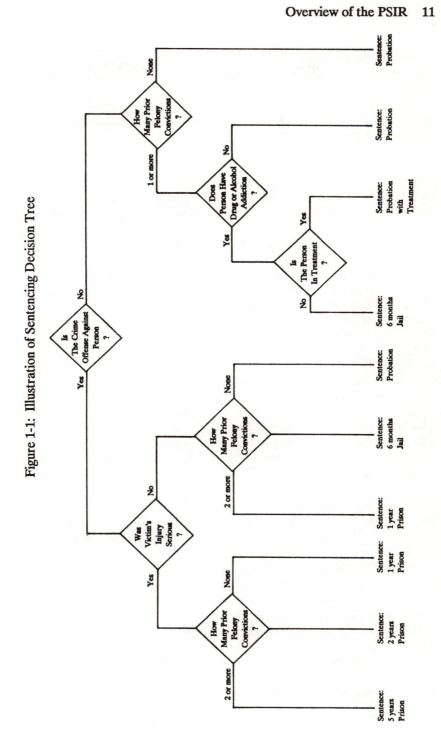

Recently, there has been a trend to limit discretion as much as possible through use of decision rules either enacted into law or established by formal policy. This trend is discussed in Chapter 3. Despite these attempts to reduce discretion, it is unlikely that discretion can ever be totally eradicated. There are several reasons why discretion will remain an important element of judicial decisions regardless of efforts to control it.

Goal Ambiguity

There is no consensus about the appropriate goals of sentencing; indeed, there is a multiplicity of goals, as we discuss in Chapter 4. The existence of goal conflict means judges need discretion to sort through the conflict. Different sanctions are required to support different goal orientations, and the judge must have latitude to choose when the circumstances of a case call for a shift in goal emphasis. In some cases, aspects of the criminal act may call for a heavily punitive sanction, while in other cases the special circumstances of the offender will call for leniency in support of rehabilitation. Some reformers have tried to codify these goal shifts in the form of "aggravating and mitigating" factors in the sentencing decision, but inevitably these attempts either leave out important considerations or result in broad, vague generalizations.

Some people have argued it is not correct to think of a single goal or rank order of goals as guiding most complex decisions. Instead, it is more common to think of "maximization" strategies which call for emphasizing a particular goal as much as possible without directly contradicting other important goals. For example, a judge may try to select sentences that rehabilitate offenders so long as those sentences do not seem ludicrous in light of the seriousness of crime.

Human Differences

Differences among offenders are often so subtle and complex that they require room for judgement as to the correct sentence. While it is intuitively convincing that equivalent crimes deserve equal punishment, an offender's situation colors virtually any judge's sentencing decisions. For instance, the offender's age often will become a consideration, especially for the very old and very young. Frequently, personal factors such as the offender's attitude, expressed by willingness to make reparation, and the offender's living situation will influence the decision. Personal factors become even more important as the offender's risk to society is considered.

It is impossible to formalize these differences into a legal code or a policy statement. These differences are often too numerous to effectively cover all possible situations in the law. Judges are left with the discretion to take these factors into account in ways that reflect shifting and competing goals.

Uncertainty

In any operation that deals with people, there is always an element of uncertainty. In criminal justice, uncertainty is more than an element, it is a constant fact of life. No matter how high the offender's apparent risk, there is always a chance his most recent crime will be his last. No matter how promising the prospects for rehabilitation, any offender may lapse into recidivism.

It is the responsibility of the judge to confront the uncertainty that attaches to each sentencing decision. This is a difficult task, involving the weighing of competing goals in light of the complex and subtle factors involved in the case, all the while knowing that some level of uncertainty must apply. It is not possible to structure the uncertainty of each and every decision. The judge must have discretion.

The Limits of Law

At least theoretically, it might seem that these various factors could still be codified into the penal law, thereby eliminating a need for discretion. To do so would be an enormous legislative undertaking. Consider the mathematical realities: If only 10 factors are to be considered important, and each factor only has two possible values (such as "married" or "unmarried"), that leaves a total of 210 possible combinations of factors, or over 1,000 possible arrangements of factors. While, in reality, not all possible combinations of factors are important (of what importance is the person's marital status if the crime is multiple homicide?), there are certainly more than 10 factors (often taking more than two possible values each) that commonly arise as important in sentencing. That is why when a major commission attempted to codify a set of non-discretionary sentences for the crime of assault, an entire book was required, and even that did not receive the full support of every member of the commission![1]

For these reasons, discretion will never be fully eradicated from judicial decisions. The simple fact is that too little is known about how various factors influence goal achievement to advocate a uniform set of criteria for sentencing. That is not to say that good decisions are impossible, but merely that good decisions require discretion. The need for discretion also leaves open the possibility of a bad decision. How is the judge to sort out the good decisions from the bad? That is the role of the PSIR: to provide information that improves the quality of sentencing.

The Need for Information at Sentencing

The major problem facing judges is the uncertainty involved in all sentencing decisions, except the most extreme cases. Anything that helps to reduce the uncertainty of a decision is considered information. The role of information in sentencing is discussed in Chapter 5. Here, we summarize the types and importance of information contained in the PSIR.

Crime Seriousness

The seriousness of the current offense is always a primary consideration. People generally assume that the crime's seriousness is important because of a desire to punish serious offenders. It seems unjust to most people when a person convicted of a serious crime (or conversely, a trivial offense) receives punishment out of proportion to that received by other offenders. Recently, it has become apparent that the crime's seriousness is important for a more subtle, but related reason: the credibility of the system is at stake. Nothing makes the criminal justice system seem more unfair to the general public than when offenders receive punishments in ways clearly inappropriate to the crimes's seriousness. Bob Dylan's famous song, *Lonesome Death of Hattie Carroll*, is a biting critique of a rich man's six-month sentence for the murder of a black housekeeper. Similarly, George Jackson's book, *Soledad Brother*, is a searing attack on the system which gave Jackson a life term for taking money out of an open gas station cash register. If the system is to remain justifiable in people's eyes, it must impose sanctions and treatments commensurate with the nature of the crime.

Usually, statutory definitions of crimes evaluate the crime's seriousness, at least as reflected in the minds of legislators who passed the law. Often, offenses are placed into "classes" which reflect a very rough ordering of seriousness; if nothing else, the sentencing provisions indicate legislative rankings of seriousness.

The penal code language is seldom specific enough to inform the judge of every crime's seriousness. The same assault statute may apply equally to a brutal stranger-victim assault and a victim-precipitated, spontaneous action between acquaintances. Most people would agree that these crimes are of inherently different seriousness. That is why the PSIR must provide detail about the crime, for the judge needs to consider questions that go beyond the statutory definitions. What were the offender's intentions in committing the act? Was the crime committed in an unusually serious manner; was the act's inherent injuriousness balanced by mitigating factors? Questions such as these can be answered only through an investigation of the actual nature of the offense.

With the advent of the victim's movement in criminal justice, the nature of the crime has become more important. PSIRs now often include a careful assessment of the financial and personal impact of the crime on the victim. It has also become increasingly accepted that the victim ought to be informed of the sentence imposed by the judge.

Offender Risk

The assessment of the offender's risk of committing a new offense is one of the most sensitive functions of the PSIR. The concern is an obvious one: "Will this offender commit a crime again, or is the current offense the last one for this individual?" Predictions of future behavior are precarious, and the potential errors weigh ominously on the PSIR writer's mind.

It is simply not possible to predict future offenders' behavior with 100% accuracy; there is always a potential for prediction error. In making predictions, two types of errors can occur. These are illustrated in Table 1-1. One kind of error occurs when the judge wrongfully believes the offender will never commit another crime. In this case, the offender is placed under a low-security status (such as probation, or work-release) and goes on to commit a new crime. This kind of error undercuts the system's ability to control crime. As citizens become disillusioned with the system's performance, this error also leads to distrust of the criminal justice system. The other error occurs when the judge mistakenly believes the offender will commit a crime. Here, offenders are placed in close custody (such as prison), when placement in a less secure setting would be just as safe. The result of this error is prison crowding and, ultimately, a system that is too intrusive in punishment of offenders. The system appears to be unjust in its treatment of offenders.

One characteristic of these errors is very important: False negatives are much more visible to judges than are false positives. When a person who has been sentenced to low custody commits a new crime, the judge who gave the sentence almost always learns about the error. There is no equivalent way for a judge to learn that a close-custody case should have been released because it is a false positive. Studies have demonstrated conclusively that many offenders in secure custody could safely be moved to much less controlling environments without threat to the community.[2]

Because false negatives are more visible to judges than false positives, there is often a tendency to "overpredict" risk, that is, to believe risk is present when it is not, because this leads to fewer visible errors. PSIR writers are often very conservative in their predictions in order to avoid taking chances that may lead to false negatives. One consequence of prediction conservation is an increase in the ratio of false positives to false negatives, to the point that overprediction results in many more false positive errors than false negatives.

Table 1-1 Types of Prediction Errors and Their Consequences

		Actual Outcome	
		Crime	No New Crime
Predicted Outcome	New Crime	Correct	False Positive (Type II)
	No New Crime	False Negative (Type I)	Correct

Consequences of False Negative	Consequences of False Positive
Unprevented crimes	Prison crowding
Costs to victims	Injustice to offender
Loss of system credibility	Loss of system credibility

The natural tendency to overpredict new crimes in order to minimize false negatives has led some experts to suggest that the problem is not to predict crimes but to "assess risk." Risk assessment differs from prediction in that a definite prediction is not made about any offender; instead, assessments are made of the *probability* a given offender will commit future crimes. The purpose of risk assessment, then, is not to determine which offenders will commit new crimes (that is the prediction approach) but, rather, which offenders are more (or less) likely to engage in such behavior, knowing that a completely accurate prediction can never be made. The PSIR writer then advises the judge on a course of action in light of the assessment of the offender's general risk level (the probability of a new crime). A "low-risk" offender is a person with a low probability of committing a new crime; conversely, a "high-risk" offender has a high probability. However, some low-risk offenders will commit crimes, just as some high-risk offenders will stay crime-free.

Studies show that the probability of a given felony offender being convicted of a new crime is between 15 and 30%.[3] Thus, the most appropriate assumption for any individual offender is that the person will not be convicted again; this will be correct 70-85% of the time. However, all the errors of such actions will be false negatives, with the serious consequences mentioned earlier, and the pressures to overpredict.

A recently developing body of research has found that various factors are associated with an offender's risk level. Some of these are intuitively sensible: prior record, substance abuse and lifestyle stability.   Several researchers have developed "risk screening instruments" which are based on studies of factors that are related to the probability of new criminal behavior.[4] Figure 1-2 shows just such an instrument.

Evaluations of risk screening instruments have drawn several conclusions about their applicability to the investigation process. First, risk screening instruments help to reduce the problem of overprediction, because investigators often overestimate the actual risk an offender represents. It is typical, for example, for an investigator to see an offender as moderate-high risk when, in reality, the offender is moderate-low risk. Second, a risk screening instrument developed as a result of studies conducted on one population of offenders does not necessarily transfer well to other populations.[5] For instance, an instrument valid in Ohio may not be useful in Texas. Third, these instruments are usually more successful in identifying low-risk offenders than high-risk offenders. It is common for the low risk offenders to have a 5% or less probability of new crimes, while even the best instruments identify highest risk group with only a 50% chance of reoffending.

The use of risk assessments has underscored the importance of information for decisionmaking. It is necessary for the writer to put the offender's risk level into context, and to aid the decisionmaker in avoiding the types of errors that are made in estimating an offender's future behavior.

Figure 1-2

WISCONSIN ASSESSMENT OF OFFENDER RISK

Select the appropriate answer and enter the associated weight in the score column. Total all scores to arrive at the risk assessment score.

SCORE

Number of Address Changes in Last 12 Months (Prior to incarceration for parolees)	0 None 2 One 3 Two or More	_____
Percentage of Time Employed in Last 12 Months (Prior to incarceration for parolees)	0 60% or more 1 40%-59% 2 Under 40% 0 Not applicable	_____
Alcohol Usage Problems (Prior to incarceration for parolees)	0 No interference w/functioning 2 Occassional abuse; some disruption of functioning 4 Frequent abuse; serious disruption; needs treatment	_____
Other Drug Usage Problems	0 No interference w/functioning 1 Occassional abuse; some disruption of functioning 2 Frequent abuse; serious disruption; needs treatment	_____
Attitude	0 Motivated to change; receptive to assistance 3 Dependant or unwilling to accept responsibility 5 Rationalizes behavior; negative; not motivated to change	_____

continued

Age at First Conviction (or Juvenile Adjudication)	0 24 or older 2 20-23 4 19 or younger	_____

Number of Prior Periods of Probation/Parole Supervision (Adult or Juvenile)	0 None 4 One or more	_____

Number of Prior Probation/Parole Revocations (Adult or Juvenile)	0 None 4 One or more	_____

Number of Prior Felony Convictions (or Juvenile Adjudications)	0 None 2 One 4 Two or more	_____

Convictions or Juvenile Adjudications for: (Select applicable and add for score. Do not exceed a total of 5. Include current offense.)	2 Burglary, theft, auto theft or robbery 3 Worthless checks or forgery	_____

Conviction or Juvenile Adjudication for Assaultive Offense within Last Five Years: (An offense which involves the use of a weapon, physical force or threat of force.)	15 Yes 0 No	_____

Offender's Circumstances

The uncertainty in sentencing is partly a product of variations in the individual offender's circumstances. While it is true to say that each offender is unique, this is not a very helpful observation. The decisionmaker is interested in making inferences about the offender's likely response alternative decisions. To do so, consideration must be given to the characteristics the offender possesses that are similar to those of other offenders. A track record of experience is built by observing personal characteristics similar to (or contrasted to) other offenders and learning how those offenders behave.

It is not that each offender's circumstances are treated as unique; rather, the person's circumstances are analyzed to find patterns or possibilities that are suggested by prior experience. This can be very complicated, since offenders' circumstances reflect a normal array of complex factors that would be true for any adult. Arriving at a confident understanding of the significance of the offender's circumstances can be difficult, because many offender's have lived lives of difficult and unusual circumstances.

For example, a person who has grown up in a broken family characterized by open hostility may have recently begun a stable relationship with a lover. This offender may be unskilled, but may also be motivated to get an education. Or, though fighting a drinking problem, an offender may have been able to sustain a good employment record. Which characteristics are the most important?

In order to sort out this kind of complexity, information is necessary. To be useful, the information must go beyond simply repeating the facts of the offender's situation; it must organize and summarize that situation in a way that has meaning for the sentencing decision. The PSIR writer must consider the significance of each aspect of the offender's life for the decision at hand, asking the question: "Given the seriousness of this crime and this offender's risk, what importance does fact 'X' (say, family relationships) have for deciding the appropriate penalty?"

Oftentimes, the crime and risk will be such that the offender's life situation has little influence on the best decision. Frequently, however, the judge faces choices that are not clear, and then information about personal circumstances becomes important. For instance, an offender's financial situation will influence the choice between restitution and community service as a condition of probation. Or the offender's employment situation will influence a decision as to whether a jail term is appropriate, if it would result in the loss of a job.

The role of the PSIR writer in dealing with the offender's circumstances is quite difficult, because often this information is of limited importance to the decision. The myriad complexities of the offender's past and current life situation must be sorted through, using professional judgement, to determine what factors are important for the judge to consider. These factors must be presented in a condensed form useful to the judge.

Sentencing Options

The final type of information in the PSIR is a summary of the sentencing options available to the judge. Because some of these options are obvious (imprison or place on probation), it is helpful for the PSIR writer to evaluate the feasibility of more creative alternative dispositions to the case. For instance, some combination of restitution and community service might be used as a punishment instead of prison, thus enabling an offender to remain in the community, work to support a family and attend a drug treatment program. Intensive probation supervision might be sufficient control to allow an otherwise jail-bound offender to remain in the community, living a law-abiding lifestyle. Immediate assignment to a work-release center often represents a sentencing option less onerous than maximum security prison for an offender who has promising work prospects.

In order to consider all the sentencing options, three requirements must be met by the PSIR writer. First, there must be a good understanding of the special circumstances of the offender. Second, there must be a familiarity with sentencing resources: the variety of services, programs and settings available for an offender, given the offender's circumstances. These often vary widely, from the most secure setting of all (the prison) to moderately secure in-patient treatment programs, to sleep-in facilities, to structured probation and so forth. Often, an effective PSIR writer will ferret out new options for dealing with offenders by putting together existing resources in new, creative ways.

Third, and of equal importance, the PSIR must have an innovative frame of reference for assessing alternatives, in light of the offender's circumstances and the available resources. It is all too common for PSIR writers to assume that the options available to the judge are limited to the few obvious alternatives listed within the criminal law. Too often, PSIR writers fail to search for creative, but appropriate sentencing options that are more fitting than the common options of prison probation. Instead, the PSIR writer should be guided by a frame of reference which seeks to minimize the amount of unproductive pain and injury suffered by offenders or their victims; they should seek creative ways to avoid both the extreme punitiveness of the prison and the often inadequate option of traditional probation supervision. It is the search for creative, appropriate sentencing options that separates the exceptional PSIR writer from the average one.

Controversies in the PSIR

Despite the unquestioned importance of the PSIR in sentencing, its use is not without problems. There are four significant difficulties with the PSIR. These are summarized below, and then are considered in more detail in the chapters which follow.

Bias

PSIR writers routinely deal with criminal behavior that is sometimes brutal, always thoughtless, often despicable. No matter how often it is repeated that the PSIR writer must remain objective and unemotionally professional in performing the job, it is always possible for personal feelings to enter into the decision. After all, PSIR writers are human, and strong personal feelings can easily develop. An otherwise professional worker who has been a victim of a burglary may carry a special dislike for housebreakers. Or personal feelings about sexual deviance may color reactions to rape or child molestation cases. These are examples of the problem of bias.

Bias can be more subtle than these obvious illustrations. A probation officer who was raised in a white, middle-class family may misinterpret a black, street-wise youth's nervous behavior in an interview as hostility toward authority, and misrepresent the offender's behavior in the PSIR. Or, an investigator may become bored with routine cases, and fail to carefully review all information and options in cases that seem, on the surface, run-of-the-mill.

To recognize that bias is natural is not to condone it. When PSIR writer's bias influences the assessment of client risk, crime seriousness, offender circumstances or sentencing options, an injustice is done. It falls upon the PSIR writer's shoulders to minimize the effects of bias on the investigation. The professional must be aware of his or her special vulnerabilities toward biases of the kinds mentioned above, and compensate for them. Whenever there is a strong emotional reaction, positive or negative, to a client or the offense, this is an indication that bias may be influencing the PSIR writer's work. While the professional must be open to the review of any work done on a case, there is a special obligation to accept supervision when the investigator's emotions have become involved. If the PSIR writer cannot accept supervision, the case should be transferred to another worker.

Irrelevance

Some critics point out that the PSIR has little or no influence on most sentencing, because other factors control these decisions. Studies show that plea bargaining determines 60-90% of all sentencing decisions. Prison crowding may make prison sentences unfeasible for all but the most serious offenders.

It is true that the PSIR is simply one of several forces that produce the sentence and often it is not the most important one. Yet it is the very existence of these many forces that makes the PSIR important. System practices such as plea bargaining do not always result in appropriate sentences. Almost always, these practices are not based on a comprehensive analysis of the offender, the crime or all the available sentencing options. The PSIR often serves the critical role of quality control on the system's ordinary processes, making certain that decisions are not irrational, and that important factors have not been overlooked. Sometimes, the PSIR makes it obvious that the plea bargain is inappropriate, and should be rejected by the court. Often, the PSIR will point out a sentencing option not considerered by the prosecutor and defender in arriving at their decision.

The Appropriateness of Discretion

A more fundamental criticism of the PSIR is that discretion in sentencing should not exist. The most eloquent writers of this viewpoint have argued that justice is violated when people convicted of the same offense are treated differently because of their personal characteristics.[6] This is a persuasive argument. Why should a person who has good prospects be treated more leniently than a person who is poor or down and out, when both have been convicted of the same crime? Giving the one offender "a break" is not much different, in practice, from penalizing the other offender for being poor. Most informed observers decry the injustice that occurs when the poor suffer in the criminal justice system because of their financial inability to afford bail or a good defense. The PSIR that considers financial and personal circumstances in making recommendations cannot help but be a disadvantage for the less fortunate citizen. It would be much better, it is argued, to eliminate the need for the PSIR entirely by eliminating discretion.

There is some truth to this claim. It is a very serious accusation that the PSIR leads to inequities in sentencing. However, the alternative (to eliminate discretion) is probably impossible to achieve, as we have shown. Studies show that decisionmakers actively seek information about offender risk, offense seriousness and offender circumstances at virtually every stage of the criminal justice system, not just sentencing.[7] To eradicate discretion would hamper the criminal justice system, and attempts to do so have resulted in serious problems for the criminal justice system.

Therefore, the PSIR must be seen as a necessary tool in the sentencing process. There is a potential for inequities to occur, and so the use of the PSIR must be carefully monitored to prevent both bias and injustices. The test of any sentencing decision about an offender is whether the decision is based on criteria that are reasonably related to valid sentencing goals: Is the investigation accurate, and does it make a fair interpretation of the options? Would a similar offender be treated similarly? Does the investigation avoid penalizing the offender unfairly simply due to his circumstances?

Who is the Client?

It is common to refer to the offender as the client in the PSIR process, but it is questionable whether the offender is always the primary client. The PSIR is being prepared for a judge who has an interest in its quality; the PSIR writer's salary is paid by government, which also has an interest in the process. Some critics argue that the needs of the offender are often taken less seriously than those of the decision maker or employer.

For example, the offender may wish to withhold from the PSIR information that is felt to be detrimental. The judge, on the other hand, may desire a conservative (non-creative) analysis of the offender's situation because this reduces judicial vulnerability toward false negatives. Government may benefit from the least expensive decision. It is common that these interests do not correspond.

In reality, there are multiple clients of the PSIR process, and their interests must be balanced. While it is important to recognize that the interests of the various clients might conflict on occasion, it is not necessarily the case that they are always incompatible. The best solution is to put together the most accurate, complete and useful report that is possible. This approach will not cater to the demands of one "client" over another.

One way of resolving the dilemma of the client is to remember that the real client is the society served by the PSIR writer. This is a society of which the government, the victim and the offender each are a part, but only a part. The larger loyalty is to the needs of a society for humaneness in official actions and fairness in the justice system. This view is not merely a parroting of the predominant social values of the day, nor is it a shortsighted advocacy of victim's or offender's rights. Instead, this approach recognizes society as a sort of superordinate client, composed of victims, offenders, citizens and laws. The aim is to conduct the PSIR process in a way that enhances the meaning and quality of society. This is not always an easy task.

Summary

In this chapter, we have reviewed the reasons why PSIRs are written to help judges sentence. There is a need for information at sentencing because of goal ambiguity, human differences among offenders, and correctional uncertainty. We then reviewed the types of information commonly contained in the PSIR. These are an assessment of the client's risk, an assessment of the crime's seriousness, a description of the offender's circumstances and a summary of the sentencing options. Finally, we described critical issues in the use of the PSIR: bias, irrelevance, discretion and client conflict.

For Further Reading:

Probation Division Administration Office of the United States Courts, *The Presentence Investigation Report*, Publication #105 (Washington, DC: Administrative Office of the Courts) April, 1984.

Paul, Keve, *The Probation Officer Investigates* (St. Paul, MN: University of Minnesota) 1960.

Notes

[1] The Twentieth Century Fund Report on Criminal Sentencing, *Fair and Certain Punishment* (New York: McGraw-Hill) 1975.

[2] National Council on Crime and Delinquency, *Corrections Plan for the State of Nevada* (San Francisco: National Council on Crime and Delinquency) 1983.

[3] Bureau of Justice Statistics, "Parole Recidivism in Selected States, " *NIJ Report* (Washington, DC: National Institute of Corrections) 1984.

[4] Marvin Bohnstedt, et al. *Screening Devices in Correctional Field Services*, (Washington, DC: National Institute of Corrections) 1979 (mimeo).

[5] Kevin N. Wright, Todd R. Clear and Paul Dickson, "The Universal Applicability of Probation Risk Assessment Instrument," *Criminology*, vol. 22 (February, 1984).

[6] See Andrew von Hirsch, *Doing Justice: The Choice of Punishments* (New York: Hill and Wang) 1975.

[7] Michael Gottfredson and Don M. Gottfredson, *Decision-Making in the Criminal Justice System* (Cambridge, MA: Ballenger) 1984.

GROUP EXERCISE

Select seven students to play specific roles debating the function of the PSIR. Assign each student one of the following "roles:" prosecution, defense, victim, criminal justice system, media, society and offender. Then have each student make a short speech on what function the PSIR should play, what information it should emphasize, and why. Then critique the different perspectives each student has taken.

DISCUSSION QUESTIONS

1. What type of error is more "expense," type I or type II? Why?

2. Can two offenders and crimes ever be *exactly* alike? Why or why not?

3. If you were given the assignment of eliminating discretion from the criminal justice system, how would you go about it?

4. Should the PSIR give more weight to evaluating the seriousness of the crime or the circumstances of the offender? Why?

Chapter 2
Sentencing Purposes and the PSIR

The purpose of the PSIR is to help the judge arrive at a good decision about an offender's correctional status. This decision implies some purpose or rationale. If an offender is sent to prison, it is for some *reason*; if an offender is kept in the community, there is some *purpose* behind that decision.

Whether Franklin's five year sentence with two years suspended is a good decision depends a great deal on what the sentence is supposed to accomplish. If Franklin is dangerous, and the sentence is supposed to protect society, then it may be too short. If Franklin is simply a bumbler in need of help, then it is probably too severe. Some will wonder if this sentence is too short (or long) to serve as a deterrent to others. The point is that the correct response to Franklin's crime depends greatly on what goals one has in mind in choosing the response.

In this chapter, we provide a critical review of the various rationales that are used to justify an offender's sentence. It makes sense to ask, "Why should we punish an offender at all?" Since the act of punishment is to do harm, it seems reasonable to ask why promoting harm against fellow citizens is a good idea. After all, it seems to be in society's interest to promote *less* pain for its citizens, rather than more.

There are four general reasons that are commonly given for a sentence, knowing that it results in pain or harm to a fellow member of society. The first is thought to be "non-utilitarian," the others are referred to as "utilitarian" justifications.

> Retribution (Desert): Punishment is appropriate because (and only when) the person has committed a crime. By virtue of that crime, the offender is deserving of blame and condemnation.

> Deterrence: Punishment is the only (or best) way to set an example for others that the action taken by the offender is wrong. Punishment is done to persuade others not to offend.

> Incapacitation: The criminal act also produces pain and harm and society must protect itself from this conduct. Punishment is designed to keep law-abiding citizens safe from those who are prone to harming them.

Rehabilitation: Society has an obligation to help offenders learn how to live law-abiding lives, even if these actions are temporarily painful.

Upon reading these justifications, it is common to think, "I agree with all of them." However, these four general justifications of punishment are not simple ideas. In fact, they are complex and sometimes confusing rationales for the act of punishment. In order to understand the sentencing decision, it is important to sort out how these various justifications "work" in practice.

Much has been written about these common justifications, and each has a strong coterie of advocates. The following section expands on the definitions of these justifications, and provides some of the more salient arguments of proponents for each one, quoting from some of the more noted advocates.

A Review of the Four
Major Justifications of Sentences

Retribution (Desert)

Retribution, the classical justification of punishment, has been described as a "non-utilitarian" purpose because it rejects the claim that "future benefits" should result from a punishment:

Benefits, such as the rehabilitation of offenders, the protection of society ...or, even more, the deterrence of others are welcome, of course. But they are not necessary, nor are they sufficient, for punishment, and they are altogether irrelevant to making punishment just.[1]

Punishment is justifiable simply and precisely because a person has offended, has broken the legal requirements of the society. Punishment under these circumstances is a means of reaffirming the social order. In the word of John Rawls,

...the purpose of the criminal law is to uphold basic natural duties, those which forbid us to injure other persons in their life and limb, or to deprive them of their liberty and property, and punishments are to serve this end. They are not simply a scheme of taxes and burdens designed to put a price on certain forms of conduct and in this way to guide man's conduct for mutual advantage.[2]

Though this connotes a utility of social order, the social order *per se* is not the motivator of punishment, for retributive punishments must be given in response to an offense, even when it can be established that the punishment of the offender has no effect on the stability of the social order.

This version of punishment is not the same as the common belief that the offender must "pay a debt" to society, for the debt is owed in reverse. By making a law, society has itself made a promise both to those who break the law and to those who obey. Society is obligated to carry out its promise. Retribution should not be construed as "official revenge," for vengeance is harmful to the social order because vigilantism is a denial of the social order. Retributive punishments negate the need for vengeance.

Translated into a system of penal sanctions, retribution requires that similar acts be dealt with by similar punishments and that the severity of the sentence be related to the amount of harm done by the offense. Therefore, retributionists have found themselves supporting the recent sentencing reforms of determinate and mandatory sentencing described in Chapter 4.

One of the difficulties with retribution is divesting the criminal law of its utilitarian purposes. Legislative versions of fixed-sentencing proposals have resulted in substantially longer sentences without a reciprocal increase in judicial control over sentencing.[3] The reason for this is often the hidden inclusion of other utilitarian purposes within the framework of the law, principally incapacitation and general deterrence. Commonly, a draconian sentence is justified as "deserved," even though it is so long because the authorities want to incapacitate the offender and make his punishment a lesson to others.

Practically, it is difficult to argue for the adoption of a sentencing framework which rejects utilitarian ideals. Given the current level of public concern about crime, it is unlikely that much support would be given to a punishment model which bases its fundamental justification on "punishment for crime" with no express regard for future crime rates. On the other hand, the retributionists claim that if a punitive sanction based on the values of retribution results in reformation of the offender or deterrence of other offenders, this is all to the good. It is just that the carrying out of punishment itself cannot be justified by these ends; the only permissible justification is to punish based on the crime alone.

The problem for retributionists is to deliver in reality a sanction system that is not contaminated by utilitarian ends.

General Deterrence

The oldest utilitarian purpose of punishment is deterrence, a point of view whose genesis is generally attributed to Jeremy Bentham. The thrust of this view

...is that punishment is a technique of social control which is justified so long as it prevents more mischief than it produces. At the point where the damage to the criminal outweighs the expected advantage to the rest of society, it loses that justification.

[The advantage produced by punishment]

...is that it serves to deter potential offenders by inflicting suffering on actual ones....The technique works by threat...and we punish only that that technique may retain some effectiveness in the future.[4]

Critics of deterrence have argued that in order for the "threat" to be workable, one must accept a rationalistic view of humankind, in which the prospective offender carefully calculates the ratio of costs to benefits of the planned crime before acting. Critics of deterrence believe it overestimates the rationality of most human decision-making; however, proponents argue that deterrence works for seemingly non-rational offenses because it works as a disincentive. The prospective criminal may not expressly calculate the costs of a crime, but the fact that the act is a crime and may result in punishment serves as a threat, nonetheless. People often make choices based on desires to avoid unpleasant experiences, without calculating those desires. Moreover, there is a power of sanctions for deterring conduct by setting a moral tone and defining a moral order which will guide citizens' conduct regardless of crude calculations of personal gain.

Another commonly erroneous criticism of deterrence is that it justifies extremely severe sanctions for offenders in order to create stronger disincentives. This is not necessarily the case, as Andenaes points out:

It was never a principle of criminal justice that crime should be prevented at all costs. Ethical and social considerations will always determine which measures are considered "proper."[5]

The effectiveness of a deterrence depends on the certainty and severity of the punishment. Evidence increasingly indicates that the former may be more important than the latter.[6] However, our ability to increase the certainty of punishment is seriously hampered by limitations on the ability to apprehend violators.

A more fundamental criticism of deterrence is that it punishes people, not for what they have done, but because others might want to behave similarly. This raises a difficult dilemma for deterrence as a sole justification of punishment; is it just to punish a specific offender because of others' predilections toward criminality? As a result, recent writers have said deterrence is useful only in combination with retributive justifications of punishment.[7]

Incapacitation

Incapacitation as a rationale for punishment has recently grown in popularity. This philosophy argues that the punishment should be designed to eliminate the convicted offender's capacity to commit another offense. Some people make the important distinction as to whether the act to be prevented through control should include all criminal offenses, or only those involving risk or actual physical harm to others.

A basic component of an incapacitation system is the use of risk assessment methods which identify those who must be incapacitated and determine when the risk is abated sufficiently to end the control measures. Many scholars believe there has been a failure to develop an acceptable means of predicting dangerous behavior.[8]

A perfect ability to predict is not necessary to establish an incapacitative system, however. In fact, for some, it is in part the failure of prediction that is used to justify an incapacitative model:

> ...Society at a minimum must be able to protect itself from dangerous offenders...it is a frank admission that society really does not know how to do much else. The purpose of isolating (or, more accurately, closely supervising) offenders is obvious: whatever they may do when they are released, they cannot harm society while confined or closely supervised.[9]

A common tendency of this point of view is to see all offenders as potential repeaters. As a result, the typical remedy is some form of imprisonment for virtually all offenders and particularly lengthy terms for violent offenders. Prison, though, is not the only incapacitative device available. Because incapacitation places value on restricting the *physical ability* of the offender to repeat an offense, chemotherapy, pre-frontal lobotomies, castration and electronic surveillance devices are all incapacitative measures that do not involve prison. Some of these methods are so extreme as to be morally reprehensible.

A final issue in incapacitation involves burden of proof or, stated in a positive manner, the value placed on liberty. Some would argue that the offender has, by the offense committed, proven beyond a reasonable doubt the propensity to offend and is therefore a risk requiring incapacitation. Other writers believe that the state is obligated to take utmost care in deciding to intervene in citizens' lives and argue that the state must make any incapacitation measure as non-punitive as possible.[10] When incapacitating, the state must be limited to the least intrusive measure reasonably constituted to be effective.

Regardless of the various incapacitation arguments, a final moral problem exists: the punishment is being given, not for what the offender has done, but for what the offender is believed likely to do in the future. One is left to wonder whether a free society can tolerate such extensive state power, particularly when there is such a large potential for errors in judgment using this approach.

Rehabilitation

Rehabilitation is a general term which refers to a change in the offender, produced by the nature of the punishment, which results in a commitment by the offender to refrain from criminal acts. The decision to refrain could be motivated by various characteristics of the punishment: fear of being caught and punished again; insight into emotional causes for criminal behavior; the creation of legitimate opportunities for social living which result from skills learned while being punished, etc. The key requirement is that the offender *chooses* to refrain from new crimes (rather than being prevented, which is an incapacitative concept), and the nature and extent of punishment was selected precisely to influence the offender in making that choice.

This rationale might be best described as "individualized punishment," a concept that has had a variety of themes over the years. The earliest germinations for this approach were contained in the writings of Lombroso who argued that there are innate differences between criminals and law-abiding persons.[11] This position leads to the conclusion that, in order to achieve specific crime prevention, the amount of punishment ought somehow to reflect the type of criminal being punished.

In later years, the discussions of physical characteristics gave way to a focus on the mental/emotional status of the criminal, and led to the "treatment" approach to handling offenders. This model presents crime as the product of some underlying disorder which must be understood and treated in order to effectively prevent crime.

In recent years, the focus of rehabilitation has changed yet again to include societal/environmental characteristics, such as poverty and disadvantage, which make crime-free living difficult for individual offenders no matter how stable their emotional makeup. This approach to rehabilitation attempts to make offenders more viable members of the citizenry (for example, through useful employment) and, by improving community acceptance of ex-offenders, "reintegrate" the criminal back into society.

Whatever rehabilitation approach one prefers (punishment, treatment or reintegration) each requires the law to provide for differential handling of offenders based on their characteristics (rather than the offense) in order to apply the sanction in a way that will help the offender to choose to obey the law in the future. That the various approaches still compete for primacy in the rehabilitative aim is illustrated by the commonly held belief that some criminals need to be taught a lesson (punishment) while others need help (treatment) in order to ensure they will stay out of trouble.

Questions have been raised about the appropriateness of rehabilitation. Critics argue that the heavy emphasis on treatment in recent years has led to abuses of power, where the rehabilitation rationale becomes an excuse for unwarranted intrusions into an offender's personal affairs, family life and even political opinions in order to "remake" him into a good citizen.[12] Nevertheless, it is difficult to conceive of sentencing and corrections without at least some emphasis on positive programs for offenders.

How Well Does Punishment Achieve Its Purposes?

It is one thing to justify a punishment on the basis of some abstract purpose, but punishments that do not achieve their purposes are hollow. For example, if rehabilitation is the purpose of a particular sentence, then how justifiable is it to punish an offender if rehabilitation is not going to occur?

In the last decade, a great deal of research has been done on the effectiveness of punishment, and there have been some surprises in the results of the studies. The research provides an important perspective on punishment aims.

Retribution

The philosophy of retribution is difficult to evaluate because it is nonutilitarian, making no claims as to the results of punishment. The sole intention is to punish sufficiently to serve as adequate retribution for an offense.

This approach to punishment is undermined by the extreme prison sentences common to the U.S. penal law. Prison sentences handed out in the United States are much longer than other industrialized, Western societies. They compare more closely with sentences in the Soviet Union and South Africa than other "free" allied nations.[13] The sentences that may be under many sentencing codes in the U.S. are of such magnitude that prosecutors are frequently reluctant to use their full force.[14] The result is a system of on-the-books penalties which, though seldom used in practice, serve to undermine the legitimate symbolic significance of the actual penalties commonly imposed.

Two problems affect our ability to promote a just system of retributive punishments: prison overcrowding and misleading sentencing practices. Both are symptoms of a criminal justice system that has become used to promising much more punishment than it can afford to mete out.

In the 1980s over forty states have faced prison crowding so serious that courts have intervened to order changes in prison administration. It is not a coincidence that this extreme crowding has followed a national trend of more severe punishment. The pressure for increasingly more severe punishments has had the ironic impact of forcing the justice system to take back the punishments it has promised to provide. Prisons are simply too full to accommodate all the criminals, and many offenders who are legally subject to severe punishments receive sentences that are significantly lower than the law allows. It is common for a person who commits a crime allowing a ten year term to receive, instead, a three-year sentence and to serve only one year.

When this happens the system seems to lack retributive credibility because people are not punished as the law seems to say they should be. It is easy for the public to lose confidence in the system. The fact that many sentences allowed under the penal code are excessive is often obscured by the pressure for severe punishments.

Deterrence

Deterrence is a very basic value that many people hold about how society ought to operate; many people say "I believe in deterrence," as though a simple belief were enough to justify punishment as effective. Nevertheless, there is a solid body of evidence on the effectiveness of punishments in deterring crime.

A simplified summary of this literature is that there is good evidence that some punishment is more of a deterrent than no punishment, but an increase in the amount of punishment does not always produce an equally strong increase in deterrence. As the severity of a punishment increases, the requisite deterrent potential of any further increase becomes less and less to the point that the deterrent value of extreme punishments is only negligibly higher than a lesser level of punishment.[15] Often, the overall deterrent value of criminal punishments is only marginal, and is insignificant in magnitude. In other words, deterrence is not an extremely effective purpose of criminal punishments, although evidence suggests the fact that the criminal law promotes some deterrence.

One of the main reasons deterrence is not powerful is that so many crimes go unpunished. One researcher estimated that less than 1% of the robberies in California result in a conviction for a crime,[16] and other studies show that fewer than 1 out of 20 crimes result in incarceration.[17] As was true for retribution, the facade of severity in contemporary U.S. punishments also distorts the deterrent potential of punishments.   In a recent survey of empirical deterrence research, for example, Tullock points out that most of the researchers counted reported crimes resulting in imprisonment as "punishment," while all other cases (including convictions leading to probation) were counted as "no-punishment."[18] This sort of approach confuses the certainty of punishment with what is actually a measure of "severity."

For one thing, the sheer power of apprehension and conviction has some deterrent impact independent of punishment severity.   Moreover, the belief that community supervision is not punitive is rooted in a naive understanding of such activity.   The restrictions on liberty associated with probation are sufficiently undesirable to deter a substantial portion of would-be offenders. The additional marginal increase in deterrence provided by systematic prison penalties might only be negligible.

The ultimate issue, really, is "how much punishment is enough?"   Presumably, one could increase all punishments to life imprisonment, thereby creating some increase in the deterrent power of the law, but, aside from intolerable financial costs and rapidly diminishing returns, the penalty would simply be too extreme.   The philosophical limits of the criminal law create boundaries on the deterrent capacity of that law.

Incapacitation

The incapacitative function has a long tradition in corrections.   Achieving this purpose has traditionally been associated with the imprisonment of the offender.   Studies of the incapacitative power of imprisonment produce ambivalent findings, however.   One study of the effects of a mandatory five-year sentence for all felons in Franklin County, Ohio, found a reduction in violent crime of less than 10%.[19] A similar study of Denver County, Colorado, estimated a much higher rate of crime prevention, but agreed with the Ohio study that a five-year term would lead to at least a tripling of prison population.[20] Studies of the actual effect of mandatory sentences have shown they are not very effective at crime prevention, since they are often subverted by criminal justice officials.[21] In fact, there is little evidence that across-the-board stiff penalties result in large amounts of crime prevention.

One reason this is true is that a minority of convicted offenders commit new crimes.   Most offenders do not recidivate, and this is true, even for prior repeaters.[22] All mandatory incarcerative sentences inevitably result in the imprisonment of many offenders who would otherwise remain crime-free.

For this reason, many researchers have tried to develop prediction methods that identify the offenders who are most likely to commit crimes, and then incarcerate them. However, these approaches have not been able to identify serious recidivists with much more than a 50% accuracy.[23] That is why attempts to incapacitate offenders so often result in serious overcrowding: many of the offenders are locked up erroneously.

Nevertheless, it is unlikely that prediction can ever be fully eliminated as a basis for sentencing, and so the problem is how to control the prevalence of error under predictive methods. Of all areas in criminology, the prediction area is receiving some of the greatest attention from both researchers and policymakers.[24] Yet, to date, it is fair to say that any currently available predictive method based on risk assessment will result in substantial levels of erroneous decisions.

Rehabilitation

Rehabilitation has been the most popular purpose of punishment, at least for the professionals in the field, for most of the last fifty years. Only recently has it come under question as a justification of punishment.

The rehabilitative ideal is currently under a great deal of criticism because of a widely accepted belief it has failed. Though some empirical evidence has recently been presented in support of a generally better success rate for those placed on probation (compared to those incarcerated)[25] and those released on parole (compared to mandatory releases),[26] the landmark findings of Lipton, Martinson and Wilkes[27] surveying evaluative studies of over 200 correctional treatment programs have served as a springboard for a critical re-evaluation of the utility of the rehabilitative model for correctional programming.

In fact, the conclusions of Lipton, et al., (which are not much different from that of other researchers who have summarized the effectiveness of treatment[28]) do not support a wholesale rejection of rehabilitative purposes. More than anything else, these efforts have served to clarify and improve the sophistication of the questions regarding rehabilitative programs.

For example, research clearly serves to question the legitimacy of the so-called "medical-model," which makes sometimes untenable assumptions regarding the etiology of a criminal's lawbreaking behavior. On the other hand, direct-service rehabilitative models which focus on financial and employment services are only recently being subjected to useful evaluation; the early results are mixed but give some reason for optimism in this area.[29] Likewise, it is now reasonably clear that provision of uniform treatment programs coercively applied "shotgun style" to a population of offenders is "at best, wasteful"[30] since the programs have "helped some, hurt some and had no effect on others."[31] The interaction effect observed between type of treatment and type of client suggests that future rehabilitative programs may need to put more stress on "individualized punishment" rather than abolishing it.

For the most part, the evaluations of treatment programs question the successfulness of prison-based rehabilitation. Either through increased prison treatment or increased prison punishment,[32] evidence suggests there is little long-term impact on success rates after release. Studies instead show that effective rehabilitation programs are not oriented toward overly broad "counseling" of offenders, but instead focus on changing specific behavioral problems of clients by providing short-term change programs in community-based settings.[33]

Even though there is some reason to think that it is possible to rehabilitate some offenders under some conditions, the limits of rehabilitation must be faced straightforward: even the most effective programs produce limited total effects. Most offenders' behavior is left unaffected by treatment programs.

Reconsidering the Purposes of Punishment

This is not a promising picture for sentencing in the U.S. It is simple to summarize what has been stated thus far: There are four traditional purposes of punishment, and studies show that there are serious shortcomings in our capacity to achieve those purposes through punishment. Most offenders are neither deterred, incapacitated nor rehabilitated through our current practices. This may lead the casual observer to suggest we need to try harder with offenders, to punish them more, but this idea is naive on two grounds. First, there is virtually no evidence that moderate increases in punishment will have a significant impact on levels of achievement of any of the three utilitarian purposes of punishment. Second, the corrections system in the U.S. is already so seriously overcrowded that any proposal for a widespread increase in the severity of punishments is untenable in almost every system in the country.

Besides, if punishments in general are not extremely effective as methods of crime control, then it seems irrational to advocate *more* punishment. The only possible justification for more punishment would seem to be retributive values. Yet we have already seen that, in the U.S., more retribution is carried out with offenders than in virtually any other Western, democratic society. The call for more and more punishment of offenders is uninformed and counterproductive.

This becomes a critical consideration in the development of the PSIR. Usually, the sentencing decision seeks to achieve either deterrence, incapacitation or rehabilitation. The thought process of the PSIR writer often goes something like this: Can this offender be rehabilitated? Is the punishment enough to deter others? How much punishment is deserved? When approached in this way, there is a tendency to advocate severe penalties, because the intent is to select a punishment that achieves all the purposes.

A different approach is what is called "the least restrictive alternative." Here the decisionmaker seeks not to achieve some affirmative purpose, but to avoid over-punishment of the offender. Instead of asking "How much punishment is necessary to achieve my purposes?" the decisionmaker constantly seeks to avoid imposition of unnecessary punishments. The decisionmaker asks "Is it possible to justify punishing this offender less severely?"

The "least restrictive alternative" approach is useful because it is consistent with what is known about the effectiveness of punishment. It is based on a recognition that governmental restrictions on citizens' freedom are a threat to a free society, and should occur only when absolutely necessary. The fact that punishment so often fails to achieve useful purposes suggests that the criminal law does best when it does least.

Summary

In this chapter we have reviewed the four major philosophies of sentencing: retribution, deterrence, incapacitation and rehabilitation. Retribution is a non-utilitarian philosophy, in that it seeks to punish the offender based solely on the seriousness of the crime. The other philosophies are utilitarian in that they seek to achieve some reduction in crime through punishment. Each philosophical position has conceptual limitations as a justification of punishment, and research on the effectiveness of punishment suggests that none of the four philosophies is without its problems. In terms of the PSIR, the main question seems to be whether the sentence seeks to be severe enough to achieve all the aims, or to be limited in its severity to the least restrictive necessary sentence.

For Further Reading:

Hyman Gross and Andrew von Hirsch, eds., *Sentencing* (London: Oxford) 1981.

Herbert Packer, *The Limits of the Criminal Sanction* (Stanford, CA: Stanford University Press) 1968.

H.L.A. Hart, *Law, Liberty and Morality* (Stanford, CA: Standford University Press) 1963.

Notes

[1] Ernest van den Haag, *Punishing Criminals: On an Old and Painful Question*, Basic Books, New York, 1975, p. 25.

[2] John Rawls, *A Theory of Justice*, Belknap Press, Cambridge, MA, 1971, p. 314.

[3] Todd R. Clear, "Neo-Retributionism, Correctional Policy and the Determinate Sentence," *Justice System Journal*, vol. 11, (Spring) 1978, pp. 63-87.

[4] Stanley L. Benn and Richard S. Peters, *Social Principles and the Democratic State*, MacMillan, New York, 1959, p. 121.

[5] Johannes Andeness, "The General Preventive Effects of Punishment," *University of Pennsylvania Law Review*, vol. 114, no. 3, 1961, p. 955.

[6] Gordon Tullock, "Does Punishment Deter Crime?" *The Public Interest*, vol. 36, no. 2, 1971, p. 103.

[7] Andrew von Hirsch, *Doing Justice: The Choice of Punishments*, (NY: Hill and Wang) 1975.

[8] *Ibid.*

[9] James Q. Wilson, *Thinking About Crime*, Basic Books, New York, New York, 1975, p. 173.

[10] von Hirsch, *Doing Justice*.

[11] Robert M. Carter, Richard A. McGee and E. Kim Nelson, *Corrections in America*, J.B. Lippincott, Philadelphia, PA, 1975, p. 5.

[12] American Friends Service Committee, *Struggle for Justice*, (New York: Hill and Wang) 1974.

[13] Richard A. Salomon, "Lessons from the Swedish Criminal Justice System: A Reappraisal," *Federal Probation*, vol. 40, no. 3, 1976, p. 40.

[14] Arthur Rosset and Donald R. Cressey, *Justice By Consent*, J.B. Lippincott, Philadelphia, PA, 1976.

[15] Alfred Blumstein, et al., *Research on Incapacitation and Deterrence*, (Washington, DC: National Academy of Sciences) 1984.

[16] Peter Greenwood, *Selective Incapacitation*, (Santa Monica, CA: Rand) 1983.

[17] Bureau of Justice Statistics, *Report to the Nation on Crime: The Data*, (Washington, DC: National Institute of Justice) 1985.

[18] Tullock, "Does Punishment."

[19] Steve van Dine, Simon Dinitz and John P. Conrad, "The Incapacitation of the Dangerous Offender: A Statistical Experiment," *Journal of Research in Crime and Delinquency*, vol. 14 (January) 1975, pp. 22-34.

[20] Joan Petersilia and Peter Greenwood, "Mandatory Prison Sentences: Their Effects on Crime and Prison Populations," *Journal of Criminal Law and Criminology*, vol. 69 (Winter, 1978) pp. 604-615.

[21] U.S. Department of Justice, *The Nation's Toughest Drug Law: Evaluating the New York Experience*, Final Report of the Joint Committee of New York Drug Law Evaluation (Washington, DC: U.S. Government Printing Office) 1978.

[22] *Report to the Nation*.

[23] Andrew von Hirsch and Don M. Gottfredson, "Selective Incapacitation?" *NYU Law Review*, vol. 28 (Spring) 1985, pp. 117-136.

[24] Al Blumstein, et al., *Criminal Careers*, (Washington, DC: National Academy of Sciences) 1986.

[25] Ted Bartell and L. Thomas Winfree, "Recidivist Impacts of Differential Sentencing Practices for Burglary Offenders," *Criminology*, vol. 15, no. 3, 1977, p. 387.

[26] See William H. Moseley, "Parole: How is it Working?" *Journal of Criminal Justice*, vol. 5, no. 3, 1977, p. 185 and Robert Martinson and Judith Wilks, "Save Parole Supervision," *Federal Probation*, vol. 41, no. 3, 1977, p. 23.

[27] Douglas Lipton, Robert Martinson and Judith Wilks, *The Effectiveness of Correctional Treatment*, Praeger, New York, 1975.

[28] See Wilkins, *Evaluation*; James Robison and Gerald Smith, "The Effectiveness of Correctional Programs," *Crime and Delinquency*, vol. 42, no. 1, 1971, p. 67; and Walter C. Bailey, "Correctional Treatment: An Analysis of One Hundred Outcome Studies," *Journal of Criminal Law, Criminology and Police Science*, vol. 62, no. 2, 1966, p. 153.

[29] See Kenneth Lenihan, "Financial Aid for Released Prisoners: An Experiment in Reducing Recidivism," paper presented to the meetings of the American Society of Criminology, Atlanta, GA, November 19, 1977; Robert Evans, "The Labor Market and Parole Success," *Journal of Human Resources*, vol. 3, no. 2, 1968, p. 207; and "An Analysis of the Federal Bonding Program," Contract Research Corporation, Belmont, MA, September, 1975 (mimeo).

[30] Marguerite Q. Warren "All Things Being Equal," *Criminal Law Bulletin*, IX, no. 2, 1973, p. 483.

[31] *Ibid*, p. 482 see also Ted Palmer, "Martinson Revisited," *Journal of Research in Crime and Delinquency*, vol. 12, no. 2, 1975, p. 230.

[32] Don M. Gottfredson, Michael R. Gottfredson and James Garofalo, "Time Served in Prison and Parole Outcomes Among Parolee Risk Categories" *Journal of Criminal Justice*, vol. 5, no. 1, 1977, p. 1 and Kassebaum, Prison.

[33] Bob Ross and Paul Gendreau, *Effective Corrections*, (Toronto: Butterworths) 1982.

GROUP EXERCISE

Construct a criminal justice system that is entirely based on the idea of deterrence. Be creative and imaginative in describing the roles and practices of police courts and corrections. Now do the same thing for the idea of rehabilitation. Based on your descriptions, identify some of the limitations that the criminal justice system faces in adopting any philosophy.

DISCUSSION QUESTIONS

1. If rehabilitation is an important value, what should be done about offenders who resist change? Why?

2. What are some other ways to incapacitate offenders besides incarceration? Are they realistic? Why or why not?

3. Some people do not like the idea of retribution, but many reformers argue that retribution is the most advantageous philosophy from the *offender's* point of view. How could this be true?

4. Why is it so difficult for the criminal justice system to adopt a clear philosophical orientation? Is it a good idea to do so?

5. People say plea bargaining is like a "game." How is the game played? What are the rules? What happens when someone "breaks" the rules?

6. Which is better, presumptive sentencing or sentencing guidelines? Why?

Chapter 3
The Sentencing Decision in Practice

When Judge Thurston sentences John Franklin, he almost certainly has some philosophical orientation that helps him select the sentence, just as the prosecutor and defender argued philosophy in reaching a negotiated plea. Yet neither the judge nor the attorneys are free to select whatever sentence best fits their philosophical orientation.

One constraint on sentencing is the law itself. Judge Thurston's sentence must be legal, in that it must be both consistent with the Constitution of the United States, and it must fall within the bounds of the penal code of Alabama. The U.S. Supreme Court, in its interpretation of the Constitution, and the Alabama legislature, in its lawmaking, set limits within which Judge Thurston must stay in selecting a sentence.

A second constraint is the sentencing process itself. While it is common to think of judges as independent arbiters of prosecutor-defense adversarial relations, this is not a fully accurate view of the sentencing process. The court is a bureaucracy. Judge Thurston cannot afford to antagonize the attorneys who practice law in his courtroom, or they could retaliate by filling his already logged calendar with motions and other due process to the point that the workload becomes unmanageable. Likewise, Prosecutor Jarvis and Defender Wholford are forced to work together in disposing of cases, because neither has the time or interest to go to trial on every case.

In this chapter we explore sentencing in practice by evaluating the role played by the constraints of law and court bureaucracy in the sentencing process. We then draw implications of this practice for the PSIR.

Sentencing Law

Sentencing Information

In recent years, experts on sentencing have engaged in a debate about the legal underpinnings of the sentencing decision. In part, the debate concerns the philosophies of sentencing which were discussed in the preceding chapter: utilitarian vs. non-utilitarian philosophies. Utilitarians believe that the imposition of a penalty on an offender should result in a specific benefit to general society in the form of reductions in the amount of crime. Non-utilitarians believe that an individual's propensity for crime should not be a basis for sentencing offenders, instead the penalty should reflect only the harm done by the crime. Utilitarians believe a wide range of information ought to be considered in sentencing offenders, as long as the information helps determine the best sentence for achieving crime control. By contrast, non-utilitarians would carefully restrict the information considered at sentencing only to that which describes the seriousness of the crime.

The issue is more than a technical debate; courts have been asked to review the appropriateness and applicability of certain information for the sentencing decision. The answer has obvious significance for the PSIR. If only a few salient facts regarding the crime may be considered at sentencing, then the PSIR is an entirely different document than if it is to be a broad review of the offender's background and current situation.

In general, the courts have taken an ambivalent stance. Many courts have affirmed that the sentencing decision must reflect the crime's seriousness,[1] but at the same time the sentencing judge is free to consider other facts or circumstances that, in the judge's opinion, help to determine the correct sentence. More recently, courts have been more permissive, ruling that crime prevention may be an explicit consideration in sentencing particular kinds of offenders,[2] in detaining juveniles before sentencing[3] and in determining whether a person should be paroled.[4] In determining a person's proneness to criminality, the court may consider a wide range of factors as they pertain to the offender's situation.

Although there has been no direct test of the issue, the only factors that are not appropriate to consider in sentencing are those that would lead to patently invidious discrimination against whole classes of offenders: race, sex, age or income.[5] Other factors such as employment history, substance abuse and social history are more permissible. In short, the law of sentencing is undeveloped with regard to the information judges may consider.

The Eighth Amendment

One limitation on sentencing comes directly from the Constitution of the United States: the 8th Amendment, which prohibits "cruel and unusual punishments." The 8th Amendment has been very narrowly applied by the courts. To be unconstitutional, a penalty must be *both* cruel *and* unusual. Thus, a chain-gang might seem cruel to most people, but if it is a usual practice, it is not a violation of the constitution.

More recently, courts have broadened the applications of the 8th Amendment to include sentence disparities. Thus, if virtually all offenders convicted of a minor crime receive probation, a prison term may be unconstitutional even if it is allowed under the law, when there appears to be no reasonable rationale for the sentence. In a sense, the courts have started to apply a combination of utilitarian and non-utilitarian values. To be constitutional, a sentence must conform to prior practice (that is, not violate a sense of fairness) but also must be logical in terms of other criteria relating to crime control.

Sentencing Codes

Sentences must conform to a statutory structure which defines the offense and publishes its penalties. Frequently statutory structures grade offenses into broad categories, sometimes called classes. (See Table 3-1) The advantages of offense grading are logic and simplicity: the code is more rational; the penalties applied to offenses are more reasonable and reflect better the relative seriousness of all crimes. The alternative is to have a separate statute for each crime. When this approach is used, offense types are often quite confusing, with even thousands of crimes on the books, each with its own statutory penalty, sometimes having little relationship to the seriousness of other crimes. The complexity of a non-graded statutory structure also makes it more difficult to determine sentencing recommendations in the PSIR.

Table 3-1 Typical Grading System for Offenses

Felony Class	Type of Crime (typical examples)
1	First Degree Murder, Felony Murder
2	First Degree Rape, Arson, Armed Robbery
3	Burglary, Aggravated Assault
4	Theft, Drug Sale, Conspiracy
5	Petty Theft, Drug Possession

There are five types of sentencing systems used in the United States. They are indeterminate, presumptive, determinate, mandatory and guidelines. Each sentencing system is designed to control judicial discretion in particular ways. A discussion of these systems follows.

Indeterminate sentencing. Indeterminate sentencing systems are designed to leave some sentencing discretion in the hands of a parole board. These systems vary widely in the amount of discretion they give to the judge. Under the broadest indeterminate sentencing structures, judges have very little discretion. All offenders receive prison sentences of zero to life, with the parole board determining when to release them. The only choice available to the judge is whether to choose probation or prison. This type of indeterminacy, called "true indeterminacy," is very rare. Currently, no states practice this system, and in recent history, only California experimented with it for a few years during the 1950's and 1960's. True indeterminacy has fallen out of favor because most people think it leaves much too much discretion to the parole board and often results in unreasonable disparities in sentencing.

A lesser form of indeterminacy is more common, in which the judge establishes a sentence range within which a parole board determines actual time served when it releases an offender. Thus, there is a minimum term (the minimum sentence to be served by the offender), and a maximum term (the time past which he or she may not be held). These terms are often altered due to the offender's performance in prison, but the judge's sentence sets the outside parameters of the punishment.

The provisions of the indeterminate statute determine the amount of discretion the judge may exercise in establishing the sentence range. In some systems, the judges select both the minimum and the maximum term from within specified ranges, while in other systems either the maximum or the minimum term is set by law, and the judge selects the other. Table 3-2 illustrates these systems.

Table 3-2 Indeterminate Sentencing Systems

Felony Class	Truly Indeterminate	Indeterminate* Min.	Max.	Partially Indeterminate** Min.	Max.
1	0-Life	5-20	25-Life	5-20	Life
2	O-Life	2-5	10-25	2-5	20
3	0-Life, Probation	1-2, Probation	2-5	1-2 Probation	10
4	O-Life, Probation	0-1 yr., Probation	2-3	0-1 Probation	5
5	0-Life, Probation	0-6 mos., Probation	1-2	0-6 mos. Probation	3

*Judge chooses within range of minimum and maximum terms.

**Judge selects minimum term. In other systems judge would select maximum and *minimum* would be fixed.

Indeterminate systems are often thought of as high discretion systems, but this is not necessarily the case. Often, the judge faces only a single, major choice: probation or incarceration. The sentencing choices within those parameters are often much more limited than the word "indeterminacy" suggests.

Indeterminate systems are most popular among those who support utilitarian theories of punishment. The parole board is free to release the offender when he or she is "ready" to live a crime-free life in the community. In selecting the punishment, there is usually some leeway for the judge to choose a sentence that fits the offender's circumstances, particularly the level of risk to the community and potential for rehabilitation.

The role of the PSIR in an indeterminate structure is first to assist the judge in choosing between probation and incarceration. If incarceration is chosen, the PSIR is used in selecting the appropriate term of incarceration. The PSIR writer is usually free to consider a wide variety of information in preparing the report, in order to present the best plan for handling the offender.

Presumptive sentencing. Indeterminate sentencing has been widely criticized because it often results in sentencing disparity. Many reformers have argued that the judge should establish a specific amount of time that the offender must serve before release. This is often referred to as "fixed" sentencing.

One of the problems with fixed sentencing systems is that criminal acts covered by the same statute often differ dramatically. A calculated beating of a defenseless elderly woman and a barroom fist-fight following an argument are both battery, but most people would agree they are acts deserving different punishments. To accommodate differences in criminal acts, but still avoid the disparities of indeterminacy, some legislatures have turned to the concept of "presumptive sentencing," illustrated in Table 3-3. Presumptive sentencing systems require the judge to select a specific term of punishment from within a range. There is a specific sentence "presumed" to be appropriate for the offense, unless the case has "aggravating" factors (viciousness, premeditation, prior criminality, etc.) which call for extending the term, or mitigating factors (victim precipitation, rehabilitative potential, remorse, etc.) which justify reducing the presumptive term.

In the presumptive system, the PSIR is very important, because it reviews all aspects of the offender's situation and the particulars of the offense to determine the presence of aggravating and mitigating factors. These factors are then used to identify the appropriate sentence within the range.

Table 3-3 Presumptive Sentencing System*

Felony Class	Minimum Range for Mitigation	Presumptive Term	Maximum Range for Aggravation
1	10	20	40 or life
2	5	10	20
3**	3	5	10
4**	1	3	5
5**	6 mos.	1	3

*Judge selects a single term in years.
**Sentence may be waived in favor of probation.

Determinate sentencing. Those who are uncomfortable with even the limited amount of discretion given the court under a presumptive system would give the judge virtually no sentencing choices, except for the basic choice between probation and a specific term of incarceration. Table 3-4 illustrates just such a system, called determinate sentencing.

Table 3-4 Determinate Sentencing Systems

Felony Class	True Determinacy	Modified Determinacy
1	20 years	17, 20 or 23 years
2	10 years	8, 10 or 12 years
3	3 years	probation, 4, or 5 years
4	3 years	probation, 2, or 3 years
5	1 year	probation, 1 or 2 year

Currently, no sentencing system in the U.S. has a completely determinate structure. Most legislators are not comfortable with a wholesale eradication of sentencing discretion. Therefore, some systems have experimented with "modified" determinacy, in which the judge has a very limited set of sentencing choices. Modified determinacy is similar to presumptive sentencing in that the term is "fixed." However, there is no "presumed" sentence, and the judge sets the term by choosing from a set of options.

Under truly determinate systems, the only need for a PSIR occurs when the judge may choose a probation term, because the investigation will outline factors the judge should consider in making that choice. In modified determinate systems, there is more choice (although discretion is very limited) and there is a greater role for the PSIR.

Mandatory sentencing. In recent years there has been a substantially influential opinion among some citizens that too many sentences are too lenient. Regardless of the accuracy of this opinion, it has influenced some sentencing systems to adopt mandatory sentencing provisions, which require the judge to impose a sentence of imprisonment. Mandatory sentences are usually applied only to specific offenses, and may be used in determinate, indeterminate or presumptive systems. Often, in addition to the particular offense, the mandatory term only applies when the offender has a prior criminal record. Mandatory sentencing provisions are attempts to restrict judicial discretion in certain types of cases, without affecting the discretion exercised in the rest of the sentencing structure.

Even under mandatory systems there may be reasons for a PSIR. Often the judge is required to impose a minimum term of prison, say, a year, but may actually impose a much longer prison sentence if appropriate. The PSIR then provides an evaluation of whether a term longer than required is warranted.

Sentencing guidelines. The idea of sentencing guidelines came about as a result of the belief that judges need discretion to sentence offenders because many cases represented unusual circumstances. However, the bulk of offenders are "ordinary" and their cases should result in fairly predictable sentences. The plan of sentencing guidelines is to give the judge "guides" to use in sentencing: a range of time that the person should receive if the case has no unusual characteristics setting it aside from similar offenders.

Table 3-5 illustrates a sentencing guidelines system which is more complicated than other sentencing systems. Guidelines are usually in the form of a "matrix" (a two-dimensional grid) that is defined by two scales. One scale is normally an "offense" scale, in which the crime's seriousness is classified as in other sentencing systems. The other scale is an "offender background" scale that evaluates the offender's characteristics based on prior record and risk of future crime. The sentence guideline is determined by locating the cell that corresponds to the correct offense and offender background score. It is expected that the sentence guideline will be imposed about 80% of the time. However, in exceptional cases (where the crime was unusually vicious, for example) the judge could sentence outside the guideline term, as long as reasons are given.

Table 3-5: Sentencing Guidelines*

Offense Background Scale	1	2	3	4	5
		OFFENSE BACKGROUND SCALE			
A	Prison 1-2 yrs.	Prison 2-4 yrs.	Prison 3-6 yrs.	Prison 4-8 yrs.	Prison 5-10 yrs.
B	Jail 1-3 mo.	Jail 3-6 mo.	Prison 1-2 yrs.	Prison 2-4 yrs.	Prison 3-6 yrs.
C	Probation	Probation	Jail 1-3 mo.	Jail 2-5 mo.	Jail 3-6 mo.
D	Probation	Probation	Probation	Jail 1-3 mo.	Jail 2-5 mo.

*Appropriate sentence falls within range in table.

The role of the PSIR in guidelines systems can be very important. If 20% of the cases are expected to fall outside the guidelines, then it is through the PSIR process that those "exception" cases must be identified.

Which Sentencing System is Best?

Like beauty, the value of a sentencing system lies in the eye of the beholder. However, studies of sentencing find that sentencing systems differ in the degree to which they achieve certain purposes. Sometimes the central intentions of a sentencing system are extremely difficult to achieve because of the nature of the sentencing process.

People who support indeterminate sentencing do so largely because it allows the parole board to take the offender's rehabilitation into account in determining the time of release from prison. Many advocates of indeterminancy believe the law works as an incentive for the offender to take responsibility for self-reform: It has been said, "When the offender holds the key to his own cell door, he will give more effort toward unlocking it." However, many offenders become bitter when they are unable to convince the parole board to release them. Instead of aiding rehabilitation, the indeterminate sentence often fuels the feeling that the system is unjust, arbitrary and vindictive.

Determinate and presumptive sentencing are designed to solve the problem of disparity. Here again, the results have been less than totally successful. Evaluations of some determinate and presumptive systems have found they had little impact on disparity, due to the prosecutor's charging discretion and judicial sentencing discretion.[6] Other studies have found that determinate systems have reduced disparity, but have far from eliminated its existence.

The experience with mandatory sentences has been even more troublesome. Most studies show that, regardless of the "mandatory" law, the judicial system finds ways to avoid the full force of the legislation. One reason is that many prosecutors and judges believe the mandatory sentence is inappropriate for many routine cases. Therefore, they reduce or alter the charges to enable the defendant to receive a more lenient sentence, or they dismiss the charges altogether, causing mandatory sentencing systems often to backfire. This was found to be true in studies of Massachusetts's 5-year mandatory sentence for crimes committed with a gun,[7] as well as New York's mandatory prison term for serious drug offenders.[8]

Sentencing guidelines have a similar spotty history. One study of guidelines in Denver, Chicago and Philadelphia found that judges seldom followed the guidelines, and there was almost no evidence the guidelines altered sentencing practices in those jurisdictions.[9] One reason was that guidelines failed to take into account the plea bargaining practices in those jurisdictions.

Why do sentencing systems so often fail to achieve their aims? The answer lies in a better understanding of the various roles played by criminal justice professionals in the sentencing process.

The Sentencing Process

The judge does not act alone in determining an offender's sentence. Several actors have an influence in the sentencing decision. As we have shown, the way in which the legislature structures the penal code establishes the options available to the judge. Likewise, when illegal actions by police result in inadmissible evidence, the prosecutor is often forced to drop charges.

However, by far it is the work of the courts' officials (the judge, the prosecutor, the defender and the probation officer) who eventually determine the sentencing decision. Recent studies of sentencing find that these actors, in the performance of their roles, comprise a shifting field of influences and counter-influences that ultimately produce the sentence. This has been referred to as the "courtroom work team" notion of the sentencing process.[10]

Court Roles and Role Performance

The idea of the courtroom work team has gained acceptance in recent years because of an improved understanding of the interdependence between the judge, the prosecutor and the defense. While the formal idea of the adversary system is at least partly accurate (the courtroom officials are not all on the same side) never in the history of the U.S. has it been the case that the true "contest" (the trial) was the predominate form for determining a defendant's guilt or innocence. In as many as 85-95% of the cases, the charges against the accused are resolved by the accused person's own admission of guilt. While this may seem odd, a review of the roles and duties of the courts' officials helps to explain why this occurs.

The judge's fundamental duty is to manage the court process in such a way that the defendant's rights are not violated and that the state meets its constitutional obligations in proving guilt. However, this role definition has some built-in sources of conflict. For example, in order to ensure the defendant's rights, the judge must preside over a series of due process hearings that can require a great deal of time. Yet, one of the defendant's rights is that of "speedy trial," which means there must be a timely resolution of all charges. Because of the conflict between the pressures of time and the pressures of due process, the judge is put in a position where guilty pleas are a premium. The guilty plea is normally the most rapid way to resolve the charges against an accused, and it also entails a waiver by the defendant of certain due process rights (especially the right to trial) that contribute to delay. Thus, when most defendants plead guilty, the judge is able to perform more effectively with less role conflict.

The prosecutor is faced with a similar dilemma. While most prosecutors give at least some importance to the obtaining of a high rate of convictions and "tough" sentences for serious offenders, in fact it is the highest duty of the prosecutor to "do justice."[11] Several problems confront the prosecutor in carrying out this responsibility.

First, sentencing provisions for certain offenses are often much more severe than the facts and circumstances of the individual case warrant. This happens because legislatures write laws establishing punishments that are appropriate to the most extreme version of a crime, not the average, everyday offender. If the prosecutor were to pursue these heavy sentences, it might well be inconsistent with basic justice.

Second, the facts of the case often require that a trial be avoided in order to obtain a conviction. Sometimes key evidence is inadmissible; sometimes witnesses are unreliable; sometimes the evidentiary case is weak. When this occurs, the prosecutor is often forced to make a difficult choice:

go to trial and perhaps lose, or work for a guilty plea that will entail some punishment, if only for lesser charges.

Third, the prosecutor faces workload levels that create a pressure to avoid costly trials. In the face of those pressures, the prosecutor often must make difficult choices of which cases deserve the most time. In other cases, a guilty plea is sought.

The pressures facing the defender are more straightforward, since the role of the defender is to represent the interests of defendants in the best way possible. Because most defendants are indeed guilty of a crime similar to that charged, and because normally the evidence of guilt is strong, it is often in the defendant's interest to plead guilty in exchange for sentencing accommodations. Thus, the defense attorney enters into a process of negotiation with the prosecutor. He offers to advise the client to enter a guilty plea if the prosecutor will agree to modifications in the charges or limitations on the eventual sentence.

In the negotiation process, the defense attorney is attempting to gain more control over the eventual sentence to be imposed on the offender. This is what plea bargaining is really about: the defense agrees to serve the prosecutorial and judicial needs for avoiding trial so long as the judge and prosecutor are willing to give up some of their influence over the eventual sentence. In this way, all parties "win;" the defender better represents the client's interests, the judge avoids a trial, the prosecutor gets a conviction.

There are three general ways this is done: the "open" plea, charge reduction and sentence promise. The structure of the penal code influences which kinds of concessions most benefit the defendant. In determinate sentencing systems, the charge determines the sentence, and so, charge bargaining is most common. In broadly indeterminate systems, sentence bargaining often predominates because charges do not always determine the sentence. Tradition also plays a role, since prosecutors and defenders learn how to approach plea negotiation by observing prior practices.

The most common type of negotiation is sentence bargaining, which can take a variety of forms. Usually, the defendant is interested in avoiding a prison sentence, and will be willing to enter a guilty plea if the prosecutor will agree to a recommendation of probation (or at least not oppose it). When the crime is so serious that a sentence of incarceration is a foregone conclusion, sentence negotiations seek to limit the length of the prison term through a prosecutorial recommendation to less time than the maximum allowed under the statute.

Charge reduction is also very common. The prosecutor agrees to drop certain charges and by this action restricts the punishments the judge can impose. Usually the prosecutor remains free to recommend whatever punishment is seen fitting. Often a reduction in charges makes probation available as a sentence, and this is a sufficient incentive for the defendant to plead guilty, even if there is no guarantee the judge will impose probation.

The most subtle type of plea negotiation is the "open" plea. In this type of plea, no promise has been made as to sentence, and no changes have been made in the charges. Instead, the defendant pleads guilty, hoping the judge will take into account the defendant's contrition when imposing the sentence. Usually, the judge will do so. This is one reason plea bargaining is so difficult to eradicate. Defendants will always have the right to waive trial and enter a guilty plea, throwing themselves on the "mercy of the court," expecting some measure of leniency.

The Role of the PSIR

Because of the interdependency among judges, prosecution and defenders, it is important to have an independent assessment of the decisions made during plea negotiation. There is so much pressure on the court system to obtain guilty pleas that there is a potential for inappropriate plea agreements. It is through the PSIR that these actions are reviewed and a separate recommendation is made to the court.

The most important advantage of the PSIR is that it can take into account a broader range of information than is typically available to the attorneys. Prosecutors and defenders work with limited information (the offense, the impact on the victim) and are often unable to consider other aspects of the offender's situation. The PSIR writer may interview the victim, the defendant and others, while also reviewing the evaluations of psychologists, law enforcement personnel and representatives of social service agencies.

Not infrequently, this more comprehensive review of the facts surrounding the offender and crime will uncover information suggesting that the negotiated plea is inappropriate. When this happens, the PSIR will recommend that the judge refuse to accept the plea, because the agreement is not warranted. On other occasions, the plea negotiation may be appropriate, but the PSIR will indicate additional factors the judge should consider in setting the sentence.

Alternative Sentencing

Because the probation officer is concerned with broader information about the offender, the officer is able to evaluate a larger number of sentencing possibilities than attorneys and judges might normally consider. "Alternative sentencing" means that sentence decisions other than the standard "big three" (probation, jail or prison) are taken into consideration. Normally an "alternative" sentence will include some probation, jail or prison time, but with a difference. For example, a probation term may be coupled with residential drug treatment, or a short stay in jail may coincide with the beginning of family therapy in response to child abuse, or "shock" imprisonment may be followed by a period of intense probation supervision.

In its common meaning, alternative sentencing promotes two considerations taken in sentencing offenders: (1) Does this offender have special needs or circumstances that justify a sentence involving treatment programs or other services? (2) Are there any programs available which, if applied to this offender, would eliminate the need for institutionalization? In practice, alternative sentencing means that the vast range of programs in the community are given a priority as mechanisms to avoid costly, and often unnecessary, incarceration.

The Probation Officer's Role

In the structure of the court system, there are several natural alliances: the state is represented by the prosecutor; the defendant is represented by the defense attorney; the judge represents the impartial interests of the law. Who is the natural constituency of the probation officer who writes the PSIR? There are two schools of thought on this issue.

One school of thought follows the belief that the probation officer's client is the judge. The job of the probation officer, from this perspective, is to provide the judge with the best, most objective information available about the case. Because judges may vary in their own philosophies of sentencing, the information put together by the officer will vary to fit the individual judge's needs. From this perspective, the best PSIR is one that gives the judge useful information in an efficient manner. This is the "objective" model of probation investigation.

A second school of thought follows the belief that the probation officer is the advocate for the defendant. The idea is that the probation officer comes to know the defendant as a result of the investigation process and is therefore in the best position to determine the most appropriate sentence, given that offender's situation and the crime. The job of the PSIR writer, then, is to build a solid case for that disposition by arranging the investigation to support its recommendations, and then to advocate for the sentence. This is the "subjective" model of probation investigation.

In reality, most PSIR writers play both roles, sometimes shifting from one to the other, depending on the situation. Sometimes there is a clear reason to be subjective, to advocate for the defendant. This happens when there is an obviously preferable sentence (usually, an "alternative" sentence) that might not be considered by the judge without the PSIR writer's advocacy. Other times, there will be no clear cut sentence that is appropriate, in which case the probation officer will simply provide the information to the judge, whose responsibility it is to act. In a minority of cases, the negotiated plea will appear inadvisable, and the system itself becomes the "client," with the PSIR designed to influence the judge so that a poor decision is not made.

In Chapter 1, we argued that there is an advantage to viewing the true client of the PSIR process as society itself: the society of citizens and institutions that our law is designed to serve. In order to serve that vision of the client, it is important for the probation officer to use professional judgment in evaluating the case. The judgment will lead to some conclusions about the best way to advance the broader interests of society (which includes the interests of the court, the defendant and public) in sentencing the offender.

Summary

In this chapter we have reviewed the sentencing process as it occurs in practice. Sentencing law was presented, including the major variants of sentencing structures: indeterminate, determinate, presumptive, mandatory and guidelines. These structures establish the nature and amount of discretion available in the sentencing decision. We also reviewed the interdependencies of the judge, prosecutor and defender, as they work in the courtroom to handle criminal cases through a process of negotiation. Finally, we drew implications of this process for the role of the PSIR and the probation officer.

For Further Reading:

Nicholas Kittrie and Elyce H. Zenoff, *Sanctions, Sentences and Corrections* (Minniola, NY: Foundation Press) 1981.

Frank J. Remington, et al., *Criminal Justice Administration* (Charlottesville, VA: Michie) 1982.

Alfred Blumstein, et al., *Research on Sentencing* (Washington, DC: National Academy of Sciences) 1984.

Notes

[1] See Andrew von Hirsch, *Past or Future Crimes* (New Brunswick, NJ: Rutgers University Press) 1985.

[2] *U.S. v. D. Francesco* 449 US 117 (1980).

[3] *Siball v. Martin*, no. 82-1278 (1984).

[4] *Morrissey v. Brewer* 408 US 471 (1972).

[5] Joan Petersilia and Susan Turner, *Guideline-Based Justice Implications for Minorities* (Santa Monica: CA, Rand) 1985.

[6] John D. Hewitt and Todd R. Clear, *The Impact of Sentencing Reform* (Lanham, MD: University Press) 1983.

[7] James A. Beha, II, "And Nobody Can Get You Out: The Impact of a Mandatory Prison Sentence for the Illegal Carrying of a Firearm on the Use of Firearms and on the Administration of Justice," *Boston University Law Review*, vol. 57, no. 1 (January, 1977) pp. 96-146.

[8] U.S. Department of Justice, *The Impact of New York's Drug Law*, Report of the Joint Commissions on the Evaluation of New York's Drug Law (Washington, DC: U.S. Department of Justice) 1978.

[9] William D. Rich, et al., *Sentencing by Mathematics* (Williamsburg, VA: National Center for State Courts) 1982.

[10] James Eisenstein and Herbert Jacob, *Felony Justice* (Boston, MA: Little Brown & Co.) 1980.

[11] American Bar Association, *Standards Relating to the Prosecutor* (Chicago: American Bar Association) 1972.

GROUP EXERCISE

Frank Brown is a 37-year-old man who has admitted to car theft, having jump-started a 1987 Chevrolet on the Reliable Used Car lot. The PSIR has not presented his version (he thinks he had a good reason) nor the version of Larry Frankel, owner of the lot (who wants restitution for the car, totaled in a train/car collision). The judge is puzzled by a plea agreement that provides a suspended sentence, informal probation and no restitution.

It is the sentencing hearing. The Judge queries the Prosecutor, the Defense Attorney, the defendant and the victim. Four class members play the roles.

DISCUSSION QUESTIONS

1.   Make the case for Community Service Restitution. Why "restitution"? How can this best be accomplished? Is it punishment?

2.   Discuss house arrest. What are the advantages and disadvantages? When is it appropriate and inappropriate?

3.   Electronic surveillance: When should it be considered? When would it be inadvisable?

4.   The standards of the American Bar Association require that the defense attorney "represent the client's best interests" but that the prosecutor "ensure that justice is done." Why doesn't the prosecutor represent the victim? Is this a good way for the prosecutor to be?

Chapter 4
The Economics of Sentencing

The sentencing of John Franklin is going to cost money. It costs money to pay for judges, prosecutors and defenders, to build and maintain courtrooms. Once Judge Thurston has pronounced his sentence, it will cost money to support the probation, jail or prison operations that will deal with Franklin. If Franklin is ordered to pay a probation fee, a fine, court or attorney fees, the amount of fees will not even come close to the total costs of those operations. Whatever Franklin does not pay will be made up through tax dollars.

In fact, Franklin's case has already cost money, and it has come out of the pockets of several sources. Police resources were spent in apprehending and booking him, jail resources in detaining him, social service resources in evaluating him. These are all paid for through public revenues. Private costs were incurred by the victim, whose losses were estimated as several hundred dollars. This is not unusual; government figures suggest the average burglary results in victim losses of $200, the average auto theft over $2,000 in losses, and the average assault over $100 in damage.[1]

Now that Judge Thurston is about to sentence Franklin, he is making a decision that involves more than justice. It has considerable fiscal implications as well. As we show in some detail in this chapter, all of the sentencing options available to Judge Thurston are costly, but some are much more costly than others. If tax dollars are a precious resource, then Judge Thurston is about to make large scale resource allocation decisions, as he announces Franklin's punishment.

One way of understanding the PSIR process is that it is a resource management activity based on a recognition that the correctional system is composed of limited resources, which somehow must be allocated rationally among all correctional clients. The resource management perspective uses the PSIR to determine what level and type of resources ought to be used for a particular offender. The PSIR writer determines if the offender requires a longer or shorter sentence, whether it should be served in the community or in an institution, and by doing so, allocates the resources of those correctional functions.

Recently, it has become common to recognize that sentencing decisions must take into account the availability of correctional resources for all offenders, not just the prison evaluated in the PSIR. If an offender is assigned to prison, he or she occupies a cell that is no longer available to house other offenders. The PSIR writers cannot simply ask "What does this offender deserve?" Instead, the question is asked "What is an appropriate sentence for this offender, given available resources?" This is the essence of a resource manager approach.

The resource manager idea has become popular in recent years because many local governments have had to operate with stable or dwindling budgets, despite pressure to provide more services. In corrections, there has been a call for improved public protection, even though voters seem reluctant to pass tax initiatives that expand correctional programs, including community treatment and institutions. At every level of operation, government is more cost conscious today than in recent history.

This cost consciousness means that corrections professionals must be aware of the economics of corrections, and that this must be considered in assigning offenders to correctional programs. In this chapter, we first provide an assessment of the costs of various correctional programs and then we review ways to manage those costs. This information is important for the PSIR writer, because the recommendations in the PSIR are fiscal decisions, sometimes of great magnitude.

The Cost of Institutional Programs

People often estimate the cost of constructing prisons as ranging from $40,000 to $70,000 per cell, while operating costs range from $10,000 to $25,000 per year per inmate.[2] These figures are misleadingly low. Construction costs are actually much greater, and the estimated costs per inmate are not as meaningful as the actual dollar costs for housing those inmates, which are often much higher than per-inmate estimates would support.

One of the reasons corrections costs are misunderstood is that one or more of the four general costs of incarceration policies are frequently ignored. *Capital* costs refer to the value of land, buildings or equipment used in providing correctional services. *Operating* costs include dollars spent to operate a correctional program, paying for staff and materials. Financial costs of corrections which are paid for out of the budgets of agencies other than corrections are called *hidden* costs. An *opportunity* cost is incurred when dollars used for corrections reduce the financial support given to other government services such as schools, mental health and transportation.

Capital Costs

Capital costs refer to the amount of money it takes to build the facility that houses a correctional program, such as a prison or an office building. These costs differ depending upon the place the facility is to be located and type of facility to be built. Prisons are more expensive to build than any other type of comparable facility (such as an office building). The typical prison, because it is in a remote area, demands the construction of a complete physical plant, with special provisions for water and utilities.[3] Moreover, the costs of building a prison in an urban area are not markedly less, because of the costs of land.[4] However, nontraditional facilities (such as camps and numerous security prisons) can cost less than half the costs of a maximum security prison.[5]

Construction costs usually do not include several substantial expenses such as architectural fees, insurance and other costs. These hidden costs can raise the ultimate price of a prison by as much as 50%.[6] More often than not, a new prison has to be funded by government bonds, which are paid for (amortized) over time much as a house is paid for by a mortgage. The projected amortization of the construction debt over 40 years *quadruples* the total final cost of a prison. Furthermore, the delay between the approval of a new prison and the date of its opening can be as long as five years, so inflation will inevitably increase the new prison's final costs. For example, a prison which would have cost $75,000 (with hidden costs) in 1975, would have increased in cost to $118,000 by 1979, due to inflation. When public estimates are that a prison will cost $75,000, the actual figure to *pay* for that prison, once built, will be two to six times that amount!

Operating Costs

The costs of running a prison include both "fixed" expenditures and costs which fluctuate according to number of prisoners managed. Fixed costs include maintenance of the physical plant, custodial staff and some institutional program staff. A simple reduction in the number of prisoners does not necessarily affect operating costs, because a prison has to be staffed, heated and maintained no matter how many prisoners it houses. Other operating costs, such as food, clothing and medical care, change with the number of inmates in the prison.

Many costs of operating prisons are routinely omitted from corrections budgets. A study in New York revealed that expenditures of the Department of Correctional Services comprised only 77 percent of the actual total costs of operating the prisons. Excluded costs are fringe benefits and retirement funds, federal grant support, and other types of programs, even the cost of transporting inmates to and from hospitals.[7]

There are other hidden costs of locking people up. These include the defaulted debts, the loss of unpaid taxes and welfare costs for the dependents of inmates. A 1977 study of persons incarcerated in Indiana estimated such hidden costs may equal the total budget of the Department of Corrections.

In order to get an accurate estimate of the true operation costs in corrections, it may be appropriate to double the commonly stated figure of $10,000-15,000.[8]

Table 4-1:   A Demonstration of the Distribution of Incarceration Costs

	Estimate per cell		
Type of Cost	Maximum Security	Minimum Security	Estimated cost for new 500-cell facility to open and run for one year
Original cost per cell	70,000	23,000	35,000,000
Hidden capital costs fees, insurance, etc.			
delay (inflation)	24,000	8,000	12,000,000
amortization (over	43,000	15,000	21,000,000
original cost)	210,000	75,000	105,000,000
Operating costs			
Maintenance	17,000	28,115	8,850,000
Hidden staff costs	7,585	12,049	3,792,500
Hidden social costs	15,000	15,000	7,500,000
Opportunity costs	200	200	100,000
Industry	500	500	250,000
Land use	500	500	250,000
TOTAL	$387,985	$178,864	$193,992,500

Source: Key Decision-Makers Seminars: Manual, edited by Todd R. Clear and Patricia M. Harris, Rutgers University, School of Criminal Justice, 1981, mimeo.

Opportunity Costs

Opportunity costs occur whenever policies are followed which eliminate the feasibility of alternative choices of action which might be more efficient or more productive. For example, the land which houses a facility ties up the dollars it would provide at market value if sold.

Inmate labor in prison industries is an example of an opportunity cost because it is often a wasted resource. During 1978, New York State lost approximately four million dollars on its prison industry program because of inefficiency, inmate labor mismanagement and outdated technology.[9] Whether the recent trend toward privatization will correct this problem remains to be seen.

The most troublesome opportunity costs occur when public monies are spent on prisons and cannot be used toward other social ends. This is a particular problem for states that have spending caps preventing deficit budgeting; for these, incarceration policies often force a rearrangement of public service priorities.

Imprisonment is an expensive correctional activity, more costly than most estimates indicate. Prison policies which call for new facility construction are dramatically more expensive than most estimates suggest. To build and operate a 500-cell facility for one year may commit as much as 200 million dollars of a state's resources (see Table 4-1). This is more than 5 times the typical, per-cell construction estimate. Of this amount, the greatest portion goes to construction; less to maintenance and operation.

The decision to place an offender in prison is very costly in public funds. This is especially true given contemporary prison crowding that is serious in most states. Every time a person is recommended for imprisonment, the pressure is increased for expansion of the prison system. As Table 4-1 shows, this can become extremely expensive.

Therefore, it is a serious responsibility of the PSIR writer to explore all possible alternative sentences prior to recommending a term of incarceration. Any other approach is fiscally irresponsible.

The Costs of Alternatives

Because prisons are so expensive, most experts have searched for alternatives to incarceration. In recent years, numerous alternatives have been developed, mostly to reduce the serious crowding of prisons and jails in many states. These programs have costs as well, and it is useful to compare their costs with those of incarceration.

Pre-trial Release

The most obvious alternative to jails for pre-trial detainees is release. With the advent of Vera Institute's *Release-on-Recognizance* program in New York in the early 1970's, a long track record has developed about the costs of these programs. Inevitably, release programs are considerably cheaper than jail, costing less than one dollar per day in comparison to over $20 per day for jail. Even supervised release programs, where offenders report to justice officials while awaiting trial, cost less than one-fifth the daily costs of jail. Pre-trial release is always considerably cheaper than detention.

Community Supervision

The traditional forms of community supervision are probation and parole. The costs of probation and parole vary drastically, based on the salaries of employees and the size of the officer's caseload. Across the U.S., probation costs vary from under $100/year per offender to nearly $1,000, depending on the agency and the program. One study of 21 New Jersey county agencies found that the average annual cost of supervision varied from under $100 in some counties to over $300 in others.[10] Despite this variation, the annual costs of supervision generally run 1-5% the annual costs of incarceration, not counting the construction costs of new prisons.

In the last 5 years, many states have begun to experiment with intensive supervision caseloads. Because these programs use caseloads of 15-25 offenders per officer, they are more expensive than the traditional supervision alternative. Intensive probation supervision in Georgia is about 5-6 times as expensive as regular probation, but is still less than 1/5 the cost of imprisonment there.[11] Even the most expensive community supervision programs only cost a fraction of the imprisonment alternative.

Hidden Costs of Community Supervision

Just as prison budgets do not contain all the costs of imprisonment, probation/parole budgets fail to reflect all the costs of community supervision. Most community supervision agencies refer clients to other human services agencies, and these agencies bear the costs of services out of their own budgets. There are no reliable estimates of how much these services eventually cost, but it is a safe assumption that they do not equal the direct costs of supervision. Thus, even including these costs, community supervision is a fiscal bargain.

Some observers have questioned the long-range cost savings of community supervision by pointing out that many offenders under supervision are rearrested for crimes and have to be processed by the criminal justice system, which itself is an expensive undertaking. Some experts believe that, when new crimes are taken into account, community supervision results in a *greater* total cost than the costs of incarceration.

While the costs of new crimes must be considered in the overall picture of correction costs, community supervision may not be as expensive as many experts believe. A recent study of RAND shows that, while almost all offenders are eventually placed into supervision in the community, those who serve prison sentences prior to being paroled have higher failure rates than those who are placed directly into supervision. Even taking into account prison's incapacitative value, this study found the cost of community supervision to be so much less that prison remains an expensive alternative to probation or parole.[12]

Cost Return Programs in the Community

One fiscal advantage of community-based sentences is that offenders who live in the community can return funds to society through restitution, fines, probation fees and taxes. A study of Georgia intensive supervision found that 1000 prison-bound offenders who were diverted to probation produced revenues in excess of $1 million, revenues that would not have existed had these offenders been incarcerated.[13] A large portion of the costs of probation in several states is defrayed by fees paid by probationers to the probation department. A $10 monthly fee for 100 probationers might defray up to 50% of the costs of the probation officer's salary.

Observations of probationers paying a part of the cost of their supervision has caused corrections officials to experiment with similar programs in the prison setting: Prisoners are to be provided with jobs paying regular wages, of which a portion will be charged back to cover costs of incarceration. Evaluations of these programs are inconclusive as to whether they actually result in a saving of dollars; sometimes they even lose money and often their profits are merely "paper-profits," which fail to cover the full costs of the enterprise.[14] At this time, the most fair conclusion is that innovations in prison industry will reduce, but not eliminate, the gap in costliness between incarcerative terms and community-based terms.

The Court as Resource Manager

This summary of the costs of corrections may seem a bit tangential to the PSIR process, but it is not. Every time a judge pronounces a sentence, that decision spends tax dollars. Those who write the PSIR should consider the fiscal implications of the recommendations they make.

The main distinction in terms of costs is between an incarcerative term and a community-based sentence such as probation. The latter is always a substantially less expensive recommendation to make, and so, all else being equal, there is a fiscal reason for preferring sentences that avoid incarceration. Using a financially conservative approach, the decisionmaker asks, "Do the circumstances of this offender and offense require a substantial investment of public revenues?"

To answer this question, PSIR writers must bear in mind that government funds available for corrections are finite; no government gives the corrections system a blank check. Thus, it is incumbent on the correctional professional to reserve the most costly correctional options (imprisonment and the intensive community programs) for those offenders for whom these programs are most appropriate. That is what responsible resource management is all about.

In practice, this means that the responsible correctional worker will not assign low risk or petty offenders to jail or prison terms. While this may seem appropriate to "teach the person a lesson" or "show that the law is serious," each of these offenders takes up space that would otherwise be available for a more deserving client: a high risk offender or one who has committed a heinous crime.

The court is the central means for managing the resources of corrections. The PSIR process can be viewed as the means of placing offenders in a sentencing context. First, the PSIR writer determines how serious the offender's crime and circumstances are *compared to those of other offenders* handled by the corrections system. Then, a requisite level of resources is applied to this offender by recommending a sentence.

This approach is the reverse of what is normally thought to be the PSIR task. Most people think that the PSIR process is designed to decide what the offender is like, and how to handle him or her. But no PSIR can be done responsibly without attention to the resource context in which the sentencing occurs. The effective investigator assesses offenders in light of the types of resources that are available and the types of offenders who will require those precious resources.

Is the cost of a punishment the most important consideration? A resource manager approach to the PSIR process does not mean that money must be conserved at any cost. There are clearly occasions when the offender's risk or the seriousness of the crime require a severe sentence, one as expensive as imprisonment. Even though they are costly, these options exist because their role is sometimes in society's interest. A resource manager realizes that sometimes this money can be well spent.

Yet, the resource manager knows equally well that to assign an offender to incarceration when not called for is to squander public funds. More important than this, the decision to tie up scarce correctional resources with inappropriate offenders means that other, more deserving offenders, cannot be given the level of resources they require – they must receive lesser sentences.

Summary

    In this chapter we have presented an economic framework for sentencing decisions that is based on the idea of resource management. This idea recognizes that imprisonment is a scarce resource and very costly. When we reviewed these costs, we showed imprisonment is more expensive than is often thought, and it is much more expensive than community supervision. The responsible PSIR writer will consider the costs of various correctional options when deciding what sentence to recommend.

For Further Reading:

Todd R. Clear, Patricia M. Harris and Albert L. Record, "Managing the Costs of Corrections," *The Prison Journal*, vol. 24 (Spring) 1982.

Douglas McDonald, *The Price of Punishments: Public Spending for Corrections in New York* (Boulder, CO: Westview Press) 1980.

Study of the Economics and Rehabilitative Aspects of Prison Industry, vol. 5, *Analysis of Prison Industries and Recommendations for Change* (Washington, DC: U.S. Government Printing Office) 1978.

Notes

[1] Bureau of Justice Statistics, *Special Report: The Economic Cost of Crime to Victims* (Washington, DC: U.S. Department of Justice) April, 1984.

[2] Gail S. Funke and Billy L. Wayson, *Comparative Costs of State and Local Facilities* (Washington, DC: Correctional Economics Center) 1975.

[3] Neal M. Singer and Vickie B. Wright, *Cost Analysis of Correctional Standards: Institutional-Based Programs and Parole Volume II* (Washington, DC: U.S. Government Printing Office, 1976) p. 14.

[4] National Clearinghouse on Criminal Justice Planning and Architecture, *The High Cost of Building Unconstitutional Jails* (Champaign, Il: University of Illinois,) 1977.

[5] George P. Falkin et al., *Revising Connecticut's Sentencing Laws: An Impact Assessment* (Alexandria, VA: Institute for Economic and Policy Studies, Inc.,) 1981.

[6] Douglas McDonald, *The Price of Punishment: Public Spending for Corrections in New York* (Boulder, CO: Westview Press, 1980).

[7] *Ibid.* p. 95.

[8] Val B. Clear et al., *The Hidden Costs of Incarceration* (Anderson, In: Anderson College Press,) 1977.

[9] McDonald, pp. 44-46.

[10] *Report of the Probation Advisory Board of New Jersey*, report to the New Jersey Supreme Court, Trenton, NJ, 1985.

[11] Billie S. Erwin, *Evaluation of Georgia's Intensive Probation Supervision* (Atlanta, GA: Department of Corrections) 1985.

[12] Joan Petersilia and Susan Turner, *Prison vs. Probation in California* (Santa Monica, CA: Rand) 1986.

[13] Erwin, *Evaluation*.

[14] Martin D. Schwartz and Todd Clear, "The Privatization of Correctional Uncertainty," Paper presented to the Annual Meetings of Law and Society, Washington, DC, August, 1985.

GROUP EXERCISE

The state of Jefferson has a budget that includes the following line of items:

Transportation	$22,500,000
Education	53,000,000
Social Services	65,000,000
Retirement fund	35,000,000
Municipal Services	30,000,000

Assume that the Governor has decided to build three new 500-bed prisons without raising taxes by "borrowing" from these five line item budget areas. How much money is needed? What resistance is likely to be faced in cutting the budget? Develop a plan for funding the money from these five categories to build the prisons.

DISCUSSION QUESTIONS

1. What are all the costs of sending a person to prison who would otherwise adjust well to community supervision? What are the costs of not sending that person to prison?

2. Is money the primary consideration in sentencing offenders? What considerations are more important? Why?

3. There are many ways to fight crime other than by imprisoning offenders. Name some of them and discuss how much they cost.

Chapter 5
Information and the PSIR

In developing the PSIR for John Franklin, Probation Officer Mack Ray will apply a process he has used for years. He learned the basic process from the Supervisory Probation Officer who trained him when he was first hired. Since that time, he has revised and perfected his techniques to meet his own style as an interviewer. The basic PSIR process involves four stages: interview, investigation, verification and writing.

In the interview stage, Mack Ray will meet with John Franklin and ask him a series of questions about the crime, his background and his current situation. He will try to explain the reason for the PSIR, and he will answer any questions Franklin has, except legal questions which should be answered by Franklin's attorney. His main goal in the interview is to help Franklin to relax and provide him with accurate information, from which he may begin the investigation. Mack Ray believes the interview is the most important of the stages in the PSIR process because Ray's first impressions of the case are formed during the interview, and most of what follows will be framed by its results.

The investigation stage involves a series of telephone calls and letters. Because much of this is routine, Mack Ray has worked out a series of "form" letters that he can use to collect vital factual data from schools, employers, banks and others, if necessary. However, when dealing with victims, family and neighbors, Ray likes to interact directly, either by telephone or better yet in person, if possible. Long experience has taught him he gains a richer understanding of the case through personal contact with these people. Perhaps the most important aspect of the investigation stage is to check Franklin's criminal record.

The verification activity occurs simultaneously with the investigation stage. Ray knows that people often repeat as fact that which is really opinion or impression, and sometimes people will be led to lie in order to protect somebody or mislead the PSIR process. It is good to get two independent sources for as much information as is possible, particularly when the information might have an important bearing on the case.

It is Mack Ray's carefully cultivated habit to keep a file of notes and materials on each PSIR he has been assigned. When he sits down to draft the PSIR, he pulls out the notes and organizes them in front of him. Then he starts the final stage of the process: writing. As he writes, he keeps in mind the several constituencies who have interest in his report: Franklin, Judge

Thurston, the victim and the community. He knows a straightforward, accurate and focused report will serve the needs of all as best as is possible.

The PSIR Process in Perspective

It is important that the offender understand what is occurring from the very beginning of the PSIR process. The purpose of the PSIR should be explained: how it is prepared, what it contains, where it goes. Understanding this information can help to ease the tensions that inevitably surround the initial interview. This information is straightforward, factual and relatively non-threatening, and can be the beginning of a dialogue between the offender and the probation officer.

The PSIR process is different from the offender's other experiences thus far in the criminal justice system. Most investigators have been concerned with the offender's guilt. The focus was mostly on the facts of the case, and only secondarily on the offender. By the time the PSIR process begins, the question of guilt has been determined, and the only issue remaining is how best to sentence this offender for this offense. Of interest is the background and character of the offender, the social and personal history, prior criminal activity and so forth. The goal is to present to the judge information enabling the tailoring of the sentence to meet the goals of the law and society. In a way, the probation officer functions as the eyes, ears, arms and legs of the judge outside the court room by interviewing, investigating and verifying that which needs to be taken into account at sentencing.

The probation officer should clarify his role, reinforcing the fact that guilt has already been established. Because thoroughness and objectivity are hallmarks of a good PSIR, the probation officer at the outset is not an advocate for either the offender or anyone else, and no sentence or disposition should be favored or supported.

Offenders, victims and family members will react to the PSIR process in many different ways. The investigating officer needs to be careful not to be drawn into manipulative strategies and ploys by the offender or others which could compromise the accuracy and objectivity of the PSIR. Ultimately, the probation officer may make a recommendation to the court as to the sentence. This may be troubling to the client or to others. It helps to recognize that the recommendation is based on the totality of the information available, and thus will not be determined until the final stages of the PSIR process.

The ultimate purpose of the PSIR process is to provide information for sentencing. Yet with all the possible facts that even an average case entails, how does the PSIR writer decide what information to include? There are three major criteria for information to be useful: validity, reliability, and equity. An understanding of each is important in deciding how to write the PSIR.

Validity

When information is valid, that means its use can help the decision-maker achieve the goals of the decision. Of course, the goals of sentencing vary from case to case, even though all decisions are concerned with justice, community protection and resource management. The validity of information depends on the priority given to these goals. Having a clear understanding of goal priorities obviously is an essential requirement in accomplishing correctional goals and in selecting information that helps to achieve those goals.

The most common validity problem today occurs when sentencing decisions result in a demand for incarcerative sanctions that exceed institutional capacity. Jurisdictions are then forced to take radical ameliorative steps such as the emergency release of offenders. These reactive measures force the corrections system to accept a policy that at best is a watered-down version of the original goals and at worst is a complete reversal of them.

Validity also suffers when the policies used to make decisions do not match goals. A good example of this problem is when the system's primary goal is public protection, and yet close supervision or incarceration are given to low-risk offenders.

The lack of validity is a main source of sentence disparity (second in importance only to a lack of agreement on sentencing goals). The use of invalid information leads some PSIR writers to base their sentence recommendations on factors that are unimportant. For example, it is a common belief that the seriousness of the current offense is predictive of the offender's future behavior in the community. This is not always a valid conclusion, and the misuse of this factor can lead to disparity.

The criterion of validity has two implications for the PSIR writer. First, there must be a clear sense of the priority attached to sentencing goals from the court's perspective. Some facts about the case may have no validity, because the goals are not related to these facts. Second, the PSIR writer must be able to organize into some order the patterns of relationships of valid information to legitimate goals.

For example, if a judge places a great deal of importance on equal punishments for equal crimes, then information about the offender's employment record usually has little or no validity in determining the sentence. Likewise, the offender's intent in committing the instant offense may be more valid than the prior record, although both will have some validity. To be useful, the information in the PSIR must give the judge a valid understanding of which sentences achieve the goals.

Reliability

Reliability in sentencing means that similar offenders will be handled alike regardless of who is doing the sentencing. One way to increase reliability is to place a limit on the information used in selecting a sentence. This is one reason why many jurisdictions have developed guidelines. Without reliability in sentencing it is not possible to achieve validity, because goals will not be consistently accomplished.

Recent research has demonstrated that many correctional decisions are plagued by low reliability.[1] For too large a number of offenders, it is not possible to predict accurately which sentence will be imposed unless it is known which judge imposes the sentence. This is one type of unreliability. Another occurs when judges themselves are unpredictable in their decisions.

Unreliability occurs because there is discretion. When decisions are being made by numerous actors who may apply whatever reasoning they wish in whatever legal way they want, unreliability can be a serious problem. The best way to avoid unreliability is to use objective and unambiguous information in a consistent manner to arrive at decisions.

There is no easy way to remove unreliability from sentencing decisions. One of the reasons for this is that virtually all human behavior is unpredictable, at least to some extent, including that of offenders and judges. A second reason is subjectivity: people interpret sentencing information in different ways, even when they agree on sentencing goals. Often, a PSIR writer will consider a fact about the case unimportant, but will include it in the PSIR anyway because the judge may want to consider it.

Limiting sentencing information to a few objective facts is not a good solution to unreliability. There may be other valid information available which, if known, would improve the sentencing decision. Perhaps the only way to achieve reliability in the long run is to rely on experience to determine which information should be used in recommending a sentence, and how it should be used.

Equity

"Equity" requires that factors used in sentencing be fair, in that they do not discriminate against special groups, and their use is consistent with broader social values. The requirement of equity is not cut-and-dried. Much controversy exists over what offender factors are appropriate.

For example, few would approve of use of the "IQ" factor in sentencing an offender. Yet studies show that IQ test scores are associated with responsiveness to treatment, and it is conceivable that IQ might be an independent correlate of recidivism.[2] Therefore, a person's IQ might actually be valid information in relation to the goal of public protection because it would tend to identify which offenders can be kept safely in the community. The use of IQ as a determinate of the decision to incarcerate would be repugnant to most people, however, because it would result in discrimination against the intellectually disadvantaged. For this reason, many people are uncomfortable with the use of IQ as a variable in sentencing. For similar reasons, others resist the use of any offender demographics in sentencing.

The least inequitable information involves prior criminal history data such as convictions and incarcerations, because these behaviors represent the "free-will" choices of the offender, and they are not accidents of birth. Yet, an extreme argument can be made that even these factors are unfair, since they penalize the offender a second time for an offense for which the offender has already been punished.

In practice, there is no absolutely equitable information for differentiation of offenders other than the instant offense. Use of any other factor in sentencing results in offenders convicted of the same crime being treated differently (at least potentially) and raises questions about the equitableness of the different treatment. Yet simply relying on the offense as the only information for sentencing often leads to poor decisions. Considering factors in addition to the offense improves decision quality, even though this may raise concerns for equity. Most judges resolve this dilemma by trying to expunge directly discriminatory factors (such as ethnicity) from influencing the sentence, while paying attention to other less offensive factors (such as prior criminality).

The criteria of validity, reliability and equity help the PSIR writer to decide which facts ought to be included in the PSIR. When reviewing the sometimes voluminous notes from interview, investigation and verification, the PSIR writer can ask three questions: How much does this fact relate to the goals of sentencing (validity)? What has been done with similar information about prior offenders (reliability)? How fair is it to use this information to make a sentencing decision (equity)?

These questions will help the PSIR writer to decide what to include in the report, but that is not enough. The PSIR writer must also have an understanding of how the information will be used by the judge to arrive at a sentencing decision, in short, how that information will be processed.

Human Beings
as Information Processors

One way of thinking about the use of information in decisionmaking is to take the perspective of information theory. From this perspective, the main difficulty of sentencing is "uncertainty:" the inability to know how well a particular sentence matches the offender's behavior and circumstances, and whether the decision is likely to be effective.

Whenever human decisionmakers are faced with uncertainty, the inclination is often to gather many facts (called "signals") in order to learn as much as possible about the uncertain situation. However, all facts are not equally valuable in reducing uncertainty about a decision. For example, knowing an offender's eye color does nothing to help decide on an appropriate sentence. "Signals" that are not information are referred to as "noise." When we speak of "information," we are referring to only those signals which help reduce the overall amount of uncertainty about a decision. The problem for the human decisionmaker is first to know which signals are noise and which are information, and second to determine how the information relates to the uncertainty. What people call "misinformation" is really a situation in which noise is treated as information, or there is an erroneous understanding of the true relationship between the information and the uncertainty.

There are numerous examples of this process when people make decisions about offenders. Let us say a probation officer is struggling to decide what recommendation should be given for an offender, and the probation officer's aim is to determine whether a rehabilitative sentence is appropriate, because the offender is very young. The probation officer notes that the juvenile has a "bad attitude" (he is disrespectful of authority and rude to the officer). He decides to treat the "signal" (the juvenile's hostile attitude) as "information" suggesting that the offender will not respond to treatment. He therefore recommends a prison term.

It is possible that the probation officer is wrong in his assumption about the relationship between "attitude" and responsiveness to treatment. Many treatment programs for young offenders (positive peer culture, guided group interaction) are quite effective with hostile as well as cooperative clients. Instead of being "information," the "signal" of the offender's hostile attitude was really "noise," bearing no relationship to the goals of the decision, which were to determine whether a rehabilitative sentence should be given.

This illustration is one example of the many times a decisionmaker erroneously estimates the importance of some signal in making the proper decision. Studies show that only a small number of signals (often as few as 5, seldom more than 11) actually relate systematically to the uncertainty underlying the sentencing decision.[3] These are called "correlates" of sentencing de-

cisions. There may be other factors that occasionally relate to sentencing decisions, but not in systematic ways.

Typically, however, PSIR writers gather many more signals than the correlates prior to writing the PSIR. Often gathering additional data beyond the
"systematic" correlates can be useful. For example, the fact that an offender
was shot during the crime and became a paraplegic is a very unusual signal,
but knowing it would certainly affect the appropriate sentence. However,
much of the time, trying to use many signals beyond the correlates in making
a decision is of limited benefit, and may actually be damaging. For example,
the gathering of additional signals increases the probability that noise will be
treated as information, or that the decision-maker will erroneously interpret
the relationship between a given signal and the uncertainty.

PSIR writers often experience this when they become more and more
confused about what to recommend in a case, the more they learn about the
offender. They think of the case as "complicated." From an information theory point of view, what is happening is that many signals (some of which are
"noise") are being gathered and simultaneously treated as information of
equal value, when in reality quite a few of the signals have an ambiguous relationship to the best possible sentencing decision. When this occurs, it is
frequently helpful to take a "step back" from the case, and try to identify the
5-7 "key" correlates of the best decision. Often, the confusion will become
less serious, when less information is being used. This is why a judge asks for
a recommendation in a pre-sentence, because there is a need to simply put
all the "signals" in the PSIR into a clean "message": what should be done with
the offender?

At minimum, the desire to "gather lots of facts" about the case means
there will be redundancy in the information. This occurs when items of information relate to uncertainty in much the same way. For example, "arrests"
and "convictions," while different, are highly correlated with each other and
are related to a sentencing decision in much the same way. To a certain extent, redundancy can be useful, because studies show that human decision-
makers like redundancy in order to increase their confidence in their decisions.[4] However, sometimes false confidence occurs, when there are lots of
signals but very little information being used to make a decision. In other
words, the uncertainty in the decision remains, despite the tremendous
amount of "noise"! Too much redundancy can be damaging also, because it
leads to "information overload" in which the decisionmaker is trying to incorporate too many facts into a decision, and cannot do so. Information overload leads to frustration and an inability to arrive at a decision in which the
person has confidence.

Because of the way human beings process information, it is generally felt
that structured PSIR formats are very useful. Sometimes, when there is not

much uncertainty to a decision (for example, whether a premeditated murder offender with a prior murder conviction should be sent to prison or whether to give a first-time check forger a probation sentence), a detailed PSIR process will do little to help the decisionmaker arrive at a decision. In times such as these, when there is little uncertainty, a shorter, less detailed PSIR process and report may be appropriate.

When detailed investigations are needed, however, the investigator is often tempted to "load the report" with signals (facts about the offender's circumstances). The real challenge to the report writer is how to differentiate the important signals (information) from the rest, and to relay that to the decisionmaker. To do this, the PSIR writer must make careful use of the criteria mentioned earlier.

How Much Information is Enough?

In the PSIR process, sometimes the PSIR writer has to ask when to stop gathering information and begin to write. The question is: how does one know when this point has been reached?

There are three common tests of when to stop. One is the *confidence-level* test. When the PSIR writer becomes 90% confident that the best decision is known, the investigation process can stop and the verification process can begin to document the accuracy of that information and identify confirming data. A second approach is the *pattern* approach, in which a set of information corresponds so closely to a common pattern (or keeps being repeated in such a pattern) that a fairly complete picture is created by the facts that define the pattern. A history of 10-15 drunk-driving arrests, for example normally constitutes a pattern. The third test is the *redundancy* test: the continued search for information seems to turn up no signals that are not already known. When this happens, it is unlikely that continued investigation (information search) will turn up anything that will reduce uncertainty. Unfortunately, the sentencing decision may have to be made despite the high uncertainty.

Summary

In this chapter we have reviewed the PSIR process and the criteria for developing the PSIR. The investigation process includes four stages: interview, investigation, verification and writing. There are three criteria for including information in the report: validity, reliability and equity. Viewing the sentencing judge as a human decision maker using information theory, the task of the PSIR process becomes separating the noise from the information, avoiding overload, and reducing uncertainty.

For Further Reading:

Michael Gottfredson and Don M. Gottfredson, *Decision-Making in Criminal Justice* (Cambridge, MA: Ballinger) 1982.

M. Kaplan and S. Schwartz, eds., *Human Judgment and Decision Process in Applied Settings* (New York: Academic Press) 1975.

Notes

[1] Victor Frankel, *Law Without Order: Criminal Sentencing in the United States* (New York: Basic Books) 1971.

[2] Bob Ross and Paul Gendreau, *Effective Corrections* (Toronto: Butterworths) 1982.

[3] Michael Gottfredson and Don M. Gottfredson, *Decision-Making in Criminal Justice* (Cambridge, MA: Ballinger) 1982.

[4] H.Einhorn and S. Schacht, "Decisions Based on Fallible Clinical Judgment," in M. Kaplan and S. Schwartz, eds., *Human Judgment and Decision Processes in Applied Settings* (New York: Academic Press) 1975.

GROUP EXERCISE

Divide the class into groups of five persons. Each group should then develop a list of the ten most important items of information to include in the PSIR. Be sure to rank the items of information, from most important to least important. Compare the lists. What are the differences and similarities in them?

DISCUSSION QUESTIONS

1.   What does "uncertainty" mean? What are good ways to reduce uncertainty in sentencing?

2.   Can the probation officer ever learn the absolute truth abouta criminal incident? Why or why not? What about learning the "truth"? about the defendant?

3.   Develop some examples of "too much" information. Show how the information actually can distort the sentencing decision.

4.   What are some of the ways a PSIR writer can avoid bias? How can the PSIR writer test for bias in doing the job?

Chapter 6
The Interview

Of all the activities Mack Ray will engage in during the PSIR process, by far the most important is interviewing. The first interview will be with the defendant, but after this there will also be interviews with victims, family and others. During these interviews, Probation Officer Ray will call upon a combination of sensitivity to the interviewee, skill in communication and knowledge of criminal justice and criminology to bring out information that will be useful in the PSIR.

The Interview Process

The PSIR interview is similiar to other types of interviews in that it is focused on a particular goal (the PSIR); it is structured to elicit information that will achieve that goal. According to Raymond L. Gordon, there are eight key elements in any interview:[1]

Planning	Structuring
Interviewing Skills	Recording
Interviewing Techniques	Responses
Listening Skills	Post Interview

Planning the Interview

The PSIR writer must plan the interview before it actually begins. This makes the interview more effective and more efficient, with less wasted time, and reduces the risk of requiring an additional interview because information was missed. The probation officer must also be aware of the purpose of the interview and the objectives sought. Perhaps the most important aspect of preparation is to know the topic areas to be covered in the interview, and to have some structure to use in covering them.

A suggested interview schedule appears in Appendix B. This schedule was used to produce the PSIR on Franklin (Appendix A). Use of a standardized interview schedule such as that in Appendix B will facilitate taking organized notes for later review prior to writing the PSIR. Because the offender is likely to feel uncertain and vulnerable, the probation officer should be prepared for resistance or inhibitions on the offender's part and should be familiar with techniques to overcome these factors and facilitate communication.

Interviewing Skills

There are many skills which go into making a good interview. These can be grouped into six major categories: hearing, receiving, remembering, observing, evaluating, and regulating.[2]

Accurately *hearing* information is essential, and can be enhanced by sharpening listening skills. Just as important is *receiving* and recording of information. Much of the direction of the later investigation, as well as the content of the report, will be based on the hearing and recording the information from the offender. The human memory is limited, so the use of written notes is a good idea to aid in *remembering*.

What the offender says is important, but so are the offender's other behaviors. *Observing* body language and other visual clues can give the probation officer additional helpful information with which to assess the offender. Obvious physical signs of nervousness or hostility can serve as a cue to problems for the interviewer to confront to increase the effectiveness of the interview. Critically *evaluating* the information received is another key skill. The officer should be willing to accept a wide variety of sources and kinds of information.

A skill often overlooked in interviewing is *regulating* the offender's behavior in the interview. This is important because it establishes the authority and role of the probation officer, and helps keep the interview focused and on track. If the offender gains control of the interview by rambling or resisting, it can take much longer to complete, it may not elicit the necessary information and much relevant information may be concealed or distorted. This will lead to considerable frustration and anxiety for the probation officer.

Interviewing Techniques

Sequencing of the interview can make a difference in the offender's willingness to communicate. In general, the sequence should be: statement, question and, most importantly, the probe. The statement introduces the topic or subject, and thereby sets the direction of the dialogue. The question elicits the information from the subject. Probes are follow-up questions which seek to clarify and/or elaborate on the information obtained with the question. Probes are valuable because one question alone may not elicit the needed information, and several questions about the same topic can stimulate recall and help the flow of information. For example, the interviewer might introduce the topic with the statement, "Now I am going to talk to you about school" This would be followed by the question, "How far did you go in school?". Then a probe might be appropriate: "Why did you quit school?"

The interviewer guides the offender toward the objectives of each interview topic area through use of the probes. Probes are needed to obtain more exact information. Unlike interview topics, specific probes are not known in advance. They are unique to each interview, developed by the interviewer in response to the offender's answers, and are designed to elaborate on those answers.

Using probes, the interviewer develops a funnel sequence for questions. Each question narrows the focus of the interview, working toward specifics until the topic area is adequately covered.

The use of probes can also be a way of influencing the offender. By example and repetition, the offender can be steered toward giving relevant, candid, clear and complete responses. This helps to set the offender at ease with the investigation as well, since it soon becomes apparent that the PSIR writer is simply there to obtain the facts and present them to the court. The offender is encouraged to be straightforward, honest and forthright in answering.

The sequence of topics can also influence the interview. Starting the interview with more factual, less threatening information puts the offender at ease and helps to establish a degree of rapport for the interview. This approach increases the liklihood of obtaining reliable and accurate information on more sensitive topics. Sequencing of topics is illustrated by an interview schedule developed by the Wisconsin Bureau of Community Corrections. In the Client Management Classification (CMC) interview, the offense is the first topic covered followed by the prior record.[3] It is not until later that more sensitive subjects such as family and personal feelings are introduced. This gives the offender a chance to become comfortable with the PSIR writer before the tougher questions are posed.

The sequence of topics in the CMC interview is:

1. Current Offense
2. Prior Offenses
3. School and Vocational Adjustment
4. Family Attitudes
5. Interpersonal Relations
6. Personal Feelings
7. Plans and Problems

Another useful sequencing technique is to draw first on facts more easily recalled, such as recent employment, residence, etc., early in the interview to give the offender confidence.

Listening Skills

The interviewer must develop critical listening skills which help to determine whether the offender's responses are relevant, clear and unambiguous. It is not uncommon to encounter inconsistencies, contradictions and untruths. The probation officer must listen for these, in order to confront and resolve them when they occur. As Gordon has warned,

> The neophyte interviewer will often ask relevant questions and dutifully record the reply,...not realizing that the response is inadequate for the purposes of the interview.[4]

Listening skills are developed by focusing attention on the responses the offender is giving to the questions, including tone of voice and attitude. Is the answer evasive? Does the offender change his tone of voice or attitude while answering? Is the answer clear to the interviewer? This type of listening skill is often called "active listening", meaning that the interviewer participates in the question/answer process by asking clarifying questions and checking to make certain the answer is fully understood.

Structuring the Interview

One way in which interviewing approaches vary is the structure of the interview. Three levels can be identified.

The Questionnaire

The questionnaire is the most structured interview approach. All of the questions are carefully specified, and the offender merely has to read and answer the questions. A good questionnaire is self-sufficient, and can be mailed to the offender for completion. This amount of structure is useful in the PSIR process to obtain basic demographic and descriptive information about the offender before a more in-depth interview takes place. However, the questionnaire does not elicit information in a manner allowing probing and follow-up, and so is not useful for more sensitive and complex PSIR information.

The Interview Schedule

An interview schedule lists all the questions to be asked and specifies the wording, context and sequence of the questions. The interviewer is free to ask follow-up questions and clarify any answers given. The CMC interview described earlier is a good example of this method.

An interview schedule is useful when it is important to ask a series of specific questions. They make for more reliable assignment to classification systems for the purposes of treatment. Because specific questions are to be asked, the interview schedule allows for more reliable comparisons of offenders for use in sentencing guidelines systems.

The Interview Guide

The interview guide acts like a map for the interviewer, stating areas to be covered, but not specific questions to be asked. It provides a framework for recording the responses and keeping track of the interview progress. The guide allows the interviewer to decide how to accomplish the goals of the interview.

Interview guides leave the interviewer with latitude to adjust the nature of the interview to special circumstances of the offender. Whether the offender is resistant, especially cooperative, inconsistent or otherwise unusual, the probation officer can tailor the questions to fit the circumstances.

Use of a highly structured interview provides uniformity and consistency, ensuring that all topics are covered and nothing is forgotten. This approach is particularly useful for inexperienced interviewers or persons who do not conduct interviews on a regular basis.

Structured interviews are not as popular with experienced staff, who often do not feel the need for such detailed guidance. The experienced PSIR writer will often use an unstructured interview format, starting with a few basic questions to get into the interview. From that point, follow-up questions will flow from previous answers until all of the topic areas have been covered. This approach can be more time consuming, and it places a greater responsibility on the interviewer to cover everything.

A structured interview is useful in instances where more than the usual amount of tension or discomfort exists. This is often true with offenses which by their nature are difficult to talk about, such as child abuse, sexual abuse or extreme violence. These situations produce anxiety, and both parties may desire, even unconsciously, to finish the interview quickly or to focus away from certain items that are sensitive. A structured interview can keep the interview on target and produce a better PSIR.

Figure 6-1

Client's Name _____

ATTITUDES ABOUT OFFENSE

Could you tell me about the offense that got you in trouble?

1a.   How did you get involved in this offense?
1b.   How did you decide to commit the offense?

> **1.   Motivation for committing current offense**
> **(a) emotional motivation (e.g., anger, sex offense, etc.)**
> **(b) material (monetary) motivation**
> **(c) both emotional and material motivation**

2.   Could you tell me more about the circumstances that led up to the offense?

> **2.   Acceptance of responsibility for current offense**
> **(a) admits committing the offense and doesn't attempt excuses**
> **(b) admits committing the offense, but emphasizes excuses (e.g., drinking,**
>   **influenced by friends, family problems, etc.)**
> **(c) denies committing the offense**

3.   Looking back at your offense, what's your general feeling about it?

> **3.   Expression of guilt about** *current* **offense**
> **(a) expresses guilt feelings or spontaneous empathy toward victim**
> **(b) expresses superficial or no guilt**
> **(c) victimless crime**

Scoring Guide

1.   *A*   __*using drugs*
            __*assault (not for robbery)*
       B. __*prostitution*
            __*car theft (except for joyriding)*
       C. __*stealing primarily for peer acceptance*
            __*stealing from parents for revenge*
            __*man who won't pay alimony, primarily because he is angry with his ex-wife*

2.   *B.* __*"I would never have done it if I hadn't been drinking."*
            __*"My friends get me in trouble."*
       C. *Clients who deny committing any significant aspect of the offense are scored "C:.*
            __*client admits helping to jimmy car window but denies responsibility for removing valuables because*
            his friends removed them

3.   *A.* *Client must feel some personal shame and regret (not just verbalization to impress agent).*
       B. __*"I feel bad because now I have a record."*
            __*"People are disappointed in me." (Indicates some regret but not necessarily guilt.)*
            __*"I know it was wrong." (Emphasis on having done wrong, not on feeling bad because one has done wrong.)*
       C. __*drug usage*
            __*sexual activities between consenting adults*

Figure 6-1 *continued*

OFFENSE PATTERN

I'd like to talk to you about your prior offenses. Have you been in trouble before?
(Obtain a complete picture of client's offense style, including current offense, when scoring items 5-8.)

4a.   What prior offenses have you been convicted of?
4b.* Were you ever in trouble as a juvenile?

> 4. **Offense and severity**
>   (a) **no prior offenses (skip items 5, 6, 7 and 8)**
>   (b) **mainly misdemeanors**
>   (c) **no consistent pattern**
>   (d) **mainly felonies**

5a.   Have you ever been armed of hurt someone during these offenses?
5b.* Did you ever threaten anyone?

> 5. **Was client ever involved in offense where he(she) was armed, assaultive, or threatened injury to someone?**
>   (a) **yes**
>   (b) **no**

6a.   How did you decide to commit these offenses?
6b.   Did you plan these offenses? (Discuss offenses individually until a clear pattern emerges.)

> 6. **Offenses were** *generally*
>   (a) **planned**
>   (b) **no consistent pattern**
>   (c) **impulsive**

7.   Were you drinking or high on drugs when you committed your offenses?

> 7. **Percent of offenses committed while drinking or high**
>   (a) **never**
>   (b) **50% or less**
>   (c) **over 50%**

8.   Did you commit your offenses alone or with others?

> 8. **Offenses were** *generally* **committed**
>   (a) **alone**
>   (b) **no consistent pattern**
>   (c) **with accomplices**

Scoring Guide

4.   *Items 4, 5, 6, 7 and 8 should include juvenile offenses and serious traffic offenses (e.g., drunk driving, hit and run).*
      B.   *Should not be used if client has more than two serious felonies. (Use choice "C" or "D".)*
      D.   *Over 50% of client's convictions are felonies*

5-8. *Use current and prior offense factors to score 5 through 8.*

6.   A.   *__exhibitionist who drives around in a car looking for girls to expose himself to*
           __person who decides to commit an offense, then drinkjs to build courage
      C.   *__exhibitionist driving to wrok, suddenly saw a girl and pulled over and exposed himself*
           __person gets drunk and into bar fight

Structured interviews are also useful for special cases requiring information not contained in the routine PSIR. This is true for sophisticated financial and white collar crimes, frauds and embezzlement, computer crime and others.

Recording Information and Responses

Accurate recording of information is crucial to the interview process. Writing the PSIR ordinarily takes place some weeks after the initial interview. The wise PSIR writer takes sufficient notes to make the writing job easier.

Good recording is also important in selecting probing questions. As the notes are recorded, the interviewer should also make "probe" notes as to later follow-up questions. The less the interview is structured and the more complex the case, the greater the need for good probe notes. Probe notes should be brief, using key words, and where possible, the offender's own words. Then the interviewer can ask, "When you said '_____', what did you mean by that?"

In addition to these benefits, good recording has been shown to have a positive impact on the offender's perception of the PSIR process. Taking notes apparently shows the offender that the officer is genuinely interested in the offender and the case, and leads to increased cooperation.[5]

Responses To The Interview

The PSIR writer is likely to encounter many problems in the interview process, some of which are described below.

Resistance. Often the offender will resist all efforts by the PSIR writer to conduct the interview. When this occurs, it is important to remind the offender that the purpose of the PSIR is not to establish guilt, but to help the judge determine the sentence. There is information known only to the offender which could have a favorable impact on the sentence. Without cooperation in the interview, that information will remain unknown to the judge. It may be useful also to advise the offender that the PSIR will be completed with or without cooperation, as some courts have ruled that a PSIR must be completed despite offender refusal to cooperate.[6]

Lack of Knowledge or Recall. A common response to questions is 'I don't know' or 'I don't remember'. This is often a defense mechanism for painful, embarrassing or sensitive topics. When this happens, the interviewer should acknowledge that the topic is difficult to discuss. By showing concern and compassion, the interviewer may break through the resistance and enable the offender to discuss the topic. It may be that no amount of concern or compassion will work. In that instance, the probation officer should move on to another subject, and possibly return later to this area.

Refocusing the Question. An offender may turn a question to the interviewer by asking 'What do you think?'. This is a common way of avoiding a question. The probation officer should not be drawn into responding and instead should turn the question back to the offender, saying 'What I think is not as important as what you think'. It is important to rephrase the question in a sensitive manner, without castigating the offender or appearing secretive, but to be certain the offender answers the question.

Falsification. Some falsification will ordinarily occur in any PSIR interview. The job for the interviewer is to minimize falsehood. Three techniques for responding to falsehood are suggested by Gordon.[7]

First, if certain facts are known about the offender and the offense, this can be acknowledged at the outset of the interview. This encourages the offender not to lie about these areas. Second, the interviewer can ask leading questions which hint at what is known. This lets the offender know that falsehoods are likely to be detected. Because this approach is subtle, it is appropriate for more sensitive clients. Third, the interviewer can wait until rapport has been established, and then confront the offender about the accuracy of some answers. This last approach places the probation officers in an awkward situation if rapport is never established.

The Post-Interview

The final stage of the interview process is the post-interview. During the post-interview, the discussion is more informal, and the PSIR writer may ask for the offender's reactions to the interview and inquire about the process. This stage has several very important objectives. The PSIR writer can determine if the offender has been inhibited during the interview, and can thus evaluate the interview, both in terms of the techniques used and the quality of the information obtained. The probation officer also uses the post-interview to receive feedback on the effectiveness of interviewing techniques.

The post-interview can generate additional information. The informal nature of the interaction will sometimes produce significant and substantive information after the 'interview' has been concluded. This is known as "out the door" information because it is often obtained as one of the parties is leaving the interview site. Reluctant clients who decline to be formally interviewed will sometimes provide, willingly, important information during informal communication after the interview.

Building on the Interview

In many probation organizations, the probation officer conducting the PSIR will receive the offender for supervision should probation be the sentence. In these situations, the interview for the PSIR is the first step in the supervision process, and the probation officer has already begun to establish the supervision relationship. This is important because the first six to twelve months are the most crucial period in probation supervision.[8]

The Client Management Classification (CMC) system, described earlier, provides an illustration of how to build supervision strategies based on information obtained during the PSIR process. The CMC is an interview schedule used to gather information which is then interpreted and numerically "scored" to classify offenders into one of four supervision groups.[9] Because each supervision group is associated with a special set of supervision strategies, the probation officer can produce a good supervision plan and begin the supervision process quickly, not having to waste valuable time in trial and error. Although it was not originally developed for the PSIR process, the CMC interview elicits much of the same information one would use in assembling the personal and social history sections of the PSIR. The CMC interview is used as the structured interview for the PSIR in several agencies.

Linking supervision methods to a high quality structure such as the CMC has been shown to lead to better initial performance by probationers, particularly with regard to probationer reporting.[10] This may be attributed to the improved quality of interaction in a structured interview which focuses on the offender's personal history, feelings and concerns.

Verification and Reliability of Information

Whatever information is finally contained in the PSIR will be regarded as accurate by the court and most other readers. A major part of the PSIR writer's job is checking and verifying information given by the offender in the interview to be sure that the court is not misled. This is not always an easy task, but is an essential one if the integrity of the PSIR is to be maintained.

When information is verified as accurate, it can be presented in the PSIR as stated by the offender. However, when information given by the offender is found to be at odds with another source, the conflict needs to be re-solved. If time does not allow for resolution, or if the offender fails to change the original statements, the conflicting information should be recorded in the PSIR for the judge to consider.

Oftentimes, the information is not verifiable, owing to factors beyond the PSIR writer's control. For example, it may be impossible to verify high school records from a small town in another state. If after reasonable efforts to verify information the PSIR writer is unable to do so, a decision must be made as to the importance of the information. If the information is not criti-cal to the investigation, it may be deleted. If the information is a key part of the report, it must be included *but always identified* as "unverified". The court will then be able to decide to postpone sentencing to allow for verification, or to proceed with sentencing.

In an attempt to streamline the PSIR and at the same time keep the judge apprised of the status of the PSIR information, the Middlesex County (New Jersey) Probation Department has developed a very simple coding scheme. In the margin, alongside key items of information, a single letter code appears. (V) signifies verified information, (A) is awaiting verification and (U) is unverified information.

With this system, PSIR text need not be consumed detailing verification efforts and the results, yet the sentencing judge is aware of the accuracy of the information. If this approach is used, the sentencing judge(s) must ap-prove and the documentation must be available in the PSIR file. This way, when an attorney challenges the verification, the PSIR writer will be able to respond.

The reliability of self-reported information from criminal offenders is frequently called into question. Conventional wisdom might have it that one cannot trust an offender, who would say anything to manipulate a sentence. Recent research has cast doubt on this wisdom. A follow-up study of Wis-consin probationers found that they reported more arrests than the official records showed.[11] A RAND Corporation study of 49 habitual offenders found that the offenders accurately reported 63% of their arrests, 74% of their convictions and 88% of their convictions resulting in incarceration. The offenders also reported significantly more delinquency activity as juveniles than the official records showed.[12] Another RAND study of 2200 jail and prison inmates showed that 75% of the inmates were better than 85% accu-rate in their accounting of their criminal careers.[13] Overall, research shows that offenders provide information that is largely accurate and complete.[14] This does not mean that verification is unimportant, since a sizeable portion of the answers by offenders were inaccurate. The interview can, however, provide an excellent factual basis for the verification process.

Confidentiality

The PSIR is generally considered a confidential court document. The legal aspects of confidentiality are discussed in detail in Chapter 14. For the purposes of the interview, the offender has no rights of confidentiality in the PSIR process and Miranda warnings do not apply. Should an offender wish to withhold information, it is a choice based on personal preference, no legal right or constitutional protection exists.

In interviewing victims, witnesses and others for the PSIR, the probation officer may find that some desire confidentiality as part of their willingness to be interviewed. The PSIR writer must then assess the value of the information to the PSIR. If it is important, the PSIR writer may include it as a confidential memorandum to the court which is not disclosed to the defendant or to the attorneys, so long as the reasons for non-disclosure are given to the attorneys.

Confidentiality is a difficult area, requiring the balancing of strong competing interests which may include the safety of a person interviewed. When a confidentiality problem arises, the probation officer should *always* seek the guidance of a supervisor before proceeding.

Summary

In this chapter, we have reviewed the role of the initial interview in developing the PSIR. Eight key elements of interviewing were presented and discussed. Special problems facing the PSIR writer in interviewing were also described. The need for verification of interview information was confirmed, and the problem of confidentiality in interviews was presented.

Notes

[1] Raymond L. Gordon, *Interviewing: Strategy, Techniques and Tactics*. (Homewood, Ill.: Dorsey Press), 1975.

[2] *Ibid.*, pp. 467-469.

[3] Kenneth Lerner, Gary Arling and Christopher Baird. *Client Management Classification Strategies for Case Supervision*. (Madison, WI: National Council on Crime and Delinquency), 1986. p.4.

[4] Gordon, *Interviewing*.

[5] Gary Arling, Remarks made in CMC training session, March 22, 1982, Columbus, Ohio.

[6] *State v. Richardson*, 117 N.J. Super. 153 (1971).

[7] Gordon, *Interviewing*, p. 456.

[8] Probation Administrative Management System. *Adult Probation in New Jersey*. (Trenton, NJ: Administrative Office of the Courts), 1980, pp. 19-22.

[9] *The Client Management Classification System*. (Washington, DC: National Institute of Corrections), mimeo, n.d., 1980.

[10] Op cit. note 5.

[11] *Ibid*.

[12] Joan Petersilia, Peter Greenwood and Marvin Lavin. *Criminal Careers of Habitual Felons*. (Washington, DC: National Institute of Law Enforcement and Criminal Justice), 1978. pp. 156-161.

[13] Jan M. Chaiken and Marcia R. Chaiken. *Varieties of Criminal Behavior*. (Santa Monica, CA: RAND), 1981.

[14] *Ibid*. pp. 223-251; Kent Marquis with Patricia Ebner. *Quality of Prisoner Self Reports: Arrest and Conviction Response Errors*. (Santa Monica, CA: RAND Corporation), 1981.

GROUP EXERCISE

From a recent newspaper or a newsmagazine story, select a crime report to be read by four members of the class. In three separate interviews the member playing the role of the probation officer conducts interviews with members designated as the defendant, the victim and the arresting officer. Each should have a good imagination and use the news account as only bare bones of a more elaborate version. Point: the probation officer encounters three quite different perspectives of the same incident.

DISCUSSION QUESTIONS

1. Using a different crime story (this could be a current news source or a historical incident such as Jack the Ripper, Charles Manson, Watergate persons or Claus von Beulow) write three versions of the alleged offense as viewed by the defendant, the investigating police officer and the victim or a witness.

2. What are some of the worst mistakes a PSIR writer can make in interviewing? How can these mistakes be avoided?

Part II

The Contents of the PSIR

The production of the manuscript for the PSIR is creative writing of a very specialized kind. The indispensable ingredient is accuracy, bolstered by an informed inquisitiveness and a sensitivity to the interests of all the parties: judge, defendant, victim and society. No PSIR is likely to rise to the level of literature, but what is produced should be lucid and should make palatable reading.

There is no universally accepted format for the PSIR, and the specific requirements of the PSIR vary from jurisdiction to jurisdiction. In Chapters 7-13, the major areas of any PSIR are covered, and guidelines for obtaining, recording and reporting the information are presented. Any PSIR will include most of the informational areas covered in these chapters, and no important aspect of the offender's crime, criminal history or current situation is left out.

In each of the following chapters, the content area of the PSIR is presented. This is followed by a discussion of important problems and issues in developing and reporting the information. Illustrations are also provided in support of the discussion.

After reading each of the sections, the student may wish to turn to Appendix A to read that section in Mack Ray's report on John Franklin. An interesting exercise is to assess Probation Officer Ray's work critically, in light of the material covered in that chapter. Why would Mr. Ray present the information as he has? What has been left out of the PSIR? Why? What should have been deleted from the PSIR? Why? This critical assessment will help to underscore that the PSIR process is a skill for which several approaches might be appropriate.

Chapter 7
Criminal History

Often the most important information, and nearly always the best place to begin the investigation process, is the offender's criminal history. After all, it is the offender's criminal behavior that has created the need for the PSIR in the first place. The criminal history includes an assessment of both the current offense and the prior criminal record. The evaluation of the current offense helps the judge to determine the seriousness of the crime or crimes for which the offender is being sentenced. The prior record provides evidence about the context of the current offense, whether criminality is a life pattern for the offender or whether the crime itself is an atypical incident. This gives the judge an initial idea of the offender's risk to the community.

Current Offense

It may seem that the crime for which the offender is being sentenced is very obvious, but frequently there are several versions of the offense, and the statutory offense does not describe fully the circumstances of the crime. Therefore, the PSIR will normally include an official version on the offense, the offender's version and the victim's version. Each of these viewpoints helps to paint an accurate picture of the crime and its true seriousness.

Official Version

The official version of the offense may be handled in either of two manners. The first is a literal repetition of what is in the information filed by the State, which would read as follows:

> On or about the twelfth day of October, 1987, in Jefferson County, State of Washington, John N. Jackson did knowingly operate a motor vehicle upon a public highway, to wit: C.R. 300S, East of C.R. 475W, while in a state of intoxication.

Some jurisdictions would prefer that the description of the offense come from the police reports, which might read as follows:

> At 11:40 pm. this officer followed the subject for about 2 miles on Highway 83, during which time he failed to stop at two red blinkers

and was driving 55 in a 35 mile zone. When he saw me following, he turned quickly into a side street and I followed with my red light on. He then pulled into a driveway and stopped. When he got out of the car he was unsteady on his feet and failed a field sobriety test. I called for back-up and Officer Calhoun backed his car out of the drive, parked it on the street and we took the subject to the station, where he tested .18% on the breathalyzer.

Either version is likely to be somewhat jargonistic, but the police version often provides more information, sometimes quite graphically.

Victim's Version

Depending upon the relationship the probation officer has to the case, the victim's version should be based on an interview with the victim, if possible. If not, there usually is a deposition, testimony of the victim's statement in the file, which can be used if the victim cannot be reached in person. In many jurisdictions the opinion of the victim as to what the penalty ought to be is considered relevant and the judge wishes to review this opinion as a part of the victim's statement. An illustration follows:

He had his buddy talk to me in the shop about some archery equipment while he sneaked in the back door of my apartment and got the coins out of my dresser. I never should have told him that I had the collection, but I guess it's too late for that now. I had saved them for years and some of them had the old silver content. I learned my lesson not to tell anybody any of my business.

At the time of the police investigation, the victim indicated that there were seventeen old two-dollar bills, about fifty silver quarters and three silver dollars. The face value of this money is forty-nine dollars and fifty cents, but the Coin Mart estimates the market value at three hundred nine dollars, due to the heavy silver content of the coins and the age of the two-dollar bills.

Offender's Version

It is preferable to get the statement directly from the offender himself at the time of the interview because his perception has probably metamorphosed somewhat as a result of conversations and thoughts the offender has had since the arrest. This gives the judge an insight into present attitudes toward the crime. However, there may also be something of value in the statement made to the police at the time of the arrest; it is probably more accurately descriptive of what actually happened. If for any reason the offender is not able or willing to give his version during the interview, the police report may be used but the source should be identified.

> Well, this old guy had bugged me before about going to his room to see his coin collection. I knew that wasn't what he wanted. He wanted me to go to his room to get into my pants. The guy's gay. So when he started playing up to Frankie, I thought I'd just go up and see if he had any coins there at all. I didn't have in mind to steal anything, just look. But when I saw all that, I thought he had so many that he wouldn't miss a few of them, so I put some in my pocket. It wasn't much and he can afford it.

Seriousness of the Offense

If the offense is a violent one, it will help the judge understand the meaning if the setting is described. For battery, the appropriate sentence will be quite different if the defendant was being harassed by the victim, if it was a malicious act or if it is a unique incident unlikely ever to recur. It is wise to avoid the use of the word "aggravation" in this section because it has a specific legal meaning that could lead to misunderstanding of what you are saying.

> I still don't understand why he done it. When I saw him stopped on the side of the road, I stopped to see if he needed any help and when I got out of my car and walked back toward him, he just flew at me and knocked me down. He was a madman. I think if he had had a knife he would have killed me. He said I had been racing him, but that was not true. I don't know whether he thought I was somebody else or just what, but he almost killed me.

The illustrations show that it is often useful to quote the interview sources as closely as possible in describing the offense. This provides a more complete understanding of the offense and the feelings that exist about it.

Figure 7-1: Illustration of a Criminal History

Date	Offense	Jurisdiction	Disposition
09-15-58	Runaway	Washington Co.	Family
10-01-58	Runaway	Washington Co.	Family
01-29-59	Truancy	Washington Co.	Informal Probation
05-06-59	Incorrigibility	Washington Co.	Probation
12-12-59	Incorrigibility	Washington Co.	7 days Juv. Ctr.
03-10-60	Shoplifting	Washington Co.	Probation 6 mos.
11-11-61	Alcohol/Juvenile	Jefferson Co.	Probation 6 mos.
05-03-62	Attempted Arson	Washington Co.	Probation 1 year
06-03-62	Car Theft	Jefferson Co.	Boys' School 1 year

_____18th Birthday 05-07-63_____

Date	Offense	Jurisdiction	Disposition
08-08-63	Car Theft	Wash. Co. (Cr-63-147)	Probation 2 yrs.
10-06-63	Driving/Influence	Madison Co.	$25 fine
01-14-64	Att. Armed Robbery	Paine Co.(C 64-5)	2 yrs. + $200
05-09-66	Public Intoxication	Washington Co.	Nolle Pros.
03-01-67	Break/Enter	Washington Co.	Nolle Pros.
04-11-68	Armed Robbery	Paine Co. (C 68-93)	6 yrs. (3 susp.)
01-01-70	Public Intoxication	Washington Co.	?
07-14-71	Battery/Law Enforcement	Paine Co.(C-71-17)	4 years
12-03-73	Battery/Law Enforcement	Paine Co. (C73-37)	20 years
12-03-73	Public Intoxication	Washington Co.	30 days
03-19-84	Possession Cocaine	Jeff. Co. (CF 8431)	1 year
08-03-85	Conspiracy/Felony	Franklin Co. (CC 8529)	Dismissed
11-17-86	Armed Robbery	Franklin Co.	Instant case
03-08-87	Battery	Franklin Co.	Pending

Prior Record

Sources of Information

As the PSIR writer becomes more familiar with a case, it becomes clear where the best sources of information are about the case. In every case there is a need to check the records office of the local police, the county sheriff and the state criminal history system. In the initial interview, the PSIR writer must be aware of any indication that the offender has been in trouble in another locality within the state or in another state. In many cases, the check will turn up no record, but sometimes the information from other jurisdictions will provide a completely new view of the offender. A check of police contacts within the state may often be done directly, but interstate information probably will have to be sought through the sheriff's office, most of whom participate in the National Crime Information Center (NCIC) communications network which keeps FBI records on all arrests and convictions.

Figure 7-1 is a listing of a long criminal history "rap" sheet. Note that the record includes both juvenile and adult records. In this case, all offenses have been committed in the same state, but with such a long record, a careful check of NCIC files would likely show other criminal activity.

Verification

It would be ideal if every piece of information entered in the PSIR would be independently verified. Often criminal history data must be used without independent verification. If there is a reasonable doubt about the veracity, an item should either be excluded or cited with a notation that it is unconfirmed.

The defendant reports that he was once arrested for shoplifting in West Palm Beach, FL, but this has not been verified.

Jefferson County Police Department files show an arrest for child molesting on August 16, 1980, but the defendant asserts that he has never had an arrest for child molesting, although he does report that he was living in Jefferson County at that time. Jefferson County Police have no information other than the simple entry on his arrest card.

Schmidt was asked about the report that he had a record in Oklahoma. He denied that he had ever been in Oklahoma. However, the FBI reports a conviction for bank robbery in Tulsa on January 7, 1984, and the Tulsa Police Department confirms that it was this defendant by a match of date of birth and social security number.

In most cases the record of arrests is admissible and helps the judge form an opinion about the offender's criminal propensity. In some settings only convictions are permitted in the PSIR, however, because arrests without convictions are deemed irrelevant. Even a report of previous convictions should be verified, if possible. A photo copy of the docket sheet or the sentencing document gives convincing proof that the person was convicted of a felony. In many states, verification is a critical issue because a prior felony conviction means a mandatory prison term or consecutive sentences for multiple felonies.

The Juvenile Record

The juvenile record is not always admissible because it is considered confidential in some jurisdictions. If it is permissible in the PSIR, it is often difficult to obtain, especially where the juvenile court expunges records. Whatever evidence is available should be included, however, and often the offender will be a good source.

If the juvenile record is extensive, it is a good idea to summarize it in a separate paragraph:

At the age of thirteen, the defendant had his first arrest, for Runaway. Three months later he was picked up for shoplifting and placed on probation. While still on probation he was arrested for shoplifting and while awaiting the hearing, escaped from the juvenile detention center. At that time he was sent to Ohio Boys School for two years. When released he was placed in a state-run group home, from which he was released at the age of seventeen. Two months after his 18th birthday he was arrested for auto banditry and given a suspended sentence and two years of probation. On that occasion he was also booked for public intoxication and driving while intoxicated. After being on probation for fifteen months, he was arrested on the present charge.

Jail Time

If there is any possibility that the judge will give the defendant credit for the time spent in jail on the current charge, that information should be calculated in the PSIR. Generally speaking, the time that applies on this offense starts with the date on which the charges were read to the defendant and includes any jail time subsequent to that, including time waiting for sentencing. The statement might read like this:

> Jones was detained on a warrantless arrest on October 3, 1986, and has remained in custody. On March 4, 1987, the date set for sentencing, she will have accumulated a total of one hundred fifty-two days of jail time.

The Importance of Criminal Information

Under proper conditions, it is possible to predict accurately where a missile will land if one has the details of the early trajectory pattern. In the same way, but with far less accuracy, it is possible to predict where a criminal career will lead if one knows the early behavior pattern. With missiles and with people, unanticipated events can interrupt the course, but without the unanticipated event, predictions are reasonably accurate.

That is why the criminal history of an offender is so integral a part of the PSIR. If the defendant characteristically responds to frustration with violence, it is safe to predict that this pattern of behavior will continue. True, he may develop a more socially acceptable pattern of response, but this would be the exception, and in the absence of contrary evidence, the court does not make a leap of faith that it will occur.

The criminal history record demonstrates, in unambiguous terms, the manner in which the offender responds to the life situations with which he is faced. Everyone has been in a situation where it appeared safe to shoplift a desired item. Some resist the temptation. Others do not. The latter have it on their records. The court needs to know what the offender does when faced with a tempting situation; what has happened in the past is likely to happen in the future, as well. To forestall future shoplifting, the judge is inclined to impose a sentence calculated to discourage future shoplifting. The same applies to other criminal patterns.

Summary

People tend to be creatures of habit. The way one has responded to life situations in the past is likely to be the way one will respond in the future unless something induces a new pattern of behavior. If a sentence is formulated in the hope of breaking the cycle, of changing the reaction pattern, it is important that the court know how the offender has responded in the past. The criminal history, including juvenile years, provides a key insight into the characteristic way the defendant reacts to situations that can lead to criminal behavior.

GROUP EXERCISE

Two opposite positions can be taken. (a) It is unjust to bring up the past of an accused person because he/she may have turned their life around and straightened up, and if you give them a bad name, the person will never be able to recover. (b) The future is a projection of the past, and research has shown that persons who offended in the past are more likely to offend in the the future than those who have no police record at all. Evaluate these two policies.

DISCUSSION QUESTIONS

1.   As a judge, how would you be inclined to deal with the alleged offender who was first arrested at thirteen as a runaway (the first case quoted in this chapter)?

2.   In many jurisdictions it is customary to allow "jailtime" by giving credit on the prison sentence for time spent in jail prior to sentencing. Under what circumstances would you as judge decline to give credit?

3.   Some jurisdictions present in the PSIR show the record of all arrests, but others include only convictions. What are the advantages and disadvantages to each approach?

Chapter 8
Family History

Each of us is a product of a very complex environment; at any given time we live at the focal point of millions of converging influences. It is impossible to understand any person apart from the unique sociogenic setting in which that individual exists. One of the most important clusters of influences is the parental family.

If the client's father is a professional wrestler and the mother is a bartender, one would assume the home setting and family values to be different from that of a client whose father is an attorney and mother a music teacher. Compare either of those homes with that of a client reared in a single-parent home, with no male figure present. This is not to suggest that one setting is necessarily better, but to argue that the personal experiences carried by the clients raised in these settings would be different.

Roles are learned by observing. A boy learns how to be a man by observing males he knows, and the closest one is normally the father. The boy develops social expectancies of how a woman is supposed to behave by observing the females he knows, the closest one normally being his mother. If he marries, in the normal course of events he will perform his masculine role much as his father did, and he will expect his wife to perform her feminine roles much as his mother did. A woman is shaped by her family environment in precisely the same way, and she will recreate her mother's role and will expect her husband to perform the male role as her father did.

Many young adults feel that their parents' lifestyles are not attractive, and seek to live differently. Even then, they are creatures of their upbringing, as they try to shape lives that are a mirror-image contrast to what they saw in their parents. This has implications for the PSIR.

Much as stormy marriages occur when the partners do not agree on appropriate male and female roles, stormy lifestyles occur when young adults emulate the socially maladapted roles of parental models, or rebel against "normal" social roles. This is why it is necessary to know something about the parental home if one is to understand a client.

Parents

Relevant characteristics of parents are their education, health, disciplinary patterns, and other personal traits. Compare the social heritage of the following two clients who are being sentenced for child abuse.

Client 1.

According to the defendant, the parents were divorced when the defendant was two years old and both remarried immediately. Visitation was regarded by the father not as a right but as a duty, and the son came to dread the first weekend of each month, summer vacation and Christmas. He was made to feel an intruder in his father's house and was extremely alienated from his stepmother. When he was twelve years old his father agreed to pay for continuous summer camps, which the son accepted eagerly not because he wanted the camps quite as much as he did not want to spend the summer in misery with his father and stepmother. To pour salt in the wound, his mother frequently pointed out what his father was doing to him.

Client 2.

The defendant reports that when he was a pre-schooler, his father was killed in an industrial accident. There was an adequate financial settlement so that the mother was not forced to work outside the home to support the family, but she felt overwhelmed by the responsibilities of rearing three fatherless children, and she bought a house next door to the defendant's paternal grandparents. They maintained a close relationship with their grandchildren and the grandfather especially put extra effort in serving as a male role model for the children. He took them on outings, dressed as Santa for Christmas, attended school plays and, after he retired, spent much free time in their home.

Any attempt to rehabilitate these two persons must take into account the perceptions they have of male roles. It is not the primary task of the PSIR to diagnose or to prescribe treatment, but it is appropriate for the PSIR to assess the prospects of rehabilitation so that the sentence can be appropriate. The judge needs to know the characteristics of the client's upbringing. The first client is more clearly in need of psychiatric treatment for lingering problems in reaction to his family background than the second (who may have problems in areas other than family, however).

Siblings

Another important part of parental-home influences is the relationship with siblings. An only child often has quite different childhood experiences from a person reared in a family of five brothers and sisters. The nature of the relationships with siblings can be critical.

Sibling factors to be examined include their ages, educational attainments, criminal history and compatibility. The offender's place in the birth order is also important. The following is a rather usual account.

The defendant has three brothers and one sister, of which he is the youngest.

George, 32
Toni, 30 (Mrs. Frank Jones)
Randy, 27
Arthur, 26
Peter, 23

The defendant reports that siblings' relationships have always been compatible, allowing for customary rivalries. The sister and the oldest brother are college graduates but the younger brother dropped out of high school early. Randy had a serious juvenile record and completed his G.E.D. in State Prison (serving time for auto banditry).

There is some function to be served by including the names of siblings; professionals within the system may be helped to know that a sibling is involved institutionally. In the above example, the Classification Committee would avoid assigning the defendant to a penal facility where his brother, Randy, is serving his sentence.

Family Stability and Other Factors

Both geographical and social stability are important concepts because they reveal influences that may have had significant consequences. A child whose family moved twice every year might be exposed to insecure feelings due to frequently interrupted peer relationships or, on the other hand, might have developed skills in meeting strangers easily. The school experience, however, is likely to have been disastrous. Being uprooted from a play group may or may not exact a psychosocial price, but being wrested from a familiar teacher and from a successful classroom adjustment is almost universally at high social cost.

There are other forms of instability, as well. Family arrangements are among these. A father who comes and goes unpredictably creates problems for the other family members each time he leaves and each time he reappears. After he has left, the family scurries to reorganize itself to equilibrium without him. This involves not only financial considerations, but such relationships as discipline, supper hour, bedroom arrangements, explanations to friends, and transportation to school activities. After a while, the family has recast all of these procedures and reaches a satisfactory stasis. When he reappears, turmoil is created, all established understandings are placed in question, and new arrangements must be negotiated. In a family where the rules and roles are this unstable, the influence on the children can be serious.

Economic instability also can be permanently harmful. A family dependent upon spasmodic income sources may inculcate feelings of distrust of money or, on the other hand, overly emphasize the importance of money.

Instability in parental figures may take its toll. A child reared in a family in which the mother has a series of paramours with no stable father figure may have trouble engaging in fully responsible marital relationships. A child reared by grandparents may encounter serious inter-generational stress. A family tragedy such as the suicide of a sibling can have an indelible effect on survivors. There is no limit to the catalogue of situations in which unstable family relationships create lasting problems for people. This can be seen in the following selection from a presentence report.

> Gonzales came into the community when he was five years old. His mother and father were migrant field laborers, but they fell out of the migrant stream and stayed when the others moved on in the fall of 1969. The father worked in maintenance at a local hotel for three years, then was laid off and has not been seen since. A year later the mother took in a new companion and the defendant names three others who were shadowy male figures moving through his world at various times. His mother continued to work as housemaid at the hotel, and the family occupied the same house as long as he lived at home. He attended only one elementary school, one junior high school and one high school, but he was in a highly transient neighborhood and says that he had few neighborhood playmates who stayed more than two years.

In some instances there will be other factors that are tangentially related to the family setting. The nature of the family livelihood (e.g., father is a retailer who works evenings and weekends), the nature of the neighborhood (e.g., a military base) or an inordinately protective mother (e.g., she never allowed him to face his own mistakes) may help explain a confused adult.

Characterizing Family History

By and large, there is more insight into human behavior to be gained from studying the parental home than from any other aspect of background. It is in the crucible of family experiences that human personality is formulated. A presentence investigation is not always expected to identify the family area as the most lucid explanation of the defendant's past behavior and future potential, but in many instances, it will.

Care must be taken so that what appears to be a defective childhood home is not made into a charter for irresponsible adulthood. Knowing that the defendant saw her mother shoot her father in a jealous rage may help the court understand why she broke under stress and shot her own unfaithful companion, but the court cannot ignore the fact that she is an adult and the law forbids shooting others, even when the history of such behavior makes it understandable in context.

There are times when the family history may be seen by the court as a mitigating circumstance, which may reduce the term to be served. Most state statutes spell out what the court is permitted to view as mitigating, but in many states the language is sufficiently vague that the court has considerable leeway. The following recommendation was made in a case of escape in which the defendant's wife was having a difficult pregnancy, had previously had two miscarriages, had not been able to visit him for two months because of her condition, and did not write because both are semi-literate.

It is recommended that the court impose the minimum sentence, based upon mitigating circumstances:

(a) The defendant had a spotless record during incarceration prior to his walking away from his farm-work assignment;

(b) He was under unusual emotional pressures imposed by the failure of his wife to visit or write and his awareness that she had had two previous problem pregnancies;

(c) The defendant turned himself in the next day, after seeing his wife and reassuring himself that she was getting adequate medical attention;

(d)   Such intense devotion to family responsibilities seems to presage a good adjustment to the streets after completion of his sentence;

(e) Repetition of the circumstances is not likely to recur.

Summary

Just as the composition of the soil is of vital importance in determining the healthiness of the tree that emerges from it, the family likewise performs much the nutritive function. This is not deterministic (note the "good" families from which scoundrels have come, the "bad" families from which saints have come, and the families that have produced both types among siblings) but there is unmistakably a tendency for healthy families to produce healthy offspring, and for deficient families to produce socially maladjusted persons. For the judge to understand what makes the defendant tick, it is important to know the milieu in which early influences took root.

The basic assumption in writing a PSIR is that good homes produce good people and bad homes produce bad people, but this is not where the PSIR stops. If the home and its product are not harmonious, an explanation should be sought. The fact that the defendant appears before the court is in itself proof that something went wrong with the socializing process. It may not have been the family at fault. There may have been a neighborhood gang, a teenage broken heart, an inept teacher, a meddlesome grandparent, or an unreasonable pastor. The suggested interview schedule contains the question, "Who has had more influence on you than anyone else – for good or for evil?" The response to this question is usually rather unimaginative: mother or dad. However, on occasion a rich insight emerges in which the defendant reveals the etiology of the criminal career. When there is especially great mystery, perhaps a special appeal to the defendant will elicit inspired introspection.

GROUP EXERCISE

Three members of the class discuss their ideas of what the mother-father relationship is characteristically. One speaks as an only child in a suburban family in which the father is an attorney and the mother a political science teacher in high school. Another member plays the role of the fifth child in a family of seven children in which the father has spent most of his life in and out of jail for petty offenses and the mother has supported the family as a waitress. The third member comes from a family in which there were two children, no father and the mother tended to have short-term liaisons with live-in boyfriends.

DISCUSSION QUESTIONS

1. In your own life, what influence on your attitudes has occurred because of your sibling (or lack of) relationships? How would you be different had you had no siblings (or, if an only child, had had siblings)?

2. Can you trace patterns of interaction in your parental home that reflect the homes in which your parents grew up? How would your upbringing be different if theirs had been different?

3. Comment: You can't blame Lottie too much for her frequent shoplifting because her mother taught her how to do it and she grew up thinking everybody shoplifts.

4. If you were assigned the supervision on probation of the escapee who left the state farm because his wife was pregnant and could not visit or write, what special efforts would you make to lead him through a helpful probation experience?

Chapter 9
Social History

If a technical term may be used out of technical context, it would be true to say that everyone is a bit insane; we differ only in degree. All people have at least a pinch of paranoia, all are at times slightly schizoid, and all fight to keep under control manic/depressive impulses.

The degree to which people differ determines where they fall on the line by which society distinguishes acceptable from unacceptable conduct. Normality is not objectively defined; it is subjectively defined, and the definition varies from group to group and setting to setting.

Behavior appropriate on the beach would be bizarre in a church. A tantrum acceptable in a child is not acceptable in an adult. Women are expected to cry, but not men. What makes one "normal" is sensing the socially appropriate form of behavior for a given setting, and avoiding the socially inappropriate.

If one is a guest at a wedding reception, one is expected to take food from the food displayed. This is not expected at the supermarket, and to do so may lead to criminal charges. Some court cases revolve around the issue of whether or not the act committed by the accused was appropriate. As Oliver Wendell Holmes said, to yell "Fire!" in a crowded theatre cannot be defended as freedom of speech.

So mental health involves more than staying out of a mental institution. A "normal" person is one who understands, accepts and practices the generally approved norms of society. That is what makes him or her "normal."

A commonly ignored dimension of this, however, is the incontestable fact that nobody participates in the total, general culture; instead, people identify with only a segment of it. In that sense, all are minority people. Even the stereotypical WASP (White Anglo-Saxon Protestant) is not totally "American." He or she is also a Southerner or Northerner, teenager or senior citizen, literate or illiterate, conservative or liberal, professional or laborer, and so *ad infinitum*.

Mental/Emotional History

As is true for everyone, the offender has a mental history that needs to be placed into its context. If psychological data from school or clinic records are available, they should be used in the PSIR. It is relevant for the judge to know that at age 12 the client had an IQ score of 120. It may be even more helpful to know that it was 80.

Finding those records is not easy. In many cases the information proves unimportant, but in those cases where a person's mental/emotional history is pivotal, the client is usually able to suggest a source. School records are normal sources, but the client may recall a psychiatric report or a clinic that would also have information.

It is advisable for the client to sign a waiver to release to the court any and all records regarding physical or mental health. Many social service agencies will not divulge this information without a waiver, and sometimes they must be persuaded to do so even with a waiver. If the latter, sometimes it helps to suggest that the information may be so important that it could be necessary to subpoena the head of the agency to appear at the sentencing with the records to testify as to their content. No busy executive wants to sit in a courtroom for a few hours waiting to be called to testify. You probably will get the records you request. (See release form in Appendix C.)

This type of information is important in those cases where the court has need to know how to deal with an offender whose mental/emotional background is unusual. Often this will become apparent from a psychiatric examination that was conducted, and should be used in the PSIR (See Chapter 11).

The PSIR writer should bear in mind that the defendant probably will be reading the document, so any information that should be shielded from the offender must be cautiously phrased. If his wife revealed some family secrets but fears reprisal if he knew that she had done so, her anonymity should be guarded:

> One of the persons interviewed for this report knew the defendant in high school and reported that he had attempted suicide on at least two occasions following failure to make the varsity team. These reportedly occurred in his sophomore and senior years.

Psychiatric opinions written for professional consumption may need to be rephrased (for instance, the word "incurable" ought never be quoted so the client might read it).

Some crimes by their nature imply the need of psychiatric assessment. Arson often is psycho-sexually motivated. Child abuse frequently is socially inherited, so the early childhood of the abuser is important. Sexual assaults may have deep psychological basis, for they are usually much more power-motivated than sexual. The chronic petty thief may be exhibiting compulsive behavior rather than instrumental poverty-stricken reactions. Nearly any crime will have some roots in early or late mental problems and the PSIR writer needs to be alert to cues of this during the preparation of the PSIR. The following excerpt illustrates this:

> The defendant was extradited from Kentucky for prosecution in this case. He had resisted the marriage of his twin brother ever since the engagement. The afternoon before the evening wedding he and his brother had argued the point and they parted with angry words. The defendant hot-wired a neighbor's car, drove it until he ran out of gas, and three days later was caught siphoning fuel from a car in a used car lot. He could not recall the circumstances by which he got there, how he got the car or anything about his argument with his brother.

> Under questioning, he recalled other occasions in which he had had similar "black-out" experiences. An interview with his fifth-grade teacher revealed that on several occasions he seemed to be "absent" while sitting in class, and he had mood changes not related to observable causes. She suspected epilepsy, but upon talking to the mother ran into strong resistance, so she did not feel free to explore further although she did discuss it with the school nurse (who is no longer available). He never had a *grand mal* seizure in class.

> It is not the proper function of this investigation to diagnose psychiatric problems, but it is suggested that the Kentucky episode has overtones of the classic *fugue* form of epileptic seizure. Regardless of the sentence, professional notice should be taken of this possibility, and appropriate testing provided.

In cases where the offender's mental/emotional separation is particularly crucial, the court may wish to get psychiatric evaluation before sentencing. This often requires a waiver by the offender so as not to delay sentencing beyond the statutory time limit, but usually this is given willingly. In most states the Department of Mental Health or the Department of Correction is able to prepare such an evaluation.

Military History

It is important to know the defendant's military history, if there is one, for two reasons. First, the reason for enlistment, progress in rank, job assignment, location, nature of discharge, disciplinary action and awards all reveal something about the person. Second, if there is a military history of criminal activity, it is ordinarily a part of the service record, especially if it is a felony offense. In this case, a military felony conviction might constitute a previous felony for sentencing purposes under mandatory provisions. It should be noted that some jurisdictions would not regard it as such however. Practices vary.

In practical terms, most PSIR writers must be satisfied with the offender's version of what happened during military service without formal confirmation. Validation of the reports frequently take a longer time than is available, so unless the interview suggests otherwise, the PSIR writer probably will not seek verification. If it appears that the defendant is not fully disclosing or that there was a serious military violation, written confirmation from military records will help the judge to consider whether this is a logical part of the record.

Written confirmation of a military record can be requested by calling the central record bureau in St. Louis, MO. (314) 263-3901 for instructions on current procedures.

The offender's perception of the meaning of the military experience may provide insight into the current offense. A person charged with possession might have the following military history:

Midway in his senior year of high school, Jones enlisted in the U.S. Army. Grades and attendance had been less than adequate and, he says, the glamour of the uniform and foreign action made the army attractive. He served eighteen months in Viet Nam, emerging with a rank of E-3. Several months were spent in combat until he was seriously wounded when he stepped on a land mine. Although he now has the use of his leg, the ankle is frozen and he walks with a limp. He receives $215 per month in disability pay.

The present charge of dealing in a controlled substance is explained by the defendant as the aftermath of an addiction he developed while convalescing. Medical use of pain pills early in his hospitalization set the scene for recreational use to ease boredom during the long convalescent period, and the addiction continues.

The felony theft charge on his military record he explains in similar terms. While inactive during six months of convalescence at a military hospital in California, he and several fellow patients stole items from the commissary more for excitement than for extrinsic value of the contraband, and three were convicted of theft.

Jones has a bitter attitude toward the military experience. "They took us out of school, sent us green kids to 'Nam, gave us guns and set us up to be cut to pieces. Then when we started on dope to forget we were living in hell, they made criminals out of us. Sure, what I did on this offense was wrong and I'm sorry it happened, but it never would have happened if I had stayed in Arcadia and got a job and got married and had kids like some of my friends did. They ain't in trouble, and I am."

The defendant reports that he was never offered drug therapy while in the service or afterward.

Whether a person's military experience, such as above, ought to be taken as a mitigating factor in sentencing is an open question. If it is germane to consider the military history, its discussion should be included in a "Statement by the Probation Officer" at the conclusion of the PSIR.

Religious History

Nothing stimulates religious conversion more than adversity, and sitting behind bars makes adversity unambiguous and undiluted. Jailhouse religion is a common phenomenon in any penal facility.

The tendency of the court is to ignore a religious experience that has occurred conveniently while awaiting sentencing; indeed, some courts interpret it as an attempt to manipulate the sentencing judge, and a report of religious conversion may boomerang to the offender's disadvantage.

In interviewing an offender, the PSIR writer needs to be especially sensitive at this point. Ethics require that one's own religious perceptions not intrude, but that what the client says (both verbally and non-verbally) be faithfully incorporated in the PSIR. If a client says that Jesus appeared to her last night and told her that she was forgiven and should start a new life, this statement should be incorporated in the PSIR as accurately as possible, without judgment by the PSIR writer. It is the judge's task to interpret.

In learning of religious history, the traditional question, "What is your religion?" often generates only a short, useless, categorical answer such as "Catholic". More to the point would be "How many times did you go to church or synagogue last month [or 3 months, if need be]?" As a check, the follow-up question, asked in a casual tone of voice is, "Who is the minister [priest, or rabbi] there?" If a name comes promptly and without stumbling, verification is probably not necessary.

While skepticism of jailhouse religion is probably good to maintain, genuine religious experiences do occur in jail. Hearing the steel door slam behind you, spending 24 hours in solitude, feeling the contempt silently (or not so silently) expressed by jailers, reflecting on the disgrace brought upon family and friends: the alchemy of the situation encourages the desperate self-examination that often precedes a genuine, life changing religious experience. Religious conversion was the original intention of the penitentiary, and a modern example is provided by Watergate conspirator Chuck Colson in his prison autobiography, *Born Again*.

For sentencing purposes, how does the probation officer determine which is genuine and which is serendipitous? Just as significant, what importance should be given even to a genuine experience?

Each case must be handled on its own merits, of course, but the truly remorseful will recognize that although the religious penitence may have eliminated divine judgment against the sins of the past, the client has accrued a temporal obligation for crimes committed, and the state has not forgiven the crimes. The offender whose religious experience is genuine is better prepared to pay the debt to the state. Traditional jailhouse religion will not last five years, but a genuine religious change will last, mature and become increasingly meaningful.

Therefore, the section of the PSIR that deals with religious history may chronicle the full picture, with the realization that jailhouse religious experiences should influence the recommendation for sentencing (either positively or negatively) only in rare and carefully reasoned cases. Generally, jailhouse religion is not a good basis for leniency.

Personal Health

In most cases it is not necessary to explore early psychogenic experiences from infancy, but the PSIR writer should be alert to the unusual case where this is important. The crimes of arson, spouse violence, sexual assault, and child molesting may be rooted in early childhood experiences. If the initial interview suggests this involvement, interviews of parents, siblings, school teachers and neighbors may prove useful. These interviews may make necessary a follow-up interview with the client.

When the initial interview alerts the probation officer to the need to explore the psychiatric past, the interview should ask the client who would know about such things. If cooperative (as is normally true), names, addresses and phone numbers may be provided immediately. The PSIR writer should then ask, "Do you mind if I talk to these persons?" If permission is given it smooths the way when contacting the persons to be able to say that the client consented. It is even better to have a signed waiver. When permission is declined by the client, a preliminary letter asking the interviewee for an appointment (and setting forth the reason for the interview) may open the door. In extreme cases a court order or a deposition may be necessary.

Medical records are made available through either a specific release signed by the defendant or a court order. Especially helpful are psychiatric reports or evaluations by mental health and addiction agencies. These reports are often heavy with jargon, but there is usually a "Summary and Interpretation" section which is intelligible to informed lay persons.

The section on health includes two major areas: mental and physical. The preliminary question opens up this area by asking whether the client has ever had a serious illness or a serious injury. If so, one needs to explore the impact of those injuries.

If there is evidence of a problem with alcohol or other drugs (the client probably categorizes these separately), the interviewer should be aware that denial of any problem is common among abusers. Rather than asking, "Is alcohol a problem?" it is often more effective to say, "When did alcohol first become a problem to you?"

Many offenders have seen school psychologists or other counselors and will confuse them with psychiatrists. For interview purposes, this is unimportant. It is helpful to get the therapist's name and the dates of the interaction to make follow-up easier. Frequently the client can remember his or her age at the time better than the date, and age can then be transposed into a year.

What the judge wants to know is the sources of the offender's conduct so that a sentence can be selected which minimizes the length of the criminal career, if possible. The health portion is often relevant.

When the defendant was ten years old there was a referral to Dr. Frank Thomas, School Psychologist, who saw the child for evaluation on October 12, 1966, and again about two years later. Several tests were administered on the first visit. Dr. Thomas described his patient as of low normal intelligence, moderately disturbed as a result of insecure early parental home setting. His father deserted the family for several months at a time on a number of occasions, and when he returned he upset the low level of stability achieved during his absence. Both parents were heavy abusers of alcohol and there was some evidence of physical child abuse. In the follow-up by Dr. Thomas two years later, the child was still operating on a low level but his attendance in school had improved and his attitude in class was more cooperative.

The defendant does not recall any serious illness but has severe scarring of his face as the result of an automobile accident when he was fifteen years old. He and an unlicensed friend stole a neighbor's car and hit a tree. He reports that he seldom drinks alcohol and never uses marijuana or harder drugs. (However, he has two recent arrests for public intoxication, and charges for possession of controlled substance are pending against him in County Court for cocaine.) He denies categorically that he is an alcoholic or a drug addict. The Substance Abuse Center confirms that he completed the in-patient program last year but indicates only minimal participation in the aftercare portion. The Probation Department considered revocation but did not file because he seemed to be staying out of trouble otherwise.

Outside Interests

The most common response to the question, "What do you do with your free time?" is "I don't have any free time." This does not give much solid information, and it is usually a false statement which requires further exploration.

The person who is unable to name a free-time activity is transparently unorganized. He or she makes few personal plans and allows circumstances to determine the course of events. A good follow-up question is, "What do you most enjoy doing, when you can?" A question about reading can be followed up with a request for specifics. If the offender says that a favorite book is the Bible, it is instructive to ask when he/she read it last, and what portion. If an unfamiliar book is named, a request for the plot should reveal how genuine the claim was. The purpose of the probing is to test sincerity, not understanding of the plot; a comfortable response is reassuring that he/she does read novels. The more casual and conversational your questions, the better the interview.

Summary

There is no social litmus test that can be used to test the sociogenic resources that a client possesses, but a careful examination of the milieu in which personhood developed will give the judge some understanding of the sociopsychological baggage the offender carries.

The mental/emotional history, for example, is important because an adult who spent most of the school-age years in Special Education sections is not likely to be operating at maximum intellectual efficiency. To force such a person to get the G. E. D. as a requirement of probation might just add new frustrations to the old ones and, in the final analysis, set the client up for failure on probation.

Although it has not been demonstrated that psychoses are biologically inherited, there is evidence that they may be socially inherited in the sense that modes of reaction are learned responses, and the child of a psychotic mother may perceive psychotic response to crisis as appropriate adult behavior. Somewhat the same can be said about religious history. Institutional religion tends to be organized around crises (childbirth, puberty, marriage, death) and personal religion tends to be organized around individuals' crises. In the case of PSIR clients, this includes the ways they deal with feelings of self-doubt, guilt or fear. The judge needs to know the way in which the client employs religion to survive the trauma of the justice experience.

Most clients probably have little of great significance in their health history, but for some this can be extremely important, and the interviewer cannot know this until the interview. Born with an addiction due to pre-natal influences, onset of epilepsy for a thirteen-year-old girl, surgery for a harelip for a nine-year-old boy, or loss of a brother with AIDS; all of these constitute barriers to normal behavior and as such are quite relevant to the sentencing process.

GROUP EXERCISE

List on the chalkboard the minority role represented in the class (i.e., male, white, New Yorker, Republican, Methodist, nursing major, parent, etc.), then discuss ways in which those roles affect perceptions and behavior.

DISCUSSION QUESTIONS

1.   Without using names, describe the oddest "screwball" you know. How has he/she stayed out of trouble with the law, or how did he/she get into trouble?

2.   Think of the most brilliant mind you know, as well as the most "stupid". How do their intellectual capacities relate to social conformity?

3.   Re-read the account of the Vietnam veteran. If he were placed on your caseload, how would you deal with his sense of injustice, that he was made a criminal by the military experience?

4.   Comment: Sins can be forgiven, but crimes must be punished.

5.   Sometimes the court will set as a special condition of probation the order that the client totally abstain from alcohol. Since our society makes use of alcohol legal, how can a court order not to use it be justified?

Chapter 10
Developmental History

A person's self perception is heavily weighted by current circumstances. To some extent, all Westerners define themselves (and derive their self-esteem) from an assessment of their socioeconomic standing in society. Someone who has completed a high school education, or more, expects to be able to find meaningful and self-supporting employment. A person who has just lost a good job will probably feel some level of despair about the future. When someone faces huge debts, this can act like a psychological weight and make it difficult to find the energy to take effective action.

Current circumstances are often best understood in light of immediate past experiences. Whether an offender has been improving circumstances, or has remained in the same socioeconomic situation is an important consideration in understanding his or her response to being convicted of a crime. The question, "what would this offender's life have been like if the crime had not been committed?" will tell a great deal about the personal circumstances that surround the offender's motivation to criminality, and to respond to the conviction.

This chapter reviews some of the major public aspects of the offender's current situation: occupational history, educational history and financial circumstances.

Occupational History

Employment is a useful index of a person's social stability. A client whose livelihood is odd jobs is economically handicapped over one who has an employer, and one on the job for six months is less secure than one with the same type of job for six years.

The nature of the job is significant, as well. A person with a marketable skill is a good prospect for probation, other things being equal. However, an unskilled person in a depressed job market is not likely to find work. This has implications for the probation plan: vocational training can be encouraged, if not required.

The client who is currently employed has a good foundation for successful adjustment after sentencing. If incarceration is a likely sentence, the employed offender is a good candidate for work release. Even a temporarily unemployed person can be considered for work-release if he or she possesses a skill currently in demand.

Velasquez is currently employed as a manager of Cooks Supermarket, 29472 East Valley Road. He has held this position for fifteen months. His previous position was as district manager for a chain of fast-food restaurants, Bob's Big Burgers, but he lost that position after several warnings from top management about his abuse of alcohol. They financed a three-month in-patient treatment program but six weeks later he appeared for work under the influence of alcohol, so they fired him. He likes his present job and says that he is beginning to feel secure in it.

Educational History

The educational history is usually straight-forward but it can be revealing, especially for school drop outs. There are clients who quit school at 15 because of pregnancy, were expelled at 16 because of hitting a teacher, dropped out at 17 to enter military service, or left at any age to help support the family. Each instance is an indication of the manner in which the offender responds to a crisis.

Unless something unusual is in the record, normally it is not necessary to verify the school experience. However, where an unusual and important assertion is made, it should be verified if possible. For example:

Jones reported that she was graduated from the engineering program at Purdue University *cum laude* in 1979, and this was confirmed by the Registrar.

Familial attitudes and standards are reflected in the degree of participation by the parents in the Parent-Teacher Organization. This conveys more about the family setting than merely the fact that the parents did or did not attend PTO meetings. Only a parent committed to the proper upbringing of a child will devote afternoons and evenings to school activities.

One of the sharpest devices in the PSIR toolbox is the reading test. It is preferable to rely on professional data if available (such as the psychiatric report or the work-up provided by the state boy's or girl's school) but such information may not be available. An approximation (it is no more than that) can be determined through the use of the office reading test. This is an easily administered instrument that gives an immediate indication of whether the client is functionally illiterate or on what grade level the reading skill falls. This is a gross tool with a generous margin of error when administered by a non-psychometrist, but it can prove useful if no other source exists for this information.

Patterns of Social Participation

All people are social beings, even the most withdrawn recluse. The manner in which one responds to social stimuli is a measure of social integration. To understand a person (or to understand one's self) it is necessary to note typical response patterns to social settings.

The "loner" is a person who, given a choice to spend an evening alone or with others, will opt for the former. This may be due to feeling uncertain and uncomfortable around others or may happen because a person enjoys being alone. The thoroughly social person, on the other hand, is never alone, is always surrounded by family members or friends. Some clients state they have many friends, yet also see themselves as loners. This can happen when circumstances throw persons into groups, when they would prefer to be alone.

A client's perceived social roles help to explain behavior patterns. A person who believes he or she is a leader in groups is quite different from the person who perceives himself as characteristically a follower, especially in interpersonal relations. However, if a question about social roles is asked early in the interview, while defenses are still high, the overly cautious client may emphasize the followership role with the thought of diminished criminal responsibility. By asking about social behavior later in successful interviews, the interviewer can avoid defensive responses.

Introspective thoughts are often elicited by the question, "In your twenty-two years, what person has had the most influence on you, for good or for bad?" After finding out the person's relationship to the client (friend, teacher, parent, sibling), the follow-up question is, "If [that person] were sitting here, what would be his/her opinion of you now?" This question often results in answers providing insight into the client's current self-perception.

If the client seems willing to talk about social self-perception, a useful follow-up question is, "What is the *real* you? Underneath the false front that we all show to the world, what are you really like, down deep inside?" Many responses to this question are self-serving, but frequently the answer will reveal a great deal about the offender.

No one goes through childhood without at least some social interaction problems. Some offenders have unusual social experiences that need to be mentioned in the PSIR. This is often the case when criminality seems to occur as a result of poor self-esteem, based on social inadequacies, or if the route to crime-free living lies in improved social confidence.

When Gomez was three years old, his parents entered the migrant stream. He spent November through February in school in Texas but the rest of the year he was in public schools in Kentucky, Indiana and Michigan, rarely more than six weeks at a time. Always the stranger among his peers, he developed a withdrawn personality and felt shut out of the school world. His reading skills never progressed beyond the sixth grade level.

As a part of his literary handicap, Gomez developed a low self-image. He understandably came to regard himself as intellectually inferior, and since the other migrants shared this social handicap, he lumped them in the same category, believing that Hispanics are by nature less intelligent than Anglos.

He met his present girlfriend at a tomato-packing plant in rural Indiana. She came from a Hispanic family that had settled there a few years before, and she had completed high school. On summer evenings she visited the migrant camps with an interdenominational religious group sponsored by the Council of Churches. A major goal of the group is to enhance the self-esteem of the younger migrants and, Gomez is responding well to this through his friendship with Dolores Sanchez.

Current Financial Situation

A person's financial situation is broader than the occupational history. Obviously, if the person has been unemployed for some time, economic resources are depleted and this has implications for sentencing and for subsequent programming. It would be futile to impose a fine, and probation supervision will have to improve job skills by providing vocational training or helping the offender to find employment.

Aspects of financial health demonstrate the person's ability to operate in the economic world. An offender who has had good or steady employment for years but reports no real property and no investments probably is undisciplined in handling finances. If the offender further reports having recent models of expensive cars, it reveals a value system based on immediate gratification.

Although the spouse's income is not available to the court for fines or fees, it is relevant to the economic situation of the offender. The interviewer should be alert to signals that information on the spouse's income may be distorted. Proof of income can be requested by pay stubs or the employer can be queried.

In cases involving large amounts of restitution, such as embezzlement, it may be necessary to explore local investment institutions to see if there have been sizable deposits by the defendant or the spouse. Confidentiality may be a barrier to disclosure by the institution, but sometimes an informal conversation with the head bookkeeper will suggest whether a court order to produce the financial records would be worth the effort. If there is a doubt, a court order should be requested for every investment firm in the community. A seasoned banker might be able to suggest some other places to seek those investments that might not occur to the PSIR writer.

> Kelly is buying a house on contract. The purchase price was $22,500 and he currently owes about half of that. His monthly house payments are $110, but he has been told that the furnace is not going to last another year, and he thinks that he needs a new roof. The furnace will cost about $1,000, or payments of about $35 per month, with the roof adding another $25 to that. His wife works as a waitress three nights a week, bringing in about $150 a week. The family seems to have good money habits, tries to live within a conservative budget, but does not have any long-term savings and is not able to put away anything for the children's post-secondary education. This bothers Kelly greatly.

Summary

The way in which we have responded to life's changing situations gives a clue as to the way we are going to respond to life's changing situations in the future. In contemplating the sentencing decision, the judge needs to know what has gone on before in order to anticipate what is going to happen the day after tomorrow.

A man who has never been able to hold a job is not likely to be occupationally stable while on probation, and unemployed persons have a difficult time staying out of new trouble. Likewise, the manner in which one dealt with school stresses is indicative of the way one is going to deal with other stresses after sentencing. The meaning of a high school diploma is not just that the graduate knows history, English, algebra and social science, but probably more important is the fact that the defendant finished school. This one fact says a great deal about a person. No one goes through high school without numerous bouts with temptation to drop out. Whatever the reason for staying in school (ambition, family tradition, a wish for an affluent life, a supportive parent, an inspiring teacher) the fact that the client did actually complete the high school course is revealing of stable personality traits.

Contemporary society makes financial independence vitally important. More than the possession of dollars alone, wealth is a vehicle for self-respect that competes with all other measures. The weekly income received from a regular job is probably not as important in the scheme of things as the more subtle meanings inherent in that weekly check: someone thinks enough of me to pay me. If the boss thinks well of me, I think well of me, too. That is an overwhelmingly significant insight, and it explains why unemployed persons are less likely to succeed on probation. It is not the dollar in the pocket quite as much as it is the self-pride in the heart.

GROUP EXERCISE

Volunteers from the class recount the persons in their lives who have had the greatest influences on them (for either good or evil) and the ways in which the personalities of the volunteers have been shaped by those influences.

DISCUSSION QUESTIONS

1. Comment: A good person with a marketable skill is a good prospect for probation.

2. Aside from the obvious fact that twenty-year-old persons who dropped out of school at 16 lack certain formal knowledge, why do employers prefer to hire graduates rather than drop outs?

3. What is your philosophy of restitution? If an offender has deprived the victim of something of value, repayment is logical, but to what extent of the defendant's income? What if the probationer is unemployed? If the victim has been reimbursed by an insurance company, does the probationer repay the insurance company or is the loss just the cost of doing business?

4. In psychogenic terms relating to your family and developmental background, explain why you have been or have not been convicted of a crime.

5. Describe how someone you know (no true names) broke the law but because of circumstances (describe them) he/she was not charged, tried or convicted.

Chapter 11
Attitudes and
Psychological Summary

The preceding three chapters have described the historical content of the PSIR. Historical information includes past factual data about the offender and the offense. Sometimes the facts speak for themselves, but more frequently, historical information does not point to a single, logical sentence. As is true for most people, an offender's life circumstances are normally a milieu of positive and negative forces, each carrying some weight in determining the person's future.

One function of the PSIR is to organize the often disorganized collection of past experiences that led to the current situation, summarizing them into a meaningful current reality to which the judge may respond. This normally begins with a summary of the offender's attitudes toward the offense and his current psychological state.

Attitudes Toward Crime

Remorse is a frequently used term in judicial inquiry. A concern for remorse exists not just to exact vengeance or to permit society to say, "I told you so;" it has genuine function.

True remorse, of course, must be distinguished from being sorry to be caught. A convicted criminal who is not sorry to have committed the crime lacks a pre-condition to reformation. Without remorse, the same lack of inhibitions that led to crime in the first place continues. Motivational conditions are unchanged, and crime may well recur.

For that reason, it is a legitimate task of the PSIR to determine how genuine is the almost universal declaration, "I'm sorry I did it and it will never happen again." The PSIR writer needs a special remorse detector to measure this. Unfortunately, none has been invented. There are a few clues, but they are no more than clues.

Several times during the interview the defendant employed evasive maneuvers and inserted disclaimers at key points. "As far as I know," he said, "that is all that I had when I got it home." His eye contact was quite evasive when he discussed the way in which his brother "talked me into going into the house," and his facial muscles were tense when he described his allegedly otherwise clean history.

Such evasiveness cannot help but cause concern that the person's story is not full and complete, to "the best of his knowledge." When an offender continues to evade full responsibility for the crime, even after conviction, it suggests strongly that any remorse expressed is superficial. Here is another example:

> The defendant's story of the event was internally contradictory. Early in the interview she indicated that her husband had been fishing with friends that Friday night and she was alone in the house, but when she described the discovery of the fire, she said she had left their daughter at home with her husband. At another point in the interview she said that they did not believe in taking out insurance because "you might as well save up the premiums and insure yourself," but later she revealed that on two other occasions they had collected fire insurance. After she made that remark she made an attempt to explain that both times they had been persuaded by her husband's father to take out the insurance.

When the PSIR writer believes that the offender is being less than candid, this should be communicated to the judge, but openly, so that the offender is able to respond to it. The information offered by the defendant should be presented as close to verbatim as is possible. Then the PSIR writer may wish to comment:

> Fraley asserts that this is the only time he has driven since his license was suspended. However, the present arresting officer, who was responsible for the original arrest, says that he is sure that he has seen the car on the road various times, because he recalls noticing the "unusual flannel balls" that encircle the rear window.

The attitude toward the crime itself can be a predictor of future performance. The client who believes that the act was not really a crime, but somehow the police just went after him, or believes that everyone is doing the same act, only he got caught, which is unfair, is likely to continue behaving as before.

> I don't understand why they are doing this to me. I ain't done nothing. Everybody does it. All I did was just keep this tip board under the counter and when a customer asked, I let him play. I didn't push it. What about the paystub sweepstakes at the factory every Friday, in nearly every department. And the bingo at the Elks

and the church over there? Why, even when you go to cross the street it's a gamble; will you reach the other side? They've got me facing two years over this but they don't touch nobody else.

These are some of the more obvious examples of the lack of remorse often felt by offenders. Sometimes the evidence is less direct, such as a subtle glibness or an unrealistically enthusiastic admission of blame. The PSIR writer needs to guard against the tendency of personal biases to color the interpretation of the legitimacy of an offender's remorse. If an offender "seems" phony, but there is no direct reason for it, the PSIR writer may simply be reacting to the offender's personality style, and not the more salient attitude toward the offense. When there is no specific behavior on which to attach the PSIR writer's doubts, it is better to leave the doubts unexpressed to the judge.

Attitude Toward the Victim

The significance of the attitude toward the victim is similar to the attitude toward the crime. Where regret is genuine, there is less likely to be a repetition.

I feel awful about the lady. When I grabbed her purse, I didn't mean to hurt her. She hung on to it and then fell on the post. If I had known what was going to happen I would not have done it. I wanted to go to her and apologize but my lawyer told me I would get in more trouble, something about tampering with witnesses, but when it is over I want to tell her.

It is unlikely that this purse-snatcher will again seize a purse. There is an additional aspect to genuine regret toward the victim: the need for retribution seems less when there is a real sorrow over what has happened. The part of retribution that expresses outrage and teaches a lesson is made less important by an already penitent offender. But in some situations, of course, the offender needs the catharsis of having made restitution.

Some defendants hasten to make amends before sentencing, such as paying the victim's hospital bill or completing a substance-abuse program. These are often favorable signs because they demonstrate a willingness on the part of the defendant to accept responsibility for his/her own actions. Occasionally this is nothing more than a ploy of the defense attorney to impress the judge. Even then, the fact that the defendant complied is a sign the offender can be worked with.

Defendants who place the blame on the victim are poor risks for future situations, and they call forth the law's retributive function as a public statement and a lesson. Even where there is some validity to the claim that the victim precipitated the crime, it is not a good sign that the defendant embraces that explanation and refuses to accept responsibility for the act. Here are two examples of common rationalizations, blaming the victim:

> I know I broke the law and can't complain that they got me, but it wasn't really my fault, you know. She was only fifteen, but she was the neighborhood slut and she teased everything in pants. Always spreading her legs and wiggling herself and rubbing against you, enough to drive any man mad. She was asking for it and I gave it to her, but it was her idea and she should have been arrested for seducing me, instead.

> Sure, they got me for DUI, but it was his fault, too. They took a blood sample at the hospital emergency room and he had .23%, but mine was only .19%. If he hadn't died they would have arrested him for DUI, too. And if he hadn't been drinking there wouldn't have been any accident, because he could see me coming and would have stopped if he had been cold sober. I guess my real crime is that I lived through it and now they're charging me with Causing the Death of Another, not him. But he was drunker than I was.

In weighing the attitude of the offender toward the crime, self-criticism, when genuine, is a good sign. The person who does not lay the blame elsewhere or seek to evade personal responsibility is well prepared for rehabilitation, the first step of which is facing oneself. It is likely that the following defendant will make a good adjustment to the future.

> Well, where I made the first mistake was I got that gun from Art and took it home. I knew at the time that I had no business having a gun there, where the children and all were, but I did it anyway. I'd give everything I own if I could go back to that day. But you can't ever go back and the only thing I can do is to spend the rest of my life being careful and trying to make it up to those children. They deserve everything I can ever do for them.

Because attitudes are totally subjective things, the probation officer needs to be on the alert at all times so that interpretations are just. As indicated above, if there is some doubt about the interpretation, that perception probably ought not be included in the PSIR. The opinion of the writer is taken seriously by the judge, and a poorly founded opinion has no place in a document that is going to determine the defendant's future.

Attitude Toward the Criminal Justice System

By the time an offender has reached the PSIR stage, there have been many contacts with the criminal justice system. The intake of criminal justice is usually performed by the beat police officer. Next comes the station-house or jail personnel and perhaps a bond person. Later, the prosecutor enters the drama, then the judge and a Defense Attorney. The person preparing the PSIR report is only the latest in a succession of functionaries.

How the client has been treated by the various actors in the system will influence attitudes toward the system, but this is not the only factor. If it is the first encounter with the law, there have been social definitions communicated to the defendant by the subculture out of which he/she comes. If the background is suburban or rural, the pre-existing attitudes toward law enforcement may be rather favorable. The inner-city resident's attitudes are more likely to be antagonistic, and the police often are seen as a type of enemy. A drug-culture youth often has ambivalent attitudes: the police maintain order but also meddle in drug-related matters.

Criminal justice attitudes relate to etiology. A negative attitude toward any part of the criminal justice system suggests resistance toward social control generally, and may mean that future social restrictions are more likely to be ignored than would occur if the offender accepted social proscriptions. Respect for the law and its institutions presages future compliance with the law.

> The cops have been out to get me ever since I beat that possession charge last year. But they're too stupid. It was just blind luck that they got me this time, because my girlfriend didn't get rid of it like I told her. She got two envelopes out of my jacket pocket and flushed them while I held the cops at the door, but she didn't look in my other pocket, and they nailed me. They'll not get me like that again.

With an attitude like that, the defendant is likely to assume that he can get away with anything, since he views the police as too incompetent to catch him. He is not a good prospect for probation. On the other hand, some clients express a true respect for criminal justice:

When I sobered up the next day, Sunday, my wife told me what I had done and showed me the stuff I had brought home. I thought she was kidding! I had to believe her, though, because there was the stereo and cassettes, and in the car I found the jar of quarters. So we talked about it and decided I should take it all to the police station and ask them what to do. They were real understanding and took my statement and said they didn't have any report of a burglary like that, but they'd let me know about it as soon as the owner called and they kept the stuff.

The prognosis for this defendant, if placed on probation, probably would be good, all else being equal. He has a healthy attitude toward himself and he trusts the police.

The frequent lawbreaker who has been in and out of penal institutions often is harder to analyze. Most active offenders reach a time when they tire of incarceration and are genuinely determined not to return to prison. That is one reason why the average age of males in U. S. prisons is about twenty-five. By the time a repeat offender gets into the late thirties or forties, he/she wearies of the life inside and exerts self-control over the desire for illegal activity. This may take many years, and juveniles with heavy delinquent records may persist in criminality through their twenties.

This is why some states permit the juvenile record to be incorporated into the PSIR; it informs the judge that the defendant has had frequent and long-term association with juvenile correctional agencies, that juvenile probation has failed and that it is likely that a negative attitude toward adult probation has already been formed. It may be time to expose the offender to the clanged gate and the depersonalization of a big-time prison.

Psychiatric Evaluation

Probation officers are not psychiatrists or psychologists and must avoid performing as such. More damage can be caused by unwise treatment than a team of practicing professionals can patch up. However, psychiatric and psychological resources can be invaluable allies in diagnosis and in framing an appropriate sentence.

In Chapter 9 we discussed the construction of the mental/emotional history. This is needed for all clients, but for some who have apparent psychological problems, a more precise evaluation is needed. If the preliminary investigation leads to a suspicion of deep problems which the judge should understand fully before sentencing, a court order can be requested. To obtain this information may require a postponement of sentencing. Sometimes the behavior suggesting this need is dramatic:

> Throughout the initial interview for this report the defendant displayed unmistakable symptoms of psychological disturbance. He had missed two appointments and was an hour late for this one, offering no explanation. There was a marked nervous tic in the right shoulder, repeated as he began the answer to each new question. When he was asked to give his version of the offense he became totally immobilized, stared steadily into space and did not move a muscle for what may have been two minutes. He appeared not to hear the interviewer's voice attempting to bring him back to reality. It is obvious that this offender has a problem that the PSIR writer is not competent to diagnose, and it is equally apparent that the judge needs to know what it is before deciding the sentence. This offender should have psychiatric evaluation.

Many times there are psychiatric or psychological reports already done on the offender, and these can be useful if done recently enough. When these evaluations are written for use by a lay person, they usually provide a non-technical interpretation. If not, a professional should be asked to interpret the report so that the PSIR can be lucid for the judge.

Below is an example of a psychological evaluation:

> Schwartz was sent to State Hospital for evaluation on April 17, 1983, as a preliminary to sentencing in CS-82-431. At that time he was found to be a homosexual pedophile, with a lengthy history of non-coercive activity. He readily states his homosexual orientation. In his early high school years he attempted to date girls in a half-hearted fashion but was always turned down and eventually gave up any such attempt. In his sophomore year he began homosexual contacts with classmates and these continued throughout his high school years, approximately one time per month. After graduation from high school he obtained a job as a janitor in the local YMCA and it was at that time that his homosexual contacts with younger children began. In addition he coached a church baseball team for 11 years, a situation which brought him into contact frequently with underage children. Approximately six years ago he was confronted about this but denied everything, and his homosexual contacts of a non-violent nature continued up until his current arrest. He denies that he ever used force or threats and backed off whenever the children objected. He feels more comfortable with children than he

does with adults. At this point he appears to recognize his problem and seems to be motivated to keep his impulses under control. He states that for the past 9 months he has avoided any homosexual contact with anyone. He denies any sexual contacts with women or girls.

Current testing indicates that he functions in the average range of intelligence but is functioning at the 4th-grade level for reading and the 6th-grade level for arithmetic. Aptitude for job placement appears to be best in unskilled types of work. He does not appear to be especially particular about the type of work he does as long as he is able to keep busy.

Mr. Schwartz appears to be a markedly insecure young man who is overly eager to please others, especially those in authority. His own ego strength and sense of self-value are low. He has made some half-hearted attempts to establish heterosexual relationships but basically he is uncomfortable with even adult men. Because he feels at ease with children he is at risk for repetition of molestation if thrown among them in an unguarded fashion. He states that he has been receiving therapy for some time and that this has been helpful to him. He gives the clear impression that he is motivated to keep his impulses under control. Other than the current crimes there is no evidence of a criminal orientation. Neither does he appear to be an assaultive, hostile or a violent individual. He is not apt to thrust himself upon what he perceives to be unwilling partners.

The prognosis for rehabilitation would be enhanced under three conditions:

1.   Continued psychotherapy either on an individual basis or in a group. Group therapy appears to offer a better prognosis. Probably such treatment could be obtained at a local mental health center. Such therapy should be continued while Schwartz is incarcerated, if possible.

2.   It would be helpful to this individual if he could also be kept busy. He is apt to do a responsible job at whatever assignment local authority gives him.

3. He should avoid unsupervised regular contact with chil-
    dren, including females.

At present the subject appears to be a good candidate for continued
therapy. He recognizes that he has a problem, is motivated to control his impulses, feels supported when in a therapy group, and is
eager to avoid further incarceration. Continued therapy is apt to
reduce significantly the likelihood of recidivism.

The purpose of the Psychiatric Evaluation is to alert the judge to a condition that might be relevant to the sentence. It is obvious that the above
psychiatric report has serious implications for the sentence. Any sentence
that makes treatment unavailable is bound to be counterproductive in the
long run. The recommended sentence could include house arrest, with safeguards to see that no children of either sex were permitted to be present.
This would allow group therapy to continue. A janitorial position in a retirement center would meet the need for safe employment and a curfew.

Nature of Evaluation

The defendant has a right to be as irregular psychologically as he/she
pleases, so long as the condition does not relate to the sentence for the crime.
However, if the psychiatric evaluation reveals the need for continuing counseling, this is relevant and the judge should know it. Likewise, if in the opinion of the psychiatrist the defendant is likely to become violent, the judge
should be informed.

On the basis of the Minnesota Multiphasic Personality Inventory,
the behavioral clinician is of the opinion that McGuire could become a serious threat to the community. This, coupled with his unusual physical strength and a short emotional fuse, presents a men-
acing reality if he is permitted to remain in the community without
supervision. It is suggested that he be given the maximum term of
probation possible and that a condition of probation be psychiatric
treatment at the mental health facility.

A word of caution is in order regarding the use of psychiatric reports.
The psychological sciences are quite inexact, and relying upon one professional opinion may do the client or society a grave disservice. No behavioral
scientist is infallible, and mistaken judgments are not uncommon. All diag-
noses, and especially prognoses with respect to criminal behavior, should be

treated with caution. Candor requires PSIR writers to recognize their own fallibility, as well.

The kinds of data found in the psychiatric report vary from agency to agency and from client to client. In most cases there is an intelligence test of some sort, along with a brief interpretation of the meaning ("in the low normal range"). Usually there is a report of the results of the Minnesota Multiphasic Personality Inventory (MMPI), which is a useful screening device for personality disorders. Occasionally there is an analysis of the findings of a Rohrschach (ink blot) Test or a Binder Gestalt measure of neurological damage. If the environment is an issue, there may be a report on the Environmental Deprivation Survey/Maladaptive Behavior Record, which assesses environmental deprivation.

The press of time will preclude newly scheduled psychological evaluations except in unusual cases. Most of the psychological information available for a PSIR will be limited to tests given the client prior to the PSIR process, for which a release must be asked (See Appendix C).

Summary

An attitude is a predisposition; that is, the client is predisposed to act in a certain manner. For the presentence investigation, the presence of an attitude is predictive of future behavior consistent with that attitude.

One purpose of psychological testing is to measure attitudes scientifically. A psychologist or psychiatrist has professional skills that assess the attitudinal framework within which the client operates. In addition, the psychologist or psychiatrist will also measure intellectual capabilities and other aspects of the defendant's psyche in a manner beyond the ability of the probation officer. This may be couched in professional jargon which must be sifted for relevance and then recast in helpful form for the judge's consideration.

GROUP EXERCISE

Three or four persons from the class agree on a fairly recent or a historical case of crime that has some readily accessible description of the offender (John Hinckley, Richard Speck, Gary Dotson), and speculate on what psychological/psychiatric information would have been helpful if the sentencing judge had had it.

DISCUSSION QUESTIONS

1. Any adequately informed PSIR writer is aware of personal limitations in dealing with the psychological aspects of clients' histories. How do you feel about your limitations? In what areas are you especially vulnerable?

2. Honesty requires us to admit that we have personal hangups. Having them is not as serious if we recognize them. What handicaps do you have in your emotional baggage that will make it difficult for you to do an objective PSIR for certain people?

3. Most state systems and almost all jails lack fully adequate facilities for the treatment of criminals who have psychiatric problems. Sometimes outpatient therapy would be available if the client were placed on probation. What considerations should be included in determining the sentence in a case where treatment is necessary if the client is ever to be restored to a conforming lifestyle?

Chapter 12
Framing the Sentence:
The Plea Agreement
and the Recommendation

The ultimate purpose of the PSIR is to help the court arrive at the most suitable sentence. All the information in the PSIR is designed to frame for the court the sentencing options, and to lead, where appropriate, to the most appropriate sentence.

Because of the realities of the criminal justice system in the U.S., this involves an evaluation of the plea agreement in up to 90% of the cases. As we pointed out in Chapter 1, the PSIR writer possesses more information about the case than either of the attorneys who negotiate the plea. Moreover, the PSIR has a neutral interest in evaluating the plea, and is not tainted by representation of the state or the offender as a client.

Once the plea agreement has been assessed, it is the proper function of the PSIR to recommend a sentence to the judge. This recommendation reflects the compilation of all the data collected during the PSIR process, and is the most significant aspect of the professional PSIR writer's job. (See Appendix D for a sentencing worksheet.)

The Plea Agreement

"Plea bargaining" is an unfortunate term that has been developed by the profession and used by the general public. It suggests a number of negative overtones. Properly used, the plea agreement is advantageous to both the prosecutor and the defendant. If it is a *bargain*, someone is losing more than is proper, but there is a mutually desirable solution to the issue in the case when both sides win enough concessions to justify the agreement. This was the implication of our discussion of plea bargaining in Chapter 3. After viewing the documents in the case (police reports, the state's evaluation, supplementary interviews and so forth) the PSIR writer has information that the judge needs in order to make an informed decision. There is a special responsibility to stand between the state and the defendant and weigh the agreement in the light of the interests of society. This role does not tilt in either direction; the PSIR writer is an officer of the court, and as such, scrutinizes the agreement to guarantee the common good. In a sense, he or she represents society. It is not in the interest of society that either side give away too much, nor is it desirable that an injustice (in either direction) should occur. This becomes a subjective matter and the discussion of the agreement ought to pose whatever philosophical questions are involved.

The PSIR writer is not the system's watchdog, but instead acts as a separate set of eyes, evaluating the case. The roles of the other court actors, even when played properly, can unintentionally lead to irrational outcomes. This occurs because of the workings of the adversary system, which ordinarily works remarkably well. When a case actually goes to trial, the police have probable cause to believe the accused guilty and the prosecutor sets out to prove the guilt. The defense attorney provides the best defense against guilt. Everything legal is done toward these purposes and the parties act as adversaries, playing out a contest of skills and intentions. The judge sits above this contest and, once in possession of all the legal facts, determines whether guilt has been legally demonstrated.

In a plea agreement, none of the evidence reaches the court and no formal contest occurs. There is no trial, and any issues raised are faced only in the restrictive setting when the prosecutor and the defense attorney wrangle an agreement. There is no impartiality to a plea agreement; instead, it is an understanding developed somewhere between the interests of the two extreme adversaries.

The PSIR writer must be sensitive to his or her objective role in this process. If either side seems to be unjustly treated, it is proper for the PSIR writer to call this to the attention of the judge, who then can ask for more information to determine if the plea agreement is proper. If the judge concludes that the plea agreement is not acceptable, it is rejected and both parties go back to a new negotiation process.

If the PSIR writer recommends that the plea agreement be rejected, the reason must be made explicit. The judge, the state and the defendant all have a right to know why that which was agreed upon is not justifiable, as these two examples show:

> There does not appear to be any advantage in incarcerating the defendant. Her need is to gain control over her life, and this is not likely to occur in prison. The prospect of a lengthy therapeutic program is, without doubt, the most promising of all alternatives. It is recommended that the plea agreement for prison time not be accepted.

> If the Court were to accept the plea agreement in its bald form, the public perception of the decision could be indignant: the Court has rewarded the defendant for having achieved the status of Habitual Offender (his third felony) by awarding him free room and board

on the American Plan. The sentence enables him to begin Work Release the day he enters jail and to be free during the day to look for work without controls, as if not incarcerated. The public interpretation of the decision might diminish the impact of the habitual offender statute.

Judges have their preferences in the content of a PSIR, but a proposal of an adaptation in the agreement to make it acceptable is often appropriate. The prosecutor and the defense attorney may not be elated with this but they may also appreciate guidelines as to what the Court would accept instead of the agreement they propose. If the judge refuses to accept the plea agreement in the form submitted, the attorneys are back on square one. An example of a modification proposal follows:

It is suggested that the main thrust of the plea agreement be retained, but that conditions of probation be (1) completion of the course already begun at the Vocational School and (2) at least one meeting of Alcoholics Anonymous each week.

A Sentence Agreement

Prior to the formalization of the agreement there has been negotiation. After each side has had a chance to see the other's case in pre-trial sessions and through discovery (a legal term for the basic evidence which the opposition would have to face in court), both sides adjust their expectations until they meet somewhere between dismissing the charges and the maximum possible sentence.

There is almost no limitation to the considerations permissible, such as agreement on the part of the state to dismiss a case pending in another court or an agreement by the defendant not to visit his minor son. It is the appropriateness of unusual facets that give the probation officer the most concern.

The provision of the plea agreement that there will be no revocation of probation in the previous felony is an affront to the Court. Since it would signal to the defendant and to others on probation that it is not necessary to observe the Court's orders, it is not consistent with the interests of society or of the Wayne County Criminal Justice System that this plea agreement be accepted by the Court. The Court's authority to administer its own probation system should not be a bargaining chip in the hands of the Prosecutor.

If the defendant violated his probation, it is the Court that should determine the appropriate action.

Appropriateness of the Agreement

As indicated, the PSIR writer acts as the public conscience in evaluating a proposed plea agreement. But the manner in which this is done is delicate. Neither the prosecutor nor the defense attorney will be pleased with a rejection of the plea agreement because it implies an imbalance which reflects upon both sides, and it nullifies all their work. This action should not be undertaken lightly by the probation officer, but neither should it be avoided when circumstances require action:

> The offender continues to maintain off the record that he did not commit the crime. His minister, within ethical limits, has implied this, and his employer and academic counselor believe it. When asked in the interview for his version of the crime, he said, "I cannot tell you anything because I did not do it."

> He explains that he was eating in the fast-food restaurant next door to the laundry where the robbery occurred, when suddenly a police officer entered and arrested him. He was placed in the interrogation room, alone with a white policeman. The victim, also white, looked through the one-way mirror and identified him. No line-up including other black males was used. He had two previous felony convictions in North Carolina (verified; see attachments), and when the Prosecutor told him that upon conviction by a jury, Habitual Offender charges would be added, the defendant agreed to plead guilty. He says that two years guaranteed is preferable to the gamble that he might get thirty-two years.

> Assuming that he is correct in his assertion that he is not guilty, one can nevertheless understand his reluctance to go to trial. Having been identified falsely, he cannot trust the system for the additional thirty years at risk.

> It appears not to be in the public interest for the Court to accept the plea agreement. In view of the firm opinions of his academic counselor at the university, his employer and his minister that he is innocent of the charges, there would be serious doubt of the integrity of a system that forced an innocent man to plead guilty.

Further review of the defendant's history tends to support his contention. The two felony convictions in North Carolina were for Driving While Under the Influence and for Battery. Both occurred over seven years ago, shortly after he returned from Viet Nam. After the Battery conviction, which occurred after a drinking bout with friends, he entered the addiction in-patient program at Veterans' Hospital and moved to Michigan to finish college in a total change of environment. In his three years here, there has been no recorded offense. His academic record shows a 3.4 on a four-point scale.

There is nothing in the defendant's recent history to suggest that he is likely to have committed this offense. No weapon was found. When he was booked he had only seven dollars, thirty-two cents ($7.32), much less than the amount taken in the robbery (reportedly $48.39). The only evidence against Johnson is the identification by a white woman distraught by a recent armed robber, looking through a mirror at a lone black man seated dejectedly in the police station with a uniformed white officer guarding him. It is not surprising that she said, "Yes, that's him," but the conditions leave a reasonable doubt.

It is suggested that the Court deny the plea agreement and set the case for trial. Only in this way will the serious questions raised by the case be answered.

The rush and bustle of the court system being what it is, it is quite possible that the prosecutor and the defense attorney would not be aware of the negative recommendation of the Probation Department until shortly before the sentencing session. There should be no surprises in the court room, least of all when the parties think that all is settled. When the probation officer recommends denial of the plea agreement it is a common but important courtesy that both attorneys be informed of the fact. Since the PSIR itself contains all the information needed, no discussion is necessary; a brief phone call alerting each attorney will discharge any obligation the probation officer has to be a cooperative member of the courthouse team.

The Victim's Perspective

Because the criminal justice system provides no formal representation for the victim of the crime, PSIR writers are often tempted to take a role of representing the victim. This temptation is enhanced by a system that is impersonal and bureaucratic, in which the negotiation process appears to disregard the victim.

It is inappropriate for the PSIR writer to succumb to this temptation. The victim is not a primary client of the PSIR process. To the extent the PSIR writer is concerned about the victim, this concern can be met by diligently keeping the victim appraised of the case's progress, by informing the victim of the proposed plea agreement, and by reporting the victim's evaluation of the agreement to the judge. If the PSIR writer feels the agreement inappropriate, he or she may join the victim in recommending that the judge withdraw the plea, but this is an independent judgment that must be made regardless of the victim's input.

Calculation of Credit for Jail Time

Although credit for jail time is usually optional (depending on local law), it is a customary consideration in sentencing.

Normally, the jail time clock begins to run when the defendant is arrested on the current offense and continues as long as he/she remains in detention with each portion of a day in jail counting as a full day. The clock stops upon release on bond or Own Recognizance (without cash or security). If the defendant has not been released, the PSIR calculates time served as of the date set for sentencing, and it should be amended if there is an unanticipated delay in sentencing.

JAIL TIME

The subject was detained on a warrantless arrest on June 17, 1987, and has remained in detention. On October 4, 1987, he will have accumulated a total of one hundred nine (109) days of jail time.

State laws and court practices differ, so it is advisable to consult the judge as to how to handle irregular case histories, such as multiple arrests, re-arrests on new charges, transfer to other jurisdictions for various reasons, work-release and other arrangements. If jail credit is not included in a plea agreement, it is up to the PSIR writer to calculate it (with documentation) so that the judge can determine how much of it applies.

The PSIR Summary and Recommendation

Salient Factors in Case: Offense and Offender

Most people with legitimate access to the PSIR will read it in its entirety, but a concise statement is useful, nevertheless. This is especially true for lengthier PSIRs about complicated cases. In these cases, the judge will appreciate a brief summary that pulls the PSIR together.

> The jury found Morrison guilty of Driving While Intoxicated, a Class D Felony. This was his third conviction. Although he tested .19% blood alcohol content on the station breathalyzer, his defense is that he was not driving; he was a passenger. The arresting officer testifies that as he approached the car from the rear after he had pulled it over to the curb, he saw the two persons in the front seat exchange positions. Mr. Morrison continues to maintain that he was not driving.

> Morrison is a married white male, 28 years old, has two minor children and has been employed by General Electric for nine years as a production worker. Three years ago he completed an out-patient alcohol-therapy program. This is his third arrest for DWI in the last six years; on the previous two occasions he was fined and placed on probation for one year. In addition to the two previous DWI convictions, he has been arrested five times for Public Intoxication and twice for Reckless Driving.

Prosecutor's Perspective on the Case

Interviews with the prosecutor and the arresting officer may reveal additional relevant information which was not heard in court, either because of the guilty plea or because the information was not admissible.

This is a delicate problem, because the PSIR should not become the prosecutor's vehicle for introducing evidence of questionable validity. Evidence may be excluded from trial, or ignored in negotiations for reasons of its inherent untrustworthiness. On the other hand, the rules of evidence are greatly relaxed at sentencing, for it is assumed that a judge is able to sift through the various claims to determine a just sentence. Therefore, the judge is permitted to hear things that would not be allowed in a jury trial.

The PSIR writer, then, is expected to share with the judge anything that may be relevant to sentencing. In the case of unproven allegations, the document must be written to indicate that these claims are unproven. Three illustrations are provided below.

> The state files show that Eldridge is named in nine other burglary investigations, all of which are currently being pursued by the police. Detective Frank Gomez says that they are ready to file charges in at least three of those cases.

> Deputy Prosecutor Cayer reports that there is little doubt that the crime was committed only after a long period of planning, but that he was unable to present this fact to the court because the witness with whom Delgado plotted over a year ago was killed in an automobile accident shortly before the trial.

> According to the prosecutor, confirmed by the police, there has been a rash of theft of black walnut trees in the area. These trees attract professional loggers because they are worth up to $600 each and are rather easily cut from groves a distance away from the nearest occupied house. The prosecutor believes that a suspended sentence would signal other illicit loggers that this is a low-risk manner of earning money.

The Offender's Perspective on the Case

With equal validity, the offender may present ideas that counter the prosecutor's claims. These may center around perceived reduced accountability ("All my life my dad told me that our property line was along the row of trees"), absence of intent ("I was just wanting to remove a safety hazard") or accidental circumstances not likely to recur ("When I shot at the dog I didn't know anyone was in the yard next door. I am as sorry as anyone could be, and I have turned my gun in to the police and will never let another one in my house").

Again, these are points that the judge should be aware of and are to be presented in the PSIR, to be accepted or ignored, as the judge determines. Consider the following examples:

> Mr. Laidlaw has been treated for a serious case of asthma for at least six years, and his physician, Dr. John Peterson, expresses the

opinion that the conditions in Washington County Jail (with which Dr. Peterson is familiar; he was Jail Doctor under the previous Sheriff) could be quite threatening, even to the fatal point. His letter to this office is attached.

Burkhart testified for the state in the trial of Barry Lockheed last year. There are seven co-defendants in that case who are now serving sentences in state institutions. The Court may wish to retain Burkhart in local facilities for his own protection.

As was reported in the trial, Mrs. Merlin has a son who will be three months old at the time of sentencing. She is breast-feeding the infant. The probation officer discussed this matter with the Superintendent of Women's Prison and with the Commissioner of Correction. Both officials say that there is no correctional facility in the state that accepts small children, and the Commissioner points out that federal statutes forbid mixing minors and adults. . The Commissioner says he would refuse to accept Mary Merlin and her infant.

The Probation Officer's Recommendations

Some judges instruct their staff not to present formal recommendations, although any well-written PSIR will inevitably carry at least implicit recommendations. But most Judges want recommendations, because it helps them frame the options available. Recommendations should be as specific as possible. To say that the sentence should be minimal is not nearly as helpful as to suggest a specific amount of time. The reasoning process is streamlined if the judge has a specific figure to accept or modify.

The following is a typical simple sentence recommendation:

Recommendations

1. For theft, a Class D Felony, sentence to the Department of Correction for two years, execution of the sentence to be suspended;

2. Formal probation for two years;

3. Probation User's Fees ($50 initial fee and 24 monthly fees of $10);

4.   Fine of $100 to be paid in 90 days;

5.   Court costs of $65 to be paid in 90 days.

Many courts are now developing approaches that aim to modify the offender's behavior through non-standard sanctions. One of these is Community Service Restitution.

CSR is based on the theory that since the criminal act is committed against society, there should be some restitution to society. This is customarily performed by personal service to a non-profit agency by the offender. These programs most commonly are operated by the Probation Department and the degree of restitution is measured by hours to be worked. For example, the recommendations above could be rewritten as:

Recommendations

1.   For theft, a Class D Felony, sentence to the Indiana Department of Correction for two years, execution of the sentence to be suspended;

2.   Formal probation for two years, a special condition of probation being the completion of 100 hours of community service under the supervision of the Probation Department;

3.   Probation User's Fees ($50 initial fee and 24 monthly fees of $10);

4.   Court costs of $65 to be paid in 90 days.

Other jurisdictions have introduced creative sentencing alternatives. These are as assorted as the PSIR writer's imagination. An illustration of a creative approach is as follows:

Recommendations

1.   For theft, a Class D Felony, sentence to the Indiana Department of Correction for two years, execution of the sentence to be suspended;

2.   Formal probation for two years, a special requirement of probation being house arrest for the first six months, in which the defendant is required to be in his home within 45 minutes

after clocking out of work and until 45 minutes before clocking in, with no stops permitted between work and residence; on days when not working, no absence from the home;

3.   Probation User's Fees ($50 initial fee and 24 monthly fees of $10);

4.   Court costs of $65 to be paid within 90 days.

The recommendations ought to reflect not only the traditional sound principle that the punishment fit the crime, but also should incorporate the larger interests of social justice. On occasion these will conflict, and it is at this point that the PSIR must delineate for the judge the issues in a clear manner. There is a place for retribution and there is a place for mercy; the writer must balance these qualities, which usually are mutually contradictory, in such a way that the judge can weigh them.

No one, even Silvers herself, defends her action in committing the offense. The murder occurred after three days in which the victim had almost incessantly baited the defendant, tantalizing her in a deliberate effort to bring her to the breaking point. Their eleven-year-old son confirms his mother's statement that for days her husband continued verbal and physical abuse. In his final act, he ordered her to go to the store for a six-pack of beer and told her that if she took more than ten minutes, he would kill their son. To emphasize the point, he took the shotgun off the rack and stood it beside the door. As she started to leave for the store, he came at her with his cane and, almost reflexively, she picked up the shotgun and shot him in the chest.

For reasons not clear to the Probation Department, she did not claim self-defense nor insanity, but there seems to be at least some of each in the circumstances. Certainly, she was pushed almost beyond the point of human endurance. Neighbors interviewed for this report support this assessment of the husband's behavior during those final days.

It would be socially abhorrent to suggest that a family fight can properly be settled with a shotgun, but it is equally important that the court sentence within the full scope of what happened in this crime. A chain that is strained beyond its rated limit can hardly be blamed for breaking, and a human being who is stressed beyond human limits likewise merits special understanding. Given the unique circumstances that led to this murder, and the likelihood that they will not occur again in Silvers' lifetime, it is recommended that the minimum sentence be imposed and that Silvers be permitted to return to her son, who needs the healing presence of a mother to help him lay to rest the ugly memories of those tragic days of hate and struggle.

The Probation Plan

Recent professional literature contains several approaches to risk assessment, classification and formulation of treatment goals for probation, and this is discussed in Chapter 15. Often the supervising probation officer is expected to draft such documents when the offender starts the probation term, but some judges like to review the plan before sentencing the offender. This is especially common when the PSIR writer will be the supervising probation officer. The plan can be presented as a separate section following the recommendations.

The probation plan is usually built around two considerations: the need to punish the offender for the crime and the need to control or alleviate problems that lead to a risk of future crimes. It is convenient to refer to the former as "punitive considerations" and the latter as "risk management considerations."

When dealing with punitive issues, the probation plan seeks to demonstrate to the offender and the public that the criminal conduct was wrong and deserves punishment. Often, the punishment is designed "to teach the person a lesson." Common conditions of fines, restitution, community service and so forth are used to place a public requirement on the offender to pay some cost for the crime.

Risk management issues are quite different. In most cases, some aspect of the offender's life (companions, drug abuse, idleness) creates a probability that criminal activity may occur again in the future. These are called "risk factors," and the probation plan must try to modify or eliminate these problems.

In considering both punishment and risk, the probation plan must be conservative in its promises, doing *less* rather than *more*. A short plan effectively implemented is to be preferred over a lengthy plan that includes conditions that are unlikely to be enforced.

Punitive Considerations

This offender needs to accept responsibility for his criminal behavior. Prompt restitution payments should be required in person (not by impersonal deductions from a paycheck) through personal contact with his probation officer each payday with receipt for restitution payment in hand.

Risk-Management Considerations

Since every arrest has occurred shortly after the bars close at 2:00 AM and involve drinking, the offender should be required to be home at 10:00 PM on Fridays, Saturdays and Sundays. It is important to this offender's success that he give top priority to finding a job. Special conditions of probation are recommended as follows:

1. Enrollment in the job-search program at Regional Vocational School, to include skill assessment and training, with verified contact with at least one prospective employer daily until employed.

2. To be home by 10:00 PM each Friday, Saturday and Sunday, and remain until dawn. If there have been no compliance problems after three months, the Sunday requirement may be dropped. Three months later the Saturday requirement may be dropped and three months after that, Friday.

3. Beginning with the first full paycheck, payment to the Clerk of the Court each payday of not less than ten dollars per week, receipt to be shown to the probation officer weekly or bi-weekly, depending on pay schedule.

Summary

The criminal justice system would be paralyzed without the tool of plea agreements. If every case were to be tried, the prosecutorial and court staffs would be inundated, and chronic criminals would rarely be brought to justice. At its best, the plea agreement serves the state, the defendant and the public equally well. Each side gives a bit and each side gets a bit.

However, where there are two negotiators, it is possible for one to out-negotiate the other, and here is where the alert PSIR writer purifies the system. If the plea agreement is unfair to either side or to the interests of society, the fact needs to be brought to the attention of the judge.

The most important part of the PSIR is the recommendation. No one in the entire criminal justice system is better informed about a case than the PSIR writer. All other parties have viewed the material from a narrow perspective. The writer hears from the police, the victim, the prosecutor, the defense attorney and other sources whose input is important. Like watching a baseball game through a hole in the fence that focuses only on the shortstop, all the players in the courtroom drama have tunnel vision. It is up to the writer to assemble all relevant information, mix it properly, condense it to a manageable size, and lay it before the judge. The precipitate from that process ought to be a good set of recommendations. They should be at the point of convergence of all related factors gathered during the investigation. That is why it is called a pre-sentence investigation report. The end product is the sentence, and the recommendation is where the writer comes out after having tussled with the facts thoroughly.

GROUP EXERCISE

The defendant is a 27-year-old female, mother of two pre-school children, who has lived on the edge of criminal subculture (barmaid, part-time prostitute, stripper) but has never before been convicted of a felony. She appears to be addicted (tracks on her arms) but denies habitual substance abuse. She sold cocaine to an undercover officer, and when they searched her apartment they found an amount which is defined by state law as Dealing in a Controlled Substance, a felony. The maximum penalty is ten years and a $10,000 fine, but since she has no prior felony, it can all be suspended (with probation). Two class members engage in negotiation over the plea agreement as Prosecutor and Defense Attorney.

DISCUSSION QUESTIONS

1. You consider the plea agreement to be too lenient and go back to the Prosecutor the second time for his reasons for agreeing to it. He is indignant; he tells you it is not your job to second-guess the two attorneys, who have reached a resolution satisfactory to them. How do you handle the Prosecutor?

2. How far is it legitimate to go in a plea agreement? Sometimes quite extraneous considerations are included, as the illustration of the client who agreed not to visit his minor son. Perhaps this was a sop thrown in to appease the victim. If both sides agree, are there any practical limits beyond which the plea agreement should not go? Why or why not?

3. How do you react to the term "plea *bargain*"?

4. In a classic case, John Junior Jones was arrested in Polk County and later transferred to Ashton County on another charge. During that period, his son, John Jones, Jr., was also arrested in Ashton County and transferred also to Polk County on another charge. Birthdates and Social Security numbers on the book-in cards had been scratched out and written over several times. How would you calculate jail time credit?

Chapter 13
Special Versions of the PSIR

When all the time and material costs of a normal PSIR are added up into a single figure, the process can be seen as relatively expensive; a complicated PSIR might cost the state as much as $500 or more. In many cases, the PSIR is routine; and much of the process is really not likely to be relevant to the ultimate sentence. This has led to experimentation with innovative types of PSIR formats. In this chapter, two common innovations are explored: the short-form PSIR and the private PSIR.

Short-Form PSIR

Where used, the short-form PSIR is usually reserved for selected cases. These tend to be routine cases where a straightforward plea agreement has already settled any possible differences between the two sides, and there are apparently no serious issues to be weighed by the judge.

The short-form saves only a little time for the PSIR writer, however, because the same amount of investigation is normally required before the officer becomes convinced that there are no hidden problems. In many cases, the preparation of the short-form PSIR saves only a few minutes of dictating time for the officer and an hour or so of secretarial time.

The main savings lies in a reduction of the judge's time to read the PSIR. Rather than eight or ten pages, the short-form PSIR runs about two pages. It contains all relevant information, but in streamlined form. The following is a typical short-form PSIR. Each heading is followed by only one brief, succinct paragraph or less.

State of Oregon v. William Dale Kaufman
3SCR-86-141

BEFORE THE HONORABLE ARTHUR JAMES STEPHENS
Multnomah County Court 3
Sentencing date: April 7, 1987

Defendant: William Dale Kaufman
              1727 Washington Avenue
              Portland, OR 89507
    Date of Birth: March 15, 1949 (38 years)

Social Security: 305-01-734X
Marital Status: Divorced

OFFICIAL VERSION: Theft, Class C Felony

On or about November 12, 1986, the defendant did knowingly exert unauthorized control over the property of K-Mart, 19753 Wilson Avenue, Portland, OR, to wit: three pairs of Levi jeans, by taking said property with the intent to deprive K-Mart of the value and use thereof.

DEFENDANT'S VERSION:

I was getting ready for a new job and needed jeans and didn't have any money and I took them and got caught.

VICTIM'S IMPACT:

The stolen merchandise was recovered undamaged just outside the door of the store.

JAIL TIME:

The defendant was detained on a warrantless arrest on November 12, 1986, and was released on bond on November 15, 1986, three days later.

PREVIOUS TROUBLE:

Multnomah County and Portland Municipal Police Department files carry the following entries:

Date	Offense	Jurisdiction	Disposition
02/21/66	JD Trespass	Mult. Co.	Informal adjustment
12/11/80	Public Intoxication	Ptl.	Dismissed
11/12/86	Criminal Conversion	Ptl.	Instant offense

SOCIAL SETTING:

The defendant has a brother two years older and a sister one year younger. Parents remain married, father retired from Sears Roebuck service department. Kaufman left school at the end of the eleventh grade to take a full-time job. His marriage lasted two years, with no children. He worked for Capital Maintenance Services Co. for eighteen years (his only job), at which time they went out of business. He was unemployed about a year before he found work, which led to this attempt to shoplift jeans for his new job.

STATEMENT BY PROBATION OFFICER:

Kaufman appears to be a reasonably well adjusted, middle-aged male who felt trapped by circumstances and took an obvious way out without thinking through the consequences. He seems to be genuinely remorseful, deeply embarrassed and determined that it will not happen again. Throughout the experience he has demonstrated a good attitude toward himself and his behavior.

THE PLEA AGREEMENT:

A signed plea agreement provides that the defendant will plead guilty as charged and that he will be placed upon formal probation for two years, do forty hours of community service restitution through Offender Aid and Restoration, and pay standard Probation Fees.

RECOMMENDATION:

The Probation Department recommends that the Court accept the plea agreement and sentence as follows:

1. For Criminal Conversion, Theft, a Class C Felony, sentence to the Oregon Department of Correction for two years, execution of the sentence to be suspended;

2. Probation for two years, a special condition being forty (40) hours of community service restitution to be completed within three months through Offender Aid and Restoration.

3. Probation Fees ($ 15 per month for twenty-four months);

4. Costs of this action ($ 65).

Respectfully submitted,

George Flanders, Probation Officer
March 15, 1987

It is important to understand that the short-form PSIR is not a less responsible piece of professional work. The full armory of skills is required to produce a competent short-form PSIR; the only difference is that the writer censures what is included in the written document. If all the signs are favorable, it is not necessary to burden the judge with unnecessary information, so the writer filters it out, but not without examining that information before deciding to omit it.

The major disadvantage to the short-form PSIR is archival. If the offender returns later for a new offense, the file does not contain information which might be useful, but this is not so critical that it is worth the extra work entailed in doing a long-form. If the writer is concerned about the preservation of information, notes accumulated during the investigation can be preserved in the file. (See Appendix C for a short-form schedule.)

The PSIR in Private Practice

Although it is still far from becoming a trend, there are professionals who, for a fee, prepare investigations for clients, and submit them to the court as a supplement to the PSIR prepared by the court staff.

There are reasons for this. So much hinges upon the PSIR that, in some cases, the client needs to guarantee that his or her perspective is well presented. A harried PSIR writer facing statutory deadlines may not be able to devote as much time to researching a client's background as that client wishes. In some jurisdictions a probation officer may be assigned twelve PSIRs a week, in addition to supervising a case load of 300. Even a more "normal" load of 2 PSIRs and 80 cases simply means some work does not get done. When asked about private PSIR's one attorney remarked that he did not intend to win the case in the court room, only to lose it on the PSIR writer's desk. Attorneys like to have control over what the judge sees.

To the client, the advantage of a private PSIR is the opportunity to present his or her view in a sympathetic manner. This can be done at the time of sentencing through sworn testimony and argument, but by that time the judge may have already decided what the sentence is to be. Timing is better if the information can be presented for the judge to study in chambers well in advance of the sentencing hearing.

Even so, in most jurisdictions it probably is a better strategy for the defense attorney to get the material to the judge via the court's own PSIR. Some states require the PSIR writer to include everything the defendant asks to be included. If the favorable information comes in through the court's PSIR, there are two advantages. It has a greater aura of objectivity because it comes from an official source. Second, the PSIR writer is forced to consider the material before framing a recommendation.

The manner in which privately prepared PSIR's are processed varies, depending upon local circumstances. If the court's PSIR writer is receptive, the attorney may offer to provide the court with the social history and/or other parts in written form. This is normally presented as a service to the court, with the caveat that it would be edited by the PSIR writer.

In other settings, however, an entirely separate PSIR might be prepared. The alert attorney will anticipate the court's reaction and will avoid irritating the judge or the Probation Department with a competing document.

The privately produced PSIR is most useful when it follows the normal format used in that court, for the simple reason that the judge reads it with greater familiarity and knows where to find what he/she is looking for.

The foci of such PSIRs will usually be diminished responsibility for the crime or to build a case for therapy rather than imprisonment. In the privately produced PSIR, these options can be emphasized more than they might be by the court's staff.

Diminished responsibility arises in the history of the client or in the history of the offense. Two illustrations follow:

When McGregor was about ten years old his mother ran away with a neighbor, the father of his best playmate. In that stressful situation, his older sister revealed to him for the first time that he had been adopted and that his natural mother was the Aunt Mary about whom the family had always talked in whispers. At that point, he developed a negative attitude toward all women, from which he has never recovered. He avoids contact with "respectable" women and treats all others with contempt. His violent mistreatment of the victim in this offense stems from the perceived injustices of those early rejections by his two mother-figures.

Marie Huff explains her reason for the theft as being impulsive and irrational. Her twelve-year-old daughter had been given an assignment of homework by her favorite teacher and it was due the next morning. When she opened her paste jar she found the contents dry and unuseable. It was the end of the month and Huff was without money with which to buy paste. Feeling frustrated with the timing of the minor crisis, and resentful because her daughter's father was always late with support payments, she went to the 24-hour supermarket to get the paste for her daughter. The only size they had cost $3.29 and she had only about two dollars in her purse, which would have bought the smaller size if they had had it. Given her mood before she got to the market and finding only a large size on the shelf, her emotions overcame her good judgment and she put the jar in her coat pocket and walked out. Huff maintains that this is the first time in her life that she ever shoplifted.

Another reason for private preparation of the PSIR is to influence the sentence with a judge who does not want recommendations in the PSIR. This requires delicate wording to suggest a sentence without seeming to do so.

> The defendant freely admits to having a long-term problem with abuse of alcohol and other substances, and the near-fatality which he caused in the present offense has gotten his attention. While awaiting disposition of the charges, he has participated in Alcoholics Anonymous meetings twice weekly, but he feels insecure with AA and would like to be able to enter a residential program. His health insurance would cover the $6,000 cost at a treatment facility.

> Most substance-abuse counselors are reluctant to see a client enter a penal environment after treatment because it tends to undo all the good achieved in therapy. They much prefer (sometimes insist) that if there is to be a period of incarceration, it come before treatment. This means that a client completes a penal obligation first, takes therapy and then is released to the streets immediately, so that defenses are at their maximum and new habit forms are sealed by action.

> It appears that the minimum sentence in this case is two years. With allowance for good behavior, this translates into one calendar year. The treatment program which the defendant's health insurance provider accepts has a three-month program. If he could be sentenced to the Wayne County Detention Facility for eighteen months and furloughed to the Community Hospital Substance Abuse Program for six months, good time to be allowed in both, it would combine punishment with treatment and might restore the defendant to responsible citizenship.

In most jurisdictions the defendant is permitted to suggest a reasonable sentence to the court. Doing this in a privately produced PSIR may be acceptable, and this presents the defense with an opportunity to be creative in proposing alternatives, as the following example shows:

Recommendation

Because of the defendant's earlier criminal history, the statute provides for mandatory executed sentence for this offense. However, it is to be noted that there has not been an arrest for any reason in four-and-one-half years, and during that time the defendant has been active in community affairs (Little League, Junior Chamber of Commerce and the Emmanuel Methodist Church; see "Social History," above).

It does not appear that any desirable outcome would result from traditional incarceration. All the evidence presented supports the assertion that Jones has already been rehabilitated. In the almost seven years since the offense was committed, he has led an exemplary life, has participated fully in community affairs and has assumed more than his share of community responsibility.

In view of the fact that he already has been rehabilitated, but also regarding the fact that the statute requires an executed portion of the sentence, the defendant asks the Court to consider sentence to twenty-six weekends, from 6:00 p.m. Friday to 6:00 p.m. Sunday.

There are other situations in which the privately prepared PSIR may have value for the defendant. Because the PSIR writer is overloaded or because funds restrict research, it may not be possible to follow up on leads that could illuminate some of the issues. There are times when one additional interview might have changed the direction of the court-produced PSIR. It is then up to private counsel to provide that input. This can relate to further evaluations of either the offender or the victim, as the following two illustrations show:

Dr. Peter Franklin, psychiatrist at the Community Health Center, reviewed the tests in Allenson's file. His full report is attached to this PSIR, but in short, he is of the opinion that the behavior disorder may well be glandular in origin and that it might respond to medication, although this would require hospitalization for at least a month for fully controlled conditions.

During the trial there were unsupported allegations that the victim had a history of erratic episodes in which he appeared to tantalize and to challenge others to do violence against him. Private investigators since the trial have obtained five notarized affidavits describing seven incidents in which the victim took the initiative in challenging another person to respond violently. Those affidavits are attached to this report, along with court records for three cases similar to this one. There appears to have been a pattern of behavior in which the victim deliberately set out to goad others to the breaking point. He seems to have invited physical punishment. In that context, Mr. Jacobs, convicted in this cause, is also the victim of a plot to involve him in violence. While this does not excuse his violent response, it does help to explain why he engaged in battery against the victim.

In addition to PSIRs produced by defense attorneys, there is a new field of privately commissioned professional PSIR-writers. They are skilled specialists who bring expertise to the aid of the defendant in the same way the defense attorney does, and on the same basis, the client pays for services rendered.

One major benefit to the client is that the privately commissioned PSIR is produced without the time and budget restrictions that are inescapable for court personnel. Since the client is paying, the private investigator can devote whatever time is needed and is free to spend funds on research that the court PSIR writer cannot, such as travel to another city to secure important records.

Likewise, the privately produced PSIR is able to propose alternatives that may be more meaningful than unproductive incarceration. Although some judges may look upon the privately employed writer of a PSIR as a "hired gun," the true role is not unlike that of the defense attorney, whose motives are to represent the best interest of the client. However, the purpose of the privately prepared PSIR should not be "to get him off." Instead, it should present to the judge all relevant information and to suggest, either directly or subtly, a sentence that will better suit the defendant's needs to adjust after sentencing.

Summary

A progressive court is ready to adopt sharper tools in the administration of justice. Two recent innovations are the short-form PSIR, which condenses salient material and saves the judge from reading unnecessarily complete documents, and the private PSIR, which provides the judge with information that otherwise might not be available.

GROUP EXERCISE

Go through the long-form and short-form PSIRs at the end of this book for John Franklin. Develop a list of the differences in information contained in each. Identify ways that the differences might influence the eventual sentence.

DISCUSSION QUESTIONS

1. Is there a conflict of interest for a person to accept money from the defendant for giving the court a PSIR? What pressures does this create? Why would the court want to pay attention to such a PSIR?

2. What are the advantages to the judge of a short-form PSIR? What are the disadvantages?

3. Should the victim be able to develop a PSIR? Why or why not? If a PSIR were done for the victim, how would it be done?

Part III
The Correctional Role of the PSIR

While the main function of the PSIR is to assist the judge in selecting a sentence, this is by far not the only use to which the document is put. Because the PSIR is normally the most carefully developed investigation of the offender's circumstances, it forms the fulcrum of adjudication. The PSIR reappears as a classification document, a statistical research document and a parole planning aid, as these various needs occur.

In the case of John Franklin, for example, the PSIR will be read by the Institutional Classification Committee of the State Reformatory, and they will base their program decisions partly on the information it contains. Later, when Franklin is released to supervision, the caseworker will read the PSIR before meeting Franklin in order to get some insight on how to approach supervising him. The information in the PSIR will also be recorded in the annual statistics of the Department of Corrections and the Administrative Office of the Courts. These are but a few of the myriad decisions that depend upon high quality information in the PSIR.

In Part III, we describe the broad role of the PSIR as a central data source in corrections. We begin with a review of the law as it applies to the PSIR. We then consider the uses of the PSIR in supervising offenders in the community and managing offenders in other correctional programs. This is followed by an assessment of the administrative issues that the PSIR process raises. The final chapter is an evaluation of the future of the PSIR.

Chapter 14
The Law of the PSIR

In this chapter, the legal requirements of the PSIR are reviewed. Four major legal considerations are highlighted: the legal authority for the PSIR, content requirements for the PSIR, the disclosure/confidentiality controversy and the PSIR writer liability in preparing the report.

Legal Authority and Requirements

The laws of the states vary regarding the PSIR. Variation exists in whether the report is mandatory or optional, the types of offenses or offenders covered by the report and the content of the report.

A PSIR is not necessarily an automatic part of the sentencing process. Ordinarily, the court must order that a PSIR be prepared before the PSIR writer is authorized to begin the investigation. There are three basic legal approaches as to whether a PSIR should be ordered.

1. Twenty-three states and the federal government have laws stating that the PSIR is mandatory for all or almost all felony offenses. In some of these jurisdictions, other factors can also require that a PSIR be prepared. Examples of these factors are:

    when incarceration of a year or more is a possible disposition, or

    when the defendant is under 21, or under 18 years of age, or

    the defendant is a first offender.

2. Nine states' statutes make the PSIR mandatory in felony cases when probation is being considered as a disposition. Where probation is not being considered, the PSIR is left to the discretion of the court.

3. In seventeen jurisdictions, ordering a PSIR is entirely up to the discretion of the sentencing court.

173

The remaining jurisdictions do not have any approach specified in their statutes. In addition to statutory law, there often are other regulations in the court rules or administrative policy.[1] The following examples illustrate the diversity of requirements, statutes and rules regarding PSIRs:

New Jersey   A PSIR is required in all felony offenses, but in the misdemeanor cases, it is suggested only when incarceration is being considered.

Connecticut   A PSIR is mandatory only if the punishment includes the possibility of imprisonment for more than one year.

Pennsylvania   A PSIR is required when incarceration of more than one year is possible, or if the offender is under 21 years of age or is a first-time adult offender (the PSIR may be waived in the latter cases if the court states its reasons on the record).

The District of Columbia Superior Court   A PSIR is required unless the offender waives the investigation with the court's permission, or there is sufficient information already available to impose sentence.

California   The PSIR is mandatory for all persons convicted of a felony; for misdemeanor convictions it is left discretionary.

Arizona   The PSIR is mandated for all persons convicted of an offense punishable by incarceration for a year or more and may be ordered in other cases.

Texas   PSIRs are not mandated for any cases and, thus, are totally discretionary. Use of the PSIR in the Texas courts ranges from 10% to 95% of the cases.[2]

The general practice is to require a PSIR when serious crimes are involved. If PSIRs are mandated, typically it is for felony offenses where one year or more of incarceration is possible.

Content and Format of the PSIR

The content required in the PSIR may also vary among jurisdictions, not unlike the authority or requirement to prepare a PSIR. At least 40 jurisdictions specify the areas of information which the PSIR must cover, although this is generally very broadly defined in the statutes. Normally, the statute defines several items of content as required, but leaves the remainder to administrative policy.[3] In five states (Hawaii, Indiana, Iowa, Nebraska and South Dakota) the statutes specify the content of the PSIR in considerable detail.

In general, the overall content of the PSIR (topic areas, sequencing, etc.) depends on the policies of the organization producing them. At times, a local court will provide guidance, but this tends to be rare. Where it does occur, guidance from the court is based more on the requirements of the court for an individual case than as a matter of routine policy.[4]

One influential force in determining the content and format of the PSIR has been the Probation Division of the Administrative Office of the United States Courts, which oversees the operation of the federal probation offices. In a series of publications over the past several decades, the Probation Division has developed a comprehensive manual on the PSIR[5] which has exerted great influence on the PSIRs outside the federal system. Many agencies have chosen to adopt the federal monographs as their standard for the PSIR.

Disclosure and Confidentiality

The PSIR was long held to be a confidential court document for the judge's eyes only. Doctrines to this effect still exist in many states, and confidentiality has been the subject of long standing, heated debate. The issue is whether the availability of the completed PSIR should be restricted to the court, or to whom and under what circumstances it should be disclosed.

The arguments for confidentiality are based on the need for the sentencing court to have full and complete information for sentencing. Persons interviewed may be assured of anonymity if the report is confidential and, thus, are more willing to provide sensitive, but crucial, information. Anonymity provides a shield from reprisals and protection against potentially compromising information. This applies to private citizens, government agencies (in particular law enforcement) and social service agencies.

The PSIR writer also gains from this protection because more full and complete information, both favorable and unfavorable to the offender, may be presented in frank and objective terms. Confidentiality becomes of even more concern if the PSIR contains a recommendation for incarceration. If the court chooses to grant probation, an awkward situation can develop between the officer who recommended jail and the offender who knows that recommendation, but is placed on probation anyway. This can have a chilling effect on the process of guidance, assistance and rehabilitation which is a large part of probation supervision.

Administrators of probation agencies also claim that disclosure can significantly delay the sentencing process. Counsel may challenge the report and hearings have to be held to resolve the disputes. This also requires the PSIR writer to be in court, away from the investigative or supervisory work.

It was largely because of arguments such as this that the U.S. Supreme Court in *Williams v. New York* (337 US 241 [1940]) ruled that a PSIR is a court document and disclosure is not constitutionally required. In *Williams*, a judge imposed the death penalty despite the jury's recommendation for leniency based on statements contained in the PSIR, the contents of which were not disclosed to the defense.

Proponents of disclosure argue that it is essential to the defense that the PSIR, on which the court will rely in sentencing, be available for review and challenge. Inaccuracies and errors, if left unchallenged, might influence the judge and possibly produce a sentence which is inappropriate or even illegal in light of the true facts.

In *Townsend v. Burke* (334 US 736 [1948]) the United States Supreme Court held that a sentence cannot be based on false information, and two separate circuits of the United States Court of Appeals have held that sentencing a person based on information that is materially false is in violation of the person's due process rights (*US v. Lasky*, 592 F.2d. 560 [9th. Cir. 1979], *Moore v. US*, 571 F.2d. 179 [3rd. Cir. 1978]).

Clearly false information is a problem and can not be considered legally in determining a sentence. Yet, there are two kinds of false information. If persons interviewed fear disclosure and therefore fail to give certain sensitive information, then the PSIR is in a sense "false" because it does not include all relevant information. On the other hand, if the PSIR writer erroneously records misinformation, how can it be learned that the information is false if no one in a position to know reads the report?

In 1969, the New Jersey Supreme Court faced the issue of disclosure in *State v. Kunz* (55 NJ 128, [1969]). The New Jersy Court stated that "as a matter of fundamental fairness" the PSIR should be made available to the defendant and counsel and to the prosecutor in advance of sentencing. This allows them time to review the report for accuracy and to prepare challenges if necessary for the sentencing hearing.

However, the Court recognized the validity of some of the concerns raised by advocates of confidentiality and provided that the PSIR should be submitted to the sentencing judge prior to disclosure. After reviewing the report, the judge may delete portions which are damaging to the offender or compromise the anonymity of persons interviewed. After this review by the judge, the report is released to the defense counsel and the prosecutor. Aside from this limited disclosure, the PSIR remains the court's property,[6] as indicated by the following standard statement:

CONFIDENTIAL

> This report shall remain confidential and copies thereof shall not be made nor disclosure of the contents made to third persons, except as may be necessary in subsequent court proceedings involving the sentence imposed or disposition made.

By contrast, in California, court law provides that the PSIR is a public document for ten days after sentencing.[7] This has resulted in the newspapers running stories which quote extensively from the PSIR. In response to this pressure, an informal practice of preparing abbreviated reports has developed in at least one California county, and this has had a deleterious effect on the quality and comprehensiveness of the PSIR provided to the judges.

A more typical middle road has been taken in Arizona, where the PSIR is routinely made a matter of public record. Provisions do exist to protect some information, known as "non-disclosed" items. This applies to information which, if disclosed, may reveal a confidential source creating a life-threatening situation for victims or witnesses, or reveals a psychiatric evaluation which may jeopardize rehabilitation, or may reveal information compromising an ongoing police investigation. According to a recent report, the "non-disclosed" provision is rarely used,[8] suggesting that it is probably even more rarely abused. In those instances where it is invoked, the related items must be identified as "non-disclosed" items in the body of the report, and a statement must be entered on the court record that this information was not used in the determination of sentence.

In the federal courts, the Federal Rules of Criminal Procedure require the sentencing judge to disclose all information relied upon in sentencing. Exceptions to this rule are permitted when:

1.   Disclosure might disrupt the rehabilitation of the defendant, or

2.   The information was obtained on the promise of confidentiality, or

3.   Harm might result to the defendant or any other person.

Fed. R. Crim. P. 32(c)(3)

Third party disclosures to other than the defense or prosecution provide a different circumstance. The case of *US v. Peerless Importers* (F.2d. [2nd, Cir. 1983]) involved a request from the Attorney General of Arizona for a copy of a federal court's PSIR. The U.S. Court of Appeals for the Second Circuit held that the PSIR is a confidential document and may be released to third parties *only* when the *court itself* finds that a compelling case has been made for disclosure in order to meet the ends of justice. That decision should not be delegated to probation authorities. The Second Circuit noted that the PSIR always remains the property of the court, even when copies are in the hands of other agencies such as the Federal Bureau of Prisons (BOP) and the United States Parole Commission (USPC). Copies of the PSIR must be returned to the court when those agencies are done with it or upon request.[9]

This seemingly straightforward situation is complicated by the fact that the Bureau of Prisons and Parole Commission files *are* covered by the Freedom of Information Act (FOIA), which has provided access to federal government agency records for citizens with an interest in them (5 U.S.C. 522). This access is restricted by several exemptions, one of which is the "Courts of the United States" (5 U.S.C. 551(1)(B), 552(e)). Thus the federal courts and their probation officers are not bound by the provisions of the FOIA. This interpretation has been upheld by several Circuits of the U.S. Court of Appeals. (*Berry v. Dept. of Justice*, 733 F.2d. 1343 [9th. Cir. 1984], *Ernst & Ernst v. FDIC*, 677 F.2d. 230 [2d. Cir. 1982], *Cook v. Willingham*, 400 F.2d 885 [10th. Cir. 1968]).

Since the BOP and USPC files are accessible under the FOIA, there appears a risk that the court's control over the PSIR could be lost. At least one circuit of the U.S. Court of Appeals has ruled that absent an express statement asserting the court's continued control over the PSIR, the report may be subject to a legitimate POIA request (*U.S. v. Carson*, 631 F.2d. 1008 [D.C. Cir., 1980]). Thus, the federal courts have an affirmative responsibility to maintain control over the PSIR.

The Probation Division of the Administrative Office of the United States Courts provides a legend to be stamped on the cover of the PSIR before it is sent to the Bureau of Prisons or the Parole Commission.

CONFIDENTIAL
Property of U.S. Courts
Submitted for Official Use of
U.S. Parole Commission and
Federal Bureau of Prisons. To Be
Returned After Such Use, Or Upon Request.
Disclosure Authorized Only to
Comply with 18 USC 4208(b)(2)

The Probation Division also maintains that offenders have no right to obtain a copy of their PSIR from their probation officer. They have the opportunity to review the PSIR at sentencing, and that right of review does not include possession of a copy. The PSIR remains the property of the court.

Federal statutes govern the dissemination of agency information to other agencies under the Privacy Act (5 U.S.C. 552a). Under the Act, the subjects of most federal agency files have the right to a list of the agencies to which information from their file has been released. They also have the right to prevent the records from being used or divulged for other than their original purpose. As with the FOIA, the federal courts and their probation offices are not bound by the provisions of the Privacy Act with regard to their own files, but they must abide by the act when dealing with other federal agencies and their records. This means that federal probation files may be on the "information release" list of other federal agencies, and that permission must be sought for such information.

The Probation Division recommends that the PSIR writer utilize written authorizations for release of information from other agencies whenever possible. Authorization allows the agency with the records to release the files without being subject to suit under the Privacy Act.[10]

Legal Liability in the PSIR Process

In recent years, probation officer liability has become a prominent concern of probation officers.[11] Under state and federal law, offenders and third parties are suing probation officers for a variety of wrongs, real and imagined. There are two types of liability: tort and civil rights liability under federal statute.

Tort Liability

Many of the actions filed against probation officers are civil suits, claiming tort liability. A tort is a civilly (as opposed to criminally) wrongful act that causes injury to the person or property of another in violation of a duty imposed by law.

A tort in the PSIR area could be based on the claim that wrong or inaccurate information was included in a PSIR, causing damage to occur, such as a harsher sentence. In contrast, the victim of a subsequent crime could claim that the PSIR should have included information about a condition or behavior pattern of the offender that would have resulted in a more severe sentence that should have kept the offender in prison and prevented that person from being victimized. Other torts could include invasion of privacy, libel, slander and any range of things related to the inclusion or exclusion of information.

Civil Liability Under Section 1983

A person wronged by a PSIR writer may also seek redress under the provisions of Title 42, United States Code, Section 1983, Civil Action for Deprivation of Rights. This federal statute provides that anyone who, acting under color of law, deprives an individual of a constitutional right is liable to the injured party for actual and punitive damages. The types of suits filed under this section vary widely, covering just about every conceivable type of improper action that involves a public officer. Moreover, courts have been very liberal in allowing these suits to be filed, actually hearing cases that many might consider frivolous, even though courts are less likely to find support in such a case.

For the PSIR writer, a wide range of charges may be brought. Given the nature of the investigation, allegations would probably cover including damaging information, excluding helpful information, invasion of privacy, failure to fully investigate, bias and faulty interpretation.

Section 1983 civil rights suits are the most threatening of all because the courts provide support to indigent litigants who bring such suits and even though the dollar amount of actual damages may have been slight, the court may order punitive damages to "teach a lesson" to other officials. In extreme cases, public officials have lost their personal savings and even their homes for unusually vicious or unconscionable actions against accused criminals.

Defenses to Liability Suits

A complex body of law exists on the subject of defenses to suits for liability; what follows is only a brief review.

Immunity. Over the years, the courts have developed a series of doctrines conferring immunity to liability. These doctrines provide governmental agencies and employees with protection from liability for acts which occur while performing regular work duties.

For the PSIR writer, two types of immunity are of greatest interest: official and quasi-judicial.

> *Official Immunity* means that some government officials are protected from liability for performing their duties. This can be absolute immunity which means that any act is protected or qualified immunity, which means that only legitimate acts within the reasonable domain of the job are protected. Probation officers generally enjoy only qualified immunity.

> *Quasi-judicial Immunity* extends some of the absolute immunity enjoyed by judges to those working for the court. If the work performed is essential to the court's functioning, the umbrella of judicial immunity can cover court personnel, including probation officers.

> In a recent federal case (*Spaulding v. Neilson*, 599 E.2d. 728 [5th. Cir. 1979]) a probation officer preparing a PSIR was entitled to judicial immunity. However, the courts have held that incompetent or malfeasant performance of the job duties is not subject to quasi-judicial immunity.

Good Faith Defense. The most common defense in civil rights suits is what is known as the "good faith" defense. It has been recognized as a legitimate defense for Section 1983 cases in the federal courts since 1967. The "good faith" defense means that the PSIR writer was acting with honest intentions, under the law and in the absence of any fraud, deceit, collusion or gross negligence. The acceptance or rejection of the good faith defense is a subjective judgment and does not provide the clear protections of the various immunities.

One result of the rapid growth of suits has been the availability of insurance for government workers (such as PSIR writers) much like a doctor's professional liability insurance. Although most government officials are already covered by the state's legal powers, probation officers should be warned that in many cases if the insuring agent can show that the action of the PSIR writer was not a legitimate part of the job responsibilities, the state may eschew any responsibility to defend the individual or pay damages.

Reducing the Risk of Liability

A recent survey of all state Attorneys General sought their advice on how probation officers can best reduce their possible legal liability in connection with their work.[12] The top five answers were:

1.	Document work and keep good records	40%
2.	Know and follow departmental rules and regulations, and statutes	35%
3.	Arrange for legal counsel and seek legal advice whenever questions arise	27%
4.	Act within the scope of your duties and in good faith	20%
5.	Get approval from your supervisor if you have any questions about what you are doing	18%

This suggests that the essential core to defending against inevitable civil suits is (1) to have written departmental policy regarding the PSIR process; (2) to involve the supervisors in that process; and (3) to monitor to ensure the process is being followed. Standards for the PSIR process are essential in today's legally charged environment.

Summary

In this chapter, we have reviewed the legal context of the PSIR process. We presented the legal authority for the content and practice of the PSIR. We then discussed two critical legal issues for the PSIR field: disclosure and liability. Guidelines for resolving legal issues were presented.

Notes

[1] Harry E. Allen and others. Critical Issues in Adult Probation: Summary. Washington, DC: National Institute of Law Enforcement and Criminal Justice, 1979, pp. 107-7.

[2] Loren A. Beckley and others. *Presentence Investigation Report Program: The Final Report*. Sacramento, CA: American Justice Institute, 1981, pp. 11-146.

[3] See, for example, New Jersey Statutes Annotated 2C:44-6 b.

[4] Robert M. Carter. *Presentence Report Handbook*. Washington, DC: National Institute of Law Enforcement and Criminal Justice, 1978, p. 13.

[5] Administratice Office of the United States Courts, Probation Division. *The Presentence Investigation Report*, Publication 101, 1943; same title, Publication 103, 1965; *The Selective Presentence Investigation Report*, Publication 104, 1974; *The Presentence Investigation Report*, Publication 105, 1978, revised ed. 1984.

[6] Rules Governing the Courts of the State of New Jersey, *R.* 1:17.

[7] West Ann. Cal. Penal Code § 1203b, 3 Ops. Atty. Gen'l 391 (California).

[8] Beckley, *Final Report*, p. 105.

[9] AOUSC, *The Presentence Investigation Report*, 1984 ed., p. 30.

[10] *Ibid.*, p. 31.

[11] Further guidance of a more legal nature can be obtained from Rolando V. del Carmen's excellent work, *Potential Liabilities of Probation and Parole Officers* published by the National Institute of Corrections (Revised Edition by Anderson Publishing Co., 1985). A probation or parole officer concerned about liability should be aware that reliance on del Carmen's work alone would not be sufficient (as he so notes). Local legal counsel should be consulted for the specifics of statute and case law in each jurisdiction.

[12] del Carmen, pp. 190-1.

GROUP EXERCISE

Select a group of five students to play the role of Mack Ray, and ask them to leave the room. The rest of the class should then divide into two roles (prosecutor and defense attorney) and develop questions for Mack Ray in order to challenge different parts of the PSIR for John Franklin. Then bring the Mack Ray group back in, and put them on the "witness stand." Take turns asking questions and allow the five to develop responses to the questions. Then discuss the role of the PSIR in the adversarial process.

DISCUSSION QUESTIONS

1.   Assume that the Supreme Court just declared the PSIR unconstitutional. What arguments might it make in defense of its decision?

2.   Is there ever a time that information in the PSIR should *not* be disclosed to the defendant? If so, give examples and justifications.

3.   What should happen to a PSIR writer who knowingly puts false information in the PSIR? Who fails to verify information reported in the PSIR? Should these acts be considered a crime? Why or why not?

Chapter 15
The Role of the PSIR
in Classification
and Probation Supervision

Across the United States, thousands of offenders are received each year for probation supervision. As with any group of human beings, these probationers will be in some ways alike and in other ways, different. As such, they will certainly present challenges to the probation staff charged with carrying out the supervision.

One task which falls to the probation officer is *how* to determine *what* to do with the probationers under supervision. Some direction is provided by the court order placing the person on probation. Still more guidance is provided by the goals of the probation agency and by its policies and procedures. Even so, a substantial amount of discretion is left in deciding how to supervise the probationer.

Absent specific guidance, probation officers develop their own systems for supervising offenders. They do not treat all probationers alike. Instead, they make an assessment of each offender and assign each a priority for attention, compared to other cases on their caseload. Probation officers do not determine in the abstract how often to see a probationer. Instead, they make a rough comparison of how much attention a probationer needs *given the rest of the workload*; it is an assessment of how much time a probation officer can afford to spend on a case. This enables the probation officer to deal more realistically with what would otherwise be an unmanageable task.

This process is known as classification: cases are assigned to a group of similar cases, and the level and type of supervision of cases in that group will be somewhat similiar. Probation officers do this intuitively, because it enables them to manage their work. When classification is done by officers in an *ad hoc* manner, without guidelines, there are serious problems which emerge.

First, there is no guarantee that the criteria used by the officers will be similiar, consistent, and free of bias. Further, there is no assurance that classification decisions made independently and without review will reflect the goals and priorities of the probation organization as a whole.

This last point is particularly important. Organizations are established in the first place because there is a belief that what the organization does or provides is socially valued. Probation provides a product or service which is valued by the public, and those who administer the probation agency are responsible for ensuring that the agency is carrying out its mandated mission. They must see that the goals established for supervision are pursued consistently and uniformly. This is not possible when crucial decisions about the priorities of supervision are being made independently by individual officers without review. Without classification standards, there are as many policies for supervision as there are officers with caseloads.[1]

Classification in Probation

Over the last decade, standards for classifying cases, known as classification "systems" have become commonplace in probation and parole agencies across the country. Systems help to reduce the problems that arise with individualized approaches to classification. The adoption of formal classification systems in probation has been based on two factors. First, caseloads have continued to grow at a time when resources have remained static or diminished. The ratio of probationers to officers has ballooned. In California, Proposition 13 forced cuts in the property tax which reduced the probation budget by almost one third.[2] The fiscal crisis in New York City in the mid and late 1970s had a similiar impact on the city's probation department.[3] These examples are indicative of trends across the country as a whole.

Second, research has shown that to undertake the same supervision strategy with everyone is foolish. Not only does it commit precious resources to some offenders who don't need them, but intensive supervision for those who do not need it can actually have a negative impact on their success rate.[4] Studies show that differential treatment is significantly more effective than to treat all offenders in the same manner.[5]

The National Institute of Corrections (NIC) has played a major catalyst role in making classification commonplace. In response to many requests from the probation field, NIC promulgated a model classification system for probation based on the work of the Bureau of Community Corrections of the Wisconsin Division of Corrections. The Wisconsin model was chosen because it was exceptionally well researched, easy to use and readily transferrable to other jurisdictions with a minimum of expense. As the result of NIC's work, over 50 agencies and jurisdictions have adopted the model system, thus making it the most commonly used classification system in the country.[6]

A Model Classification System

The NIC model classification system features components that relate to the primary goals of probation supervision.[7] One goal is the reduction of the *risk* that new crimes will be committed by the probationers. The second is providing services to deal with the *needs* of the probationers for concrete assistance and guidance. The NIC classification system helps the officer make decisions about how to allocate resources among those goals of probation supervision.

Risk Assessment

Probation has the responsibility to reduce the risk of further offenses by those on probation. The classification system provides an assessment of client risk. This is accomplished with a statistically developed prediction device which provides an assessment of an offender's likelihood of committing a new offense. In Chapter 1, we have described the logic underlying risk assessment instruments. The Wisconsin Risk Assessment is shown in Figure 15-1.

Risk assessment tools use variables that are associated with the risk of a new offense and place a probationer into a group of persons with similiar risk levels. If the group's rate of reoffending is high, say 65%, the probation agency might decide to devote intensive supervision to offenders who are classified in that group. If the group has a low rate, say 5%, the agency would probably allocate minimal supervision resources to cases in that group.

Information in the PSIR is useful in completing the risk assessment instrument because it focuses on many of the same risk factors (offense, prior record, employment, education, and drug or alcohol use) and should contain verified information. With a good PSIR, virtually all the items on the risk assessment can be completed prior to the first contact with the supervising probation officer. Certain preliminary decisions can be made about the intensity of supervision and the general supervision strategy. The risk assessment can also give the sentencing judge information on how a particular offender would be supervised if the sentence is probation.

Needs Assessment

Probation agencies are also charged with helping offenders to accomplish positive personal and social adjustments. This is based on the belief that if the problems which underlie the law violating behavior can be ameliorated, then a law abiding life is more likely to occur.

Figure 15-1

Department of Health and Social Services
Division of Corrections
Form C-502 (Rev. 8/79)   State of Wisconsin

ASSESSMENT OF CLIENT RISK

Client Last	First	MI	Client Number
Name			
Probation Control Date or Institution Release Date (Month, Day, Year)	Agent Last Name		Number

Select the appropriate answer and enter the associated weight in the score column.
Total all scores to arrive at the risk assessment score.

                                                                          SCORE

Number of address changes in last 12 months: 0   None   ——
(prior to incarceration for parolees)   2   One
     3   Two or more

Percentage of time employed in last 12 months: 0   60% or more
(prior to incarceration for parolees)   1   40%-59%
     2   Under 40%   ——
     0   Not applicable

Alcohol usage problems: 0   No interference with
(prior to incarceration for parolees)   functioning
     2   Occacional abuse; some
     disruption of functioning   ——
     4   Frequent abuse; serious
     disruption; needs treatment

Other drug usage problems: 0   No interference
(prior to incarceration for parolees)   1   Occassional abuse; some
     disruption of functioning   ——
     2   Frequent abuse; serious
     disruption; needs treatment

Attitude: 0   Motivated to change;
     receptive to assistance
     3   Dependant or unwilling
     to accept responsibility   ——
     5   Rationalizes behavior;
     negative; not motivated
     to change

Age at first conviction: 0   24 or older
(or juvenile adjudication)   2   20-23
     4   19 or younger   ——

Number of prior periods of
probation/parole supervision: 0   None   ——
(adult or juvenile)   4   One or more

Number of prior probation/parole revocations: 0   None   ——
(adult or juvenile)   4   One or more

Number of prior felony convictions: 0   None
(or juvenile adjudications)   2   One   ——
     4   Two or more

Convictions or juvenile adjudications for: 2   Burglary, theft, auto
(Select applicable and add for score.   theft or robbery
Do not exceed a total of 5. Include   3   Worthless checks   ——
current offense.)   or forgery

Convictions of juvenile adjudication for
assaultive offense within last 5 years: 15   Yes
(an offense which involves the use of a   0   No   ——
weapon, physical force or the threat of force)

Probation officers make assessments of probationer needs and use these assessments to make decisions about supervision, program services, referrals, and the nature of resources to be committed to an offender. Just as with the risk assessment, many agencies have formalized the process of quantifying offender problems and needs. This is typically accomplished with a needs assessment instrument. An example is shown in Figure 15-2.

The needs assessment instrument is constructed differently than the risk instrument. Needs are not as objective as the predictor items found in the risk assessment instrument. The needs instrument is thus less precise, but not necessarily less valuable. They are typically developed by a group of experienced staff through a consensus process in which they identify and agree on need areas which should be measured. Each need item is structured to provide several levels of need severity which generally correspond to the urgency for intervention or treatment.

Use of the needs assessment provides several benefits. A standardized format ensures consistency of assessment of each offender need area. It allows the individual needs of the probationer to be ranked, one against the other, as to severity or urgency. This allows comparison of individual probationers on overall needs as well as individual need items. The needs instrument identifies areas for offender treatment and can therefore define the activities of the probation supervision process. Last, the needs assessment helps to determine the amount of supervision provided: a high need score generally calls for a greater amount of time.

A well prepared PSIR can assist in the preparation of the needs assessment. Many of the needs items are discussed in the report, often in great detail. This information provides a head start for the needs assessment, which is usually completed at or soon after the initial supervision interview. A needs assessment contributes to the supervision plan, which can again assist the judge in deciding if probation is appropriate.

Building Classification into the PSIR Process

It is rare to find the risk and needs assessment completed prior to sentencing and incorporated into the report to the judge. This is partly a result of the fact that the process was developed as a tool for the probation supervision process and has rarely been incorporated into the sentencing process. Accomplishing that merger presents some problems.

Figure 15-2

Department of Health and Social Services
Division of Corrections
Form C-502 (Rev. 8/79)

State of Wisconsin

ASSESSMENT OF CLIENT NEEDS

Client Last		First	MI	Client Number
Name				
Probation Control Date or Institution Release Date (Month, Day, Year)			Agent Last Name	Number

Select the appropriate answer and enter the associated weight in the score column. Higher numbers indicate more severe problems. Total all scores. If client is to be referred to a community resource or to clinical services, check appropriate referral box.

Academic/Vocational Skills

REFERRAL   SCORE

| -1 | High school or above school level | 0 | Adequate skills; able to handle every-day requirements | +2 | Low skill level causing minor adjustment problems | +4 | Minimal skill level causing serious adjustment problems | ☐ | _____ |

Employment

| -1 | Satisfactory employment for one year or longer | 0 | Secure employment; no difficulties reported; or homemaker, student or retired | +3 | Unsatisfactory employment; or unemployed but has adequate job skills | +6 | Unemployed and virtually unemployable; needs training | ☐ | _____ |

Financial Management

| -1 | Long-standing pattern of self-sufficiency, e.g. good credit rating | 0 | No current difficulties | +3 | Situational or minor difficulties | +5 | Severe difficulties; may include garnishment, bad checks or bankruptcy | ☐ | _____ |

Marital/Family Relationships

| -1 | Relationships and support exceptionally strong | 0 | Relatively stable relationships | +3 | Some disorganization or stress but potential for improvement | +5 | Major disorganization or stress | ☐ | _____ |

Companions

| -1 | Good support and influence | 0 | No adverse relationships | +2 | Associations with occassional negative results | +4 | Associations almost completely negative | ☐ | _____ |

Emotional Stability

| -2 | Exceptionally well-adjusted; accepts responsibility for actions | 0 | No symptoms of emotional instability; appropriate emotional responses | +4 | Symptoms limit but do not prohibit adequate functioning; e.g., excessive anxiety | +7 | Symptoms prohibit adequate functioning; e.g., lashes out or retreats into self | ☐ | _____ |

Alcohol Usage

| | | 0 | No interference with functioning | +3 | Occassional abuse; some disruption of functioning | +6 | Frequent abuse; serious disruption; needs treatment | ☐ | _____ |

Other Drug Usage

| | | 0 | No interference with functioning | +3 | Occassional substance abuse; some disruption of functioning | +5 | Frequent substance abuse; serious disruption; needs treatment | ☐ | _____ |

Mental Ability

| | | 0 | Able to function independently | +3 | Some need for assistance; potential for adequate adjustment; mild retardation | +6 | Deficiencies severely limit independent functioning; moderate retardation | ☐ | _____ |

Health

| | | 0 | Sound physical health; seldom ill | +1 | Handicap or illness interferes with functioning on a recurring basis | +2 | Serious handicap or chronic illness; needs frequent medical care | ☐ | _____ |

Sexual Behavior

| | | 0 | No apparent dysfunction | +3 | Real or perceived situational or minor problems | +5 | Real or perceived chronic or severe problems | ☐ | _____ |

Agent's Impression of Client's Needs

| -1 | Minimum | 0 | Low | +3 | Medium | +5 | Maximum | ☐ | _____ |

TOTAL   _____

One problem has to do with the inevitable fallibility of any prediction method. The problem is described in Chapter 1, but it deserves mention here. To be valid, a prediction method must be based on sound research that has demonstrated that the method works on the population to which it is being applied. Even so, there will be errors of two types: failure to identify recidivists (false negatives) and false identification of recidivists (false positives). When the judge is given a prediction, it has a built-in error factor. Yet the existence of a statistically valid predictor in a PSIR makes it difficult for the judge to go against the prediction, even though a certain portion of those predictions are known to be erroneous.

Another problem is posed by the sentencing provisions of the criminal codes of some states. These often prescribe the information that can be considered in sentencing. It may not be appropriate or legal to consider assessments of risk or need under some of these codes.

The question of validity arises as well. When validated, the assessments of risk and need are typically based on the probation population, and thus probably do not take into account the characteristics of the prison bound population. This may alter the predictive value of any risk or needs instrument for the sentencing process.

Regardless of statutory law and statistical validity, the sentencing judge may not wish to have this information for a number of reasons. It could be seen as an intrusion on the authority of the court in the sentencing process or as an inappropriate use of statistical data in a legal process. The sentencing judge may also mistrust social science methodology, and consequently be hesitant in incorporating it into the sentencing process.

Nevertheless, providing this information to the sentencing judge makes the court more aware of how probation will respond to a potential probationer, and may reduce the number of cases inappropriately sentenced. That is why, in court systems that include classification information in the PSIR, it is usually only provided as an indication of how probation would handle the case, and not as part of the sentence recommendation.

Risk and needs based classification is also useful in defining probation's workload capacity. Each case receives a workload value based on its classification. This value represents the amount of a probation officer's time that the case will require for supervision. Probation, under this workload model, has a finite capacity to accept and supervise cases, based on the total staff time. When that capacity is reached, no new cases are accepted until some adjustment is made. Probation supervision is thus viewed as similiar to the prison system, where the number of cells is limited, and when they are full, adjustments are made.

Inclusion of classification information in the PSIR can backfire, when the court uses it to tie the hands of the probation department. The judge may desire to be "tough" and set the level of supervision at a greater intensity than is prescribed by the classification system. This would result in overclassification of the case and a commitment of supervision resources that are not required.

There is also the potential that the classification decision will become embodied in the court order at sentencing. This defeats the dynamic nature of the classification process, which should be under the control of the probation department and subject to adjustment based on the probationer's rate of progress. Requiring the judge to change the court-ordered classification unnecessarily bogs down the probation supervision process.

The use of statistical prediction and standardized assessment has been relatively recent in corrections. Understanding the uses and potential abuses of these methods has not kept pace with their adoption. This has led to a "technology gap," in which the basis for modern offender classification is misunderstood or distorted. Two common mistakes are the elimination of human judgement and the inappropriate transfer of classification systems from one decision point to another.

Statistical Prediction v. Human Judgment

While the accuracy of statistical predictions has been shown to be superior to clinically based human judgments,[8] this is not to say that we should abandon human judgement in the offender assessment process. In fact, the combination of statistical prediction and human judgement has proven to be *more* accurate than either method alone.[9] The most effective classification systems allow for the probation officer to influence the classification decision through an option often called "override." An override occurs when the officer disagrees with the classification decision as prescribed by the instruments. Overrides should be reviewed by a supervisor, because this helps to ensure that the final classification is based on good information and sound reasoning. Experience has shown that overrides determine approximately 10 to 15% of the classification decisions.

Transferability of Classification Instruments

Probation and parole agencies often attempt to minimize or avoid altogether the costs involved in developing a classification system by adopting one used in another jurisdiction. This would seem to be a prudent step, particularly if the assessment instruments to be adopted were carefully developed originally. Unfortunately, classification systems may not be wholly transferable. Several recent reports detail the *lack* of transferability, especially among risk assessment instruments,[10] due primarily to the variations in offender populations.

Transfer of risk prediction instruments can only be done wisely if a validation study is done on the offender population of the adopting agency. If the study shows the instrument to be valid for the new group of offenders, then the transfer can be accomplished without the development costs. Modifications may be necessary to improve the instrument's validity; however, in some cases it is best to undertake a new risk assessment development project.

The needs assessment instrument does not present the same statistical transferability problems, but there are considerations to be observed in this area as well. One of the keys to a successful classification system is that it have validity in the eyes of the probation staff.[11] If the system lacks "face validity", the staff will not readily accept it. A needs assessment instrument from another jurisdiction may be seen by staff as lacking face validity. Since the needs assessment development process is simple, it is advisable to undertake that process if the staff are not prepared to accept another needs assessment instrument as valid.

Case Management and Case Planning

Case management is the heart of the work of probation and parole agencies. While it is probably common to hear the term caseload management, the concept used here has a much broader focus, relating to the entire supervision function as a set of organizational policies and practices.[12]

Case management has three major components (clients, goals and resources) and is defined as the process of applying agency *resources* to *clients* to achieve the organization's *goals*. Every probation agency has case management practices of some sort; some are more systematic and sophisticated, others more individualized and intuitive.

The key to an effective case management system is not its sophistication, but how well the three components "fit" together in the case management practices. Lack of fit can result from an imbalance between these three components. Are there resources available to allow the goals to be achieved, given the type of probationer? Are caseloads so large that the counseling goals of the agency cannot be met? Are there high-risk offenders that cannot be handled effectively within the heterogenous caseload structure?

Achieving the organizational fit through case management is complex and demanding. Goals need to be articulated and communicated to all staff. Resources, both human and financial, need to be quantified and examined in order to determine how they are best used. The probationer pool must also be studied and the demands they place on the supervision function must be evaluated. There are many ways to accomplish organizational fit, once goals, resources and client characteristics are known.

The components of case management are not static; they change over time. If fit is going to be maintained, changes in goals, clients and resources must be monitored and evaluated to ascertain their significance for maintenance of case management. System modification is a regular requirement of managing the probation supervision function.

The PSIR plays a key role in this process by providing the basis for defining the *client* component of the case management system. Aggregate information from the PSIR is extremely useful in documenting shifts in the clientele, among whom resources must be allocated. The concept of aggregate client information is very important. In discussions about clients, the "average client" is often used, as in "the average client is 26 years old, unemployed and black". Yet this person does not really exist, rather the characteristics of clients have been combined and averaged in a manner with limited utility. Of what use is the description of the average client if that person does not even appear in any caseload? By contrast, the aggregate client represents combined characteristics of all clients. The population can then be described in percentages or rates of these characteristics.

For example, the aggregate client population may have employment problems in 40% of the cases, drug problems in 25% and family problems in 15%. These percentages can then be converted into useful information about demands for resources and programming. If there are 1,000 cases, then the 40% with employment problems translates into 400 clients with a potential need for job training programs or specialized employment services. Similiar information can be drawn from the drug and family problem percentages. Aggregate client information is analyzed at the caseload level, the unit or divisional level or at the departmental level to give an idea of the total service demands these organizational units face.

Therefore, case management is first and foremost an organizational function, in which steps are taken to assess clients for aggregate problems and structure resource allocation strategies (such as referrals, counseling and specialized caseloads) in order to achieve the organizational goals with these clients. The PSIR helps to provide the organization with the information it needs to assess the aggregate client.

Individualized Case Management

Ultimately, the case management system results in supervision activities undertaken with individual probationers. The PSIR is a valuable tool for the supervising probation officer planning supervision activities. It provides an account of the probationer's current status, including the legal, personal and social history. This mini-biography is often enough information to meet two needs. First, it allows the case to be assigned to a probation officer with appropriate skills. Second, the PSIR gives that officer information to formulate the basic supervision strategy from which to work.

It is important for supervision to begin quickly without lost time because research indicates that the greatest risk of the probationer committing a new offense is during the first six months of supervision. That risk decreases slightly during the second six months and drops off significantly after the first year.[13] Avoiding wasted time at the outset of supervision can thus contribute to an increased likelihood of success.

Conditions of Probation

When an offender is placed on probation, conditions are attached to the order of probation. Conditions are requirements set forth by the judge that either restrict a probationer's freedom or stipulate that certain things be done by the probationer. Restrictions include curfew, abstention from alcohol or drug use, refraining from associations with certain people or frequenting particular establishments and not leaving the jurisdiction without permission. Stipulated activities include paying fines and restitution, performing community service, participating in counseling and treatment programs and obeying all laws.

There are two types of conditions: standard and special. Standard conditions apply to all probationers. Special conditions are tailored to the specific offender in an attempt to individualize the sentence and punishment to fit the needs and characteristics of the case.

Special conditions are imposed by the sentencing judge based on information contained in the PSIR. For example, curfew and restrictions on association are likely to be imposed because of information on the crime and past record contained in the PSIR. The PSIR enables the judge to fashion a sentence which facilitates accomplishing the dual goals of probation supervision: protecting the community and helping the probationer.

Supervision Objectives

In the process of planning and carrying out probation supervision, the officer formulates a strategy for supervision, often referred to as case planning. One model for case planning that has gained widespread use in recent years is Objectives Based Case Management (OBCM). This is a systematic case planning model with several features which are strongly associated with successful supervision outcomes.[14]

In OBCM, the supervising officer, normally in collaboration with the probationer, specifies a series of behavioral objectives for the probationer to work on during a set period of time. At the end of that time, typically six months, the probationer's performance is reviewed and new objectives are prepared. The supervision plan is regularly reviewed and updated, and the probationer is routinely given feedback on his or her behavior and performance on probation.

There are several reasons why OBCM has become popular. First, the focus of OBCM is on holding the offender accountable for the behavior while under supervision. Second, the objectives describe specific behavioral goals, not attitudes or other amorphous indicators. This means the objectives are specific and measurable, making it difficult to claim misunderstanding or misinterpretation. Third, since the probationer is usually involved in the formulation of the objectives, it is hard to feign ignorance of the requirements of the supervision. Fourth, the objectives are reviewed and updated regularly, providing realistic time frames for accomplishment. This means the case plan is always current.[15]

The initial supervision objectives are prepared during the first 30 days of supervision, in what is sometimes known as the "intake" period. The supervising officer interviews the probationer at least once, makes field visits to the home and possibly the place of employment, and makes other contacts in the community. Intake is designed to build on the PSIR information and give the officer a fuller understanding of the case. The PSIR is particularly important to the first interview with the offender because it provides extensive background information that facilitates the interview.

Supervision objectives are different from conditions of probation. Conditions are legal requirements imposed by the court; and they may only be modified by the judge. Supervision objectives are jointly developed goals for supervision progress. They are more limited in intent than conditions.

Objectives do not have the legal weight of conditions. It is rare for a violation of probation to be based on a failure to accomplish objectives. Failure to achieve objectives can be included with materials in support of a violation of probation based on other grounds. Unwillingness to work at agreed upon objectives could be indicative of a general uncooperativeness with probation supervision.

Normally, the objectives are developed collaboratively by the probation officer and the probationer. This is certainly not the case with court imposed conditions. This involvement in the case planning process increases the probationer's ownership and accountability for supervision outcomes.

Probationers often feel overwhelmed by the court-imposed conditions. Setting short term, achievable objectives helps to break down the seemingly unmanageable requirements of the conditions into tasks which are more reasonable. Giving the probationer tasks that can be accomplished increases the chance of overall success.[16] Helping the probationer look at a large task and break it down into smaller, more manageable units is a useful problem-solving skill, and is something which also is associated with positive supervision outcomes.[17]

The PSIR writer learns of the offender's needs for personal improvement while preparing the report. Should the judge wish to consider a probation sentence, the PSIR writer can point out to the judge problems that need to be addressed in a probation plan. It is also the PSIR writer's responsibility to differentiate the critical needs of the offender in areas of risk control and punishment from other, less central problems. The former are appropriately made part of the special conditions of probation, while the latter are rightfully left to the supervising officer to involve the probationer in working on as part of the case plan.

Summary

This chapter has reviewed the usage of the PSIR in the probation/supervision functions of classification and case management. Because the PSIR is an amalgamation of critical information about the offender, it is useful in determining the client's risk to the community and needs for assistance ; two primary concerns of probation classification. It is possible for the PSIR to inform the judge of the basic dimensions of the probation plan, based on the classification standards. Moreover, the PSIR provides the basis for developing the individual supervision plan during intake, and it serves as the data base for measuring the aggregate client, crucial to improving the organization's case management.

Notes

[1] Michael Lipsky. *Street-Level Bureaucracy*. New York: Russell Sage Foundation, 1980. Studt, Elliot. *Surveillance and Service in Parole*. Washington, DC: National Institute of Corrections, 1978.

[2] Jan M.Chaiken *The Impact of Fiscal Limitation on California's Criminal Justice System*. Santa Monica, CA: RAND Corporation, 1981.

[3] Economic Development Council Probation Task Force. *Organization Report on the New York City Department of Probation*. New York: Economic

Development Council of New York City, 1977. p.1. Citizen's Committee for Children of New York. *Lost Opportunities*. New York: Author, 1982. p.10

[4] S. Christopher Baird and others. *The Wisconsin Case Classification/Staff Deployment Project: A Two Year Followup Report.* Madison, WI: Bureau of Community Corrections, 1979. Adams, Stuart. "The PICO Project" in Johnston, Norman and others, eds. *The Sociology of Punishment and Corrections*, 2nd. ed. New York: John Wiley & Sons, 1970.

[5] Robert R. Ross and Paul Gendreau, eds. *Effective Correctional Treatment*. Toronto: Butterworths, 1980.

[6] National Institute of Corrections. *Annual Report for Fiscal Year 1983*. Washington, DC: author, 1984. p. 8.

[7] S. Christopher Baird. *Classification for Caseload Management and Staff Deployment in Wisconsin*. In the Proceedings of the 111th. Congress of Correction. College Park, MD.: American Correctional Association, 1977. pp.42-55.

[8] John Monahan. *Predicting Violent Behavior: An Assessment of Clinical Techniques*. Beverly Hills, CA: Sage, 1982. Clear, Todd R. and Vincent O'Leary. *Controlling the Offender in the Community*. Lexington, MA: D.C. Heath, 1982. pp. 38-43.

[9] Baird, *Two Year Follow-up Report*. p. 4.

[10] Kevin N. Wright, Todd R. Clear & Paul Dickson. "The Universal Applicability of Probation Risk Assessment Instruments: A Critique". *Criminology*, v. 22, n. 1. February 1984. pp. 113-134. Probation Administrative Management System. *Adult Probation in New Jersey*. Trenton, NJ: Administrative Office of the Courts, 1980. pp. 46-48.

[11] S. Christopher Baird & Larry Solomon. "Classification: Past Failures, Future Potential". *Corrections Today*, v.43 n.3. May/June 1981. p.4.

[12] Todd R. Clear and Vincent O'Leary. *Controlling the Offender in the Community*. Lexington, MA.: D.C. Heath, 1983. O'Leary, Vincent and Todd R. Clear. *Directions for Community Corrections in the 1990s*. Washington, DC.: National Institute of Corrections, 1984. Clear, Todd R. *A Model for Supervising the Offender in the Community*, a Report to the National Institute of Corrections, mimeo, 1978. Clear, Todd R. and others. *Objectives-Based*

Case Management: Final Report of the Case Management Institutes. Hackensack, NJ: National Council on Crime and Delinquency, 1980. Ch. 1.

[13] Probation Administrative Management System. *Adult Probation in New Jersey*. Trenton, NJ: Administrative Office of the Courts, 1980. pp. 19-22.

[14] Op cit, note 12.

[15] Robert R. Ross and Bryan McKay. "Behavioral Approaches to Treatment in Corrections" in Ross, Robert R. and Paul Gendreau, eds. *Effective Correctional Treatment*. Toronto: Butterworths, 1980. pp. 37-54. Reid, William J. and Laura Epstein, *Task-Centered Casework*. New York: Columbia University Press, 1972. Reid and Epstein. *Task-Centered Practice*. New York: Columbia University Press, 1977. Andrews, D.A. and Jerry J. Keissling. "Program Structure and Effective Correctional Practices" in Ross, Robert R. and Paul Gendreau, eds. *Effective Correctional Treatment*. Toronto: Butterworths, 1980. pp. 441-463.

[16] Reid and Epstein. *Task-Centered Casework*. pp. 106-116.

[17] Andrews and Keissling. "Program Structure..." pp. 457.

GROUP EXERCISE

On your caseload you have the following persons, all serving two-year, sus-pended sentences for theft. Discuss within the group the kinds of controls and the probation plan that would be most appropriate for each client and the classifications based on these characteristics.

Brian 39 years old, clerk at Sears sporting goods department, took home from the store an expensive bowling ball, married 12 years, two children, high school graduate, no prior criminal history, still working at Sears.

Fred 19 years old, stole a stereo from a neighbor's car, senior in high school but having academic problems, dating a girl he plans to marry after graduation, living with parents but working carryout at a supermarket on Fridays and Saturdays, spent one year in Boys' School.

Lucy 22 years old, shoplifted and sold a winter coat, AFDC mother of two children, never married, dropped out of school at 16 to have first baby, never held a regular job but insists that she wants to be-come self-supporting.

DISCUSSION QUESTIONS

1. Comment: It is fallacious to use the nature of the offense in the risk as-sessment because you cannot assume that everyone convicted of a given crime will or will not recidivate. For example, some first-time armed robbers will do it again and some will not.

2. If you were a judge pondering a sentence, would you want the PSIR to include a risk assessment figure? Why and why not?

3. Following up on the preceding question, would you want the probation department to have a risk assessment available when the case is assigned to a probation officer? Why and why not?

4. Justify the override system. How can abuses be avoided?

5. Elaborate: The components of case management are not static, either in terms of the agency or in terms of an individual client.

6.   Construct as long and as creative a list as you can (let your imagination work at it!) of special conditions that might be imposed by a judge in sentencing defendants with special needs.

7.   Since the objectives in OBCM are not enforceable, why would a probationer pay any attention to them?

Chapter 16
Other Users of the PSIR

In addition to being central to the sentencing process, the PSIR is the basic working document in the field of corrections. The report follows the offender through both institutional and community based correctional placements, and it forms the core around which those agencies' offender files are built. Because of the volume and depth of personal and social information it contains, the PSIR guides much of the treatment and programming for the offender in the correctional setting. The report is also a rich source of data for research about offenders and the effects of programs on them.[1]

Classification for Correctional Facilities

In both prisons and jails, sentenced inmates are assigned to housing units and involved in education, work, training, treatment programs and other formalized activities on the basis of a process known as classification. Since the beginning of institutional corrections in the early 1800s, efforts have been made to separate offenders based on characteristics or needs. Early classification systems were rudimentary, separating the youthful offender from the adult, the first offender from the chronic criminal, women from men, and the mentally disturbed from the rest of the population. There were practical as well as humanitarian bases for these decisions then, as there are now.

By the 1930s, diagnostic screening had become a standard procedure in corrections. Most prison systems operated some type of reception unit for classification of newly sentenced persons. It is in the reception facility that plans are usually made for the inmates' housing and program activities.

Shortly after an inmate arrives in the reception/diagnostic unit, classification staff review all available information on the offender in order to make their assessment. They develop a plan that is designed to meet the needs of the offender best in the context of available resources and security requirements. The classification staff rely heavily on the PSIR as part of the assessment process, because it provides a wealth of information.

The focus of the institutional classification process is basically two fold: custody needs and treatment needs. The security and custody needs of the institution are considered to be the primary of the two. Security needs are met by ascertaining whether the offender is a security risk either in terms of escape or of harm to other inmates. Most institutions try to maintain an inmate at the lowest level of security commensurate with this assessment of risk.

The National Institute of Corrections has found that most prisons *overclassify* inmates' need for custody.[2] Inmates who do not need maximum security are often housed there. This is a poor use of scarce incarceration resources, especially when most maximum security prisons in the United States are overcrowded. Overclassification also restricts management options such as furlough and work release, since most systems require a prisoner to be at a low-security classification to be eligible for such release programs.

Inmates with special custody needs requiring observation or protection are a related concern for institutional management. Those inmates with psychological problems or suicidal tendencies need to be watched closely. Homosexuals need to be protected from the general prison population. Inmates who have been or are informants and special classes of inmates such as former law enforcement officers also need protection. The PSIR is an excellent source of information to alert the classification staff to the possibility of these custody concerns. Frequently, the PSIR writer will note in the body of the report or in the recommendation whether special security arrangements will be necessary for the prisoner.

The second focus of the classification process is programs and treatment. Whenever possible within custodial requirements, institutions attempt to involve prisoners in some sort of positive activity.

If there are needs in the area of physical or mental health, an effort will be made to obtain treatment. Often offenders will exhibit chronic maladjustments, such as social incompetence, substance abuse or sexual problems, that have contributed to their criminal behavior. Treatment staff will attempt to address these problems through group or individual treatment.

If there is a training or educational need, the inmate will be assigned to a program designed to provide training or education. Because many offenders are school dropouts or have a low level of educational achievement, remedial work or GED courses are commonly recommended.

Offenders who have no work skills and lack work discipline will be assigned to vocational programs which teach useful skills for life on the outside and good work habits. Those inmates with a work record are assigned to jobs within the institution to keep them busy and use existing skills.

Classification also considers social service needs, and social workers strive to maintain family ties during incarceration. They may also recommend personal development through group and individual counseling, which is aimed at easing the reintegration of the offender back into society.

All of these needs become apparent to the PSIR writer while the report is being prepared. If the judge is considering a sentence of incarceration, the

PSIR writer needs to advise the judge of the treatment or custody considerations that will occur as a result of that sentence.

Most PSIR writers are reluctant to recommend incarceration *in order* to provide treatment, however. Research studies have consistently shown that treatment programs in total institutions are considerably less effective than comparable programs operated in the community.[3] Therefore, if treatment needs are a central consideration of a person's sentence, this usually suggests a minimization of incarceration.

Nevertheless, effective classification is crucial to a well-run institution, and is fundamental to rehabilitation. The PSIR is a key to the effectiveness of the classification decisions. It is doubtful that the necessary information would be gathered without the PSIR, since few jails or prisons are able to assign staff to the community to collect this information. That is why most require that copies of the PSIR be delivered to the institution of custody when an offender is sentenced to a term of incarceration.

The Parole Process

In most jurisdictions, the release of offenders from incarceration is governed by a system of parole. The origins of this system in the United States can be traced back to the Elmira (New York) Reformatory and the indeterminate sentence.[4] (See Chapter 3 for a discussion of the indeterminate sentence.)

The parole process has three major components – parole release, pre-release planning and supervision. In each component, the PSIR plays a vital role.

Parole Release

Almost all incarcerated offenders are released back into the community. Most are released under some type of discretionary release mechanism such as parole. The basis for the parole decision varies from state to state, but consideration is usually given to two criteria: whether enough time was served and whether the offender presents an acceptable level of risk to the community.

The discretion vested in the parole is so vast that, in practice, the parole board determines how much time the offender will actually serve. In recent years, parole discretion has come under criticism. Parole authorities have had their discretion limited, the most drastic example of which has been the abolition of parole release. Most paroling authorities have responded to criticism by adopting structured decision making systems.

Figure 16-1

ADULT
Guidelines for Decision-Making
Customary Total Time Served Before Release
(Including Jail Time)

OFFENSE CHARACTERISTICS: Severity of Offense Behavior (Examples)	OFFENDER CHARACTERISTICS: Parole Prognosis			
	(Salient Factor Score)			
	Very Good (11 to 9)	Good (8 to 6)	Fair (5 to 4)	Poor (3 to 0)
LOW Marihuana or soft drugs, simple possession (small quantity, for own use) Minor theft (includes larceny and simple possession of stolen property less than $1,000) Walkaway	6-10 months	8-12 months	10-14 months	12-18 months
LOW MODERATE Alcohol law violations Counterfeit currency (passing/possession less than $1,000) Forgery/fraud (less than $1,000) Immigration law violations Income tax evasion (less than $10,000) Selective Service Act violations Theft from mail (less than $1,000)	8-12 months	12-16 months	16-20 months	20-28 months
MODERATE Bribery of public officials Counterfeit currecny (passing/possession $1,000 to $19,999) Drugs: Marihuana, possession with intent to distribute/sale (less than $5,000) "Soft drugs," possession with intent to distribute/sale (less than $500) Embezzlement (less than $20,000) Firearms Act, possession/purchase sale (single weapon – not sawed-off shotgun or machine gun) Income tax evasion ($10,000 to $50,000) Interstate transportation of stolen/forged securities (less than $20,000) Mailing threatening communications Misprison of felony Receiving stolen property with intent to resell (less than $20,000) Smuggling/transportation of aliens Theft/forgery/fraud ($1,000 to $19,999) Theft of motor vehicle (not multiple theft or for resale)	12-16 months	16-20 months	20-24 months	24-32 months
HIGH Burglary or larceny (other than embezzlement) from bank or post office Counterfeit currency (passing/possession $20,000-$100,000) Counterfeiting (manufacturing) Drugs: Marihuana, possession with intent to distribute/sale ($5,000 or more) "Soft drugs," possession with intent to distribute/sale ($500 to $5,000) Embezzlement ($20,000 to $100,000)	16-20 months	20-26 months	26-34 months	34-44 months

Figure 16-1 (*continued*)

	26-36 months	36-48 months	48-60 months	60-72 months
Explosives, possession/transportation Firearms Act, possession/purchase/sale (sawed-off shotgun(s), machine gun(s), or multiple weapons) Interstate transportation of stolen/forged securities ($20,000 to $100,000) Mann Act (no force – commercial purposes) Organized vehicle theft Receiving stolen property ($20,000 to $100,000) Theft/forgery/fraud ($20,000 to $100,000)				
VERY HIGH Robbery (weapon or threat) Drugs: "Hard drugs," (possession with intent to distribute/sale) [no prior conviction for sale of "hard drugs"] "Soft drugs," possession with intent to distribute/sale (over $5,000) Extortion Mann Act (force) Sexual act (force)	26-36 months	36-48 months	48-60 months	60-72 months
GREATEST Aggravated felony (e.g., robbery, sexual act, aggravated assault) – weapon fired or personal injury Aircraft hijacking Drugs: "Hard drugs," (possession with intent to distribute/sale) for profit [prior conviction(s) for sale of "hard drugs"] Espionage Explosives (detonation) Kidnapping Willful homicide	(Greater than above – however, specific ranges are not given due to the limited number of cases and the extreme variation in severity possible within the category)			

NOTES:
1. These guidelines are predicated upon good institutional conduct and program performance.
2. If an offense behavior is not listed above, the proper category may be obtained by comparing the severity of the offense behavior with those of similar offense behaviors listed.
3. If an offense behavior can be classified under more than one category, the most serious applicable category is to be used.
4. If an offense behavior involved multiple offenses, the severity level may be increased.
5. If a continuance is to be given, allow 30 days (1 month) for release program provision.
6. "Hard drugs" include heroin, cocaine, morphine, or opiate derivatives, and synthetic opiate substitutes. "Soft drugs" include, but are not limited to, barbiturates, amphetamines, LSD and hashish.

Figure 16-1 (*continued*)

SALIENT FACTOR SCORE

Case Name_____   Register Number_____

Item A
   No prior convictions (adult or juvenile) = 2
   One or two prior convictions = 1
   Three or more prior convictions = 0

Item B
   No prior incarcerations (adult or juvenile) = 2
   One or two prior incarcerations = 1
   Three or more prior incarcerations = 0

Item C
   Age at first commitment (adult or juvenile) 18 years or older = 1
   Otherwise = 0

Item D
   Commitment offense did not involve auto theft = 1
   Otherwise = 0

Item E
   Never had parole revoked or been committed for a new
      offense while on parole = 1
   Otherwise = 0

Item F
   No history of heroin or opiate dependence = 1
   Otherwise = 0

Item G
   Has completed 12th grade or received GED = 1
   Otherwise = 0

Item H
   Verified employment (or full-time school attendance) for a
      total of at least 6 months during the last 2 years in the
      community = 1
   Otherwise = 0

Item I
   Release plan to live with spouse and/or children = 1
   Otherwise = 0

Total Score

The structured discretionary decisions of the parole board rely on the PSIR for information. The question of whether the punishment has been enough relies on the PSIR's description of the offense. Parole authorities use that information to help calculate whether the punishment is commensurate with the crime's seriousness. The description of the offender's role in the offense needs to be clear and accurate in order for the parole officials to calculate the amount of punishment deserved for the offense.

One of the best examples of structured decision making for parole release is the parole guidelines of the United States Parole Commission.[5] In the early 1970s, the Commission instituted the guidelines system which calculated the offender's personal circumstances (the salient factor score) and a ranking of the seriousness of the offense. These two criteria were plotted on a matrix which indicates the normal range of time to be spent in custody before parole eligibility, unless unusual circumstances existed.

This approach has been thoroughly studied and updated several times since its adoption. The salient factor score instrument and the matrix are shown in Figure 16-1.

This system has resulted in the federal parole decisions becoming more predictable. The criteria used in making those decisions have become more visible, and thus can be reviewed for fairness, accuracy and equity. Because of these advantages, many states have followed the U.S. Parole Commission in adopting guidelines systems for parole release.

Pre-parole Planning

When reviewing a case for the parole release decision, the paroling authorities consider more than just the parole guidelines. They only establish a recommended range of time to be served. Staff prepare an extensive file about the offender which allows other factors to be considered. These other factors include activities prior to incarceration and plans for the future. This file is usually prepared by the institutional parole officer, who serves a function for the parole board analogous to that of the PSIR writer for the court.

The PSIR is an important part of the parole file. It provides information about the inmate's behavior in the community prior to incarceration. This is important because it is to the community that the offender will return.

A parole plan compiled by the institutional parole officer usually includes the following:

The PSIR, including prior criminal record and previous probation and parole performance

Institutional reports on work, discipline, education and treatment

Reception/diagnostic reports

Medical and psychiatric evaluations

Previous parole plan and summaries

Field reports on suitability of planned residence, verification of employment, etc.

Parole prognosis, an evaluation by the parole officer of the offender's prospects for successful parole

The parole plan is a repeat version of the PSIR, without the same degree of verification of past behaviors, as that has already been done in the PSIR. The parole plan verifies foward-looking information: what this offender will do if released. Therefore, the offender's planned living circumstances, employment and financial arrangements are verified so that the parole board can incorporate these plans into its assessment of the offender's prognosis for successful parole.

Parole Supervision

Release on parole includes a program of supervision in the community by a parole officer. This supervision is similiar to that of probation, combining control and assistance components. In preparing the parole case plan and in carrying out the supervision, the PSIR is a valuable resource for the same reasons it supports probation classification and case management.

The usefulness of the PSIR declines with time, however. The longer an inmate spends in custody, the older and less reliable the information becomes.

The quality of the PSIR is critical, however. In jurisdictions where the PSIRs are inadequate, parole officers have to conduct what is in essence an entire PSIR prior to the offender's release in order to provide parole authorities with the information normally expected in a PSIR, and needed to support the release decision and subsequent supervision. In jurisdictions where quality PSIRs are done, substantial savings in parole planning time is realized. The value of a good PSIR to parole is evident; it saves time and duplication of effort by parole officers.

Assessment and Treatment Programs

The PSIR can also be used as a resource for assessment and treatment programs, either in institutions or community agencies. With the permission of the court, the PSIR can be released to treatment programs, therapists or counselors involved with the offender. This is particularly common if the court orders treatment or counseling.

Typical of this is a New Jersey law which requires that all offenders convicted of certain sex offenses be examined by specialists at the Adult Diagnostic and Treatment Center, which specializes in identifying and treating sex offenders.[6] A PSIR must be completed and sent to the staff before the diagnostic evaluation is done. The results of the evaluation are sent to the judge, along with the PSIR for use in sentencing.

Appellate Sentencing Review

The sentence imposed by the judge is often appealed. Until recently, appeal of a sentence was almost always the province of the defendant, but statutes of some states now allow the prosecutor to appeal what is perceived to be an inappropriately lenient sentence.

When a case is appealed, the parties submit written briefs in support of their position. In appeals of sentences, whether as too harsh or too lenient, the PSIR is usually included to provide the appellate judge with all of the facts used in determining the sentence. The PSIR is seen as presenting an objective view of the offense and the offender, which contrasts with the adversarial presentation of the facts by the parties to the appeal. The appellate courts need the PSIR as much as the sentencing judge in order to rule on the appropriateness of the sentence.

Research and Evaluation

The field of corrections has come under great fire as being ineffective. Beginning with Robert Martinson's famous 1974 pronouncement that "nothing works,"[7] critics have characterized correctional programming as ineffective and a waste of tax dollars.

Volumes have been written in support of Martinson's position[8] (which was later softened by Martinson himself)[9] as well as in support of correctional programming.

One consistent point emerging from this debate is that the evaluation studies have been so shoddy that it is very difficult to really say what works and what does not. Research designs and methodology have left a good deal to be desired, as has the information on which conclusions have rested. This was the conclusion of the National Academy of Sciences' review of offender rehabilitation research.[10]

For an evaluation to be useful, the relevant characteristics of the subjects of the treatment need to be clearly described. Individual offenders' characteristics vary greatly, and these variations may relate to the effectiveness of the treatment. Moreover, these differences may account for variations in outcomes after similiar treatment or supervision. Rigorous definition enables researchers to draw conclusions with more confidence and thus contribute more to the body of knowledge.

The PSIR contains a wealth of information on the offender, enabling researchers to identify and clearly distinguish offenders in terms of characteristics. Since the PSIR is prepared for almost all serious offenders, the availability of this information is fairly uniform. A recent study by the RAND Corporation of the effectiveness of felony probation relied heavily on data gleaned from the PSIRs.[11]

Management Information Systems (MIS)

As criminal justice agencies become more computerized, information for the computers becomes more crucial. A computer without information is useless, and one with poor information is dangerous because of the ease of access to information of questionable reliability. Ease of data collection for computerized systems is key; if it is too difficult to obtain information, staff will become less diligent in verifying its accuracy. The usefulness of the computer then declines markedly.

The PSIR usually forms the basis for establishing the file in the data base of probation and parole agencies. Compiling the MIS information is relatively painless, because the PSIR already contains much of it. With the PSIR data as a base, the management information system can provide client tracking, background characteristics, case management information and supervision outcome measures.

Management information systems allow agencies to communicate with each other with much greater ease. One county in New Jersey is experimenting with a project to link the management information systems of several agencies involved with the family court, including probation and other social service departments.[12] Case information will, for the first time, be available to multiple agencies with an interest in a particular client. Each agency will set limits based on laws and regulations about confidentiality, but information on common clients can be shared. This will naturally include some of the PSIR data.

The Juvenile PSIR

Just as the PSIR process is conducted to support sentencing in adult courts, a variation is undertaken to assist the juvenile court in decision making. While the purpose of the PSIR in the juvenile court is fundamentally the same as that in the adult court, there are differing philosophies in the two courts and the juvenile PSIR reflects its special mandate.

The separate court for juveniles evolved in the United States around the turn of the century. Social activists posited that, due to their tender years and still developing personalities, juvenile offenders needed to be treated differently than adult offenders. Juveniles could not be held accountable for their acts in the same way as adults. They were not seen as capable of the same rational decision making and choices that characterize the adult in the eyes of the law.

In addition to this diminished accountability, there was more of an emphasis on causes of delinquency in the juvenile court. Anti-social behavior was seen as the product of dysfunctional families, ineffective social institutions and a lack of healthy, positive recreation and leisure time pursuits. The focus of the juvenile court was more ameliorating problems rather than punishing bad behavior.

This philosophy is reflected in all aspects of the juvenile court. The doctrine of *Parens Patriae*, or the state as parent to the child, results in the court taking the juvenile under its authority in order to provide the missing guidance, support and love required to reform the youngster. The terminology shows this differing orientation: complaints are not filed, "petitions" are; juveniles are not convicted, a "finding" is made; rather than a sentence being imposed, a "disposition" is reached. Many matters are adjusted informally without ever reaching the court calendar.

This focus on problem identification and helping interventions is reflected in the juvenile PSIR, often called instead a "social history". The juvenile PSIR seeks to help the court in understanding the complicated array of factors precipitating this delinquency so that a rehabilitative disposition may be reached.

Thus, while the juvenile PSIR deals with the delinquent behavior and lists prior involvement with the law, these concerns are ordinarily overshadowed by the interest in personal, family and social history information.

In comparison to the adult PSIR, the juvenile report contains more detailed information on the family, including parents, siblings and any problems those individuals or the family as a whole might have; and school, including academic performance, behavior and extra-curricular activities, and the views of teachers, guidance counselors and child study teams.   The home and neighborhood are reported on, as are leisure time activities.   If any counselors or therapists are familiar with the child or the family, they are asked to provide an assessment of the child.   In short, the juvenile PSIR covers virtually the same information as the adult PSIR, but the report is written in order to help the court define the disposition that provides the most supportive method for helping the juvenile avoid further delinquency, just as a good set of parents might do.

In the last decade, some reformers have argued that the *Parens Patriae* philosophy of the juvenile court has failed, and that there should be a return to the adult model of punishment for young offenders.   In some states, violent juvenile offenders are now handled in much the same way as adults. Nevertheless, for most juvenile delinquents, the PSIR is an opportunity for the state to consider ways to curb delinquency rather than to determine the most appropriate punitive reponse.

Summary

In this chapter, we have reviewed the uses of the PSIR for functions other than sentencing.   The PSIR is used for jail and prison classification and institutional programming.   It is used in parole/release decisionmaking, parole planning and parole supervision and the PSIR is an important research and management information tool.   Finally, in this chapter we describe how the PSIR process applies to the juvenile court.

Notes

[1] Robert M. Carter. *Presentence Report Handbook*.   Washington, D.C.: National Institute of Law Enforcement and Criminal Justice, 1978. p.3.

[2] National Institute of Corrections. *Prison Classification: A Model Systems Approach*.   mimeo. n.d. p.8.

[3] Douglas Lipton, Robert Martinson and Judith Wilks. *The Effectiveness of Correctional Treatment*.   New York: Praeger, 1975.

[4] George B. Killinger, Hazel B. Kerper and Paul F. Cromwell, Jr. *Probation and Parole in the Criminal Justice System*. St. Paul, MN: West., 1976, pp. 200-209.

[5] Don M.Gottfredson, Peter B. Hoffman, Maurice B. Sigler and Leslie T. Wilkins. "Making Parole Policy Explicit" in *Crime and Delinquency*, v. 21, n. 1, January, 1975. pp. 37; United States Parole Commission Rules, 28 C.F.R. 2.1-2.59; Hoffman, Peter B. and Michael A. Stover. "Reform in the Determination of Prison Terms" in *Hofstra Law Review* v.7, n.1, Fall, 1978. pp. 89-121.

[6] New Jersey Statutes Annotated. 2C:47-1 et seq.

[7] Robert Martinson. "What Works? – Questions and Answers About Prison Reform" in *The Public Interest*. Spring, 1974, pp. 22-54.

[8] Ted Palmer. "Martinson Revisited" in the *Journal of Research in Crime and Delinquency*, v.12, n.2, July 1975. pp. 133-152. Robert Martinson. "California Research at the Crossroads" in *Crime and Delinquency*, v.22, n.2, April 1976. pp.178-191. Ted Palmer. *Correctional Intervention and Research*. Lexington, MA: D.C.Heath, 1978. Paul Gendreau and Robert R. Ross. "Effective Correctional Treatment: Bibliotherapy for Cynics" in *Crime and Delinquency*, v.15, n.4. October 1979. pp. 463-489. Robert R. Ross and Paul Gendreau. *Effective Correctional Treatment*. Toronto: Butterworths, 1980.

[9] Robert Martinson. "Viewpoint on Rehabilitation" in *The Criminal Justice Newsletter*, v.5, n.21. November 18,1974. id. "Evaluation in Crisis – A Postscript" in *Rehabilitation, Recidivism and Research*. Hackensack, NJ: National Council on Crime and Delinquency, 1976. id. "New Findings, New Views: A Note of Caution Regarding Sentencing Reform" in *Hofstra Law Review*. v.7, n.2, 1979. pp.243-258. Robert Martinson and Judith Wilkes. "Save Parole Supervision" in *Federal Probation* Quarterly, v.41, n.3, 1977. pp.23-26.

[10] Susan A. Martin, Lee B. Sechrest and Robin Redner, eds. *New Directions in the Rehabilitation of Criminal Offenders*. Washington, DC: National Academy Press, 1981.

[11] Joan Petersilia and others. *Granting Felons Probation*. Santa Monica, CA: RAND Corporation, 1985.

[12] Community Foundation of New Jersey. *Union County Family Court Data Exchange Project*. 1985, mimeo.

GROUP EXERCISE

What are special security needs of the following inmates? Discuss aspects of which the penal institution's staff should be aware and relate to the content of the PSIR.

Child molester
Attorney
Con man
Homosexual
Paranoid schizophrenic
Masochist
Juvenile waived to adult court
Informer
Former police officer
Prostitute (male and female)
Woman who murdered her own child
Alcoholic

DISCUSSION QUESTIONS

1.   Why is it common to overclassify a new inmate? How can a PSIR aid in preventing this?

2.   What special controls are needed for an alcoholic newly assigned to an institution?

3.   Develop this scenario: A woman receives a mandatory executed sentence for forgery. The PSIR writer fails to include the information that she has been treated for marginal diabetes and that the inmate suspects that she may be pregnant. Because of overcrowded conditions in the Women's Prison, the judge allows her to serve her two-year sentence (i.e., 12 months) in the county jail. What happens?

4.   In some jurisdictions the parole board considers the inmate's offense to be the crime which was originally filed against him/her, not the crime for which he/she is convicted. Is this justice? Why, and why not?

5.   Compare the two systems: What would happen in adult court if the *parens patrial* philosophy were applied and the court were seen as the

protector of the accused; what would happen in juvenile court if the principles of adult court were carried over?

6.   Why do juvenile courts often call the document a "Predispositional Report" (PDR) or "Social History"?

Chapter 17
Managing the PSIR Process

The PSIR is an important managerial tool in the operation of probation agencies. It is directly related to the efficient processing of cases through the court, and it also plays a key role in probation supervision. The PSIR is also a tangible product, more so than probation's other major function (supervision) whose work product is much less visible, except when unsuccessful.

In most probation agencies, there is a tension between the supervision function and the PSIR function. Both are important, but there are usually insufficient staff resources to complete all the reponsibilities of both functions. Priorities have to be set by management.

In the current era of decreasing resources and increasing workload, probation managers must also find ways to maintain effectiveness with only diminished resources to meet demands. Generally, supervision bears the brunt of any cuts in resources because it is less visible than PSIRs. With the PSIR, the courts make known their need for PSIRs to be completed on time for sentencing. There is no such vocal constituency for the supervision function.

Recently, renewed emphasis has been given to the importance of supervision. This has been due to studies of the ineffectiveness of the supervision provided to felony offenders on probation when caseloads are large.[1] Special programs of intensive supervision for serious offenders in small caseloads are proving to be very effective in reducing recidivism.[2] These studies have supported the argument that removing resources from supervision to keep the PSIR function on track is a counterproductive to probation in the long term.

Management Strategies

This chapter presents approaches to management of the PSIR process. The first section of the chapter is a description of recent approaches to streamline the PSIR process and thus salvage resources. The second section describes the backbone of good PSIR management: training.

Short-form Reports

The most commom approach to reducing the resource demands of the PSIR is to move to a reduced format with certain designated, less serious offenses such as misdemeanors, or lesser felonies committed by first offenders.

The strengths and weaknesses of the short-form PSIR were discussed in Chapter 13, but the total savings realized with the short-form are often only marginal. This has led managers to experiment with other approaches.

Paraprofessionals and Volunteers

Some probation agencies have recognized that much of the work of preparing a PSIR is routine information gathering and does not require professional judgment or discretion. These agencies have hired non-professionals to assist the probation officer in preparing the PSIR, including lower paid, less extensively educated or experienced paraprofessionals; volunteers, who are unpaid; and student interns from local colleges and universities. The probation officer is relieved of much of the mundane PSIR work if assisted by others, and can spend time more productively on interviewing, reviewing and analyzing information, composing reports and documenting recommendations to the court. Paraprofessionals verify information, collect records and make follow-up contacts.

Use of alternative staff in this way makes the professional officer more of a supervisor of the PSIR process instead of being the person carrying it out. Those with a talent for supervising paraprofessionals can be identified from among probation officers, and potential probation officers may emerge from the ranks of the paraprofessionals. The benefits of this system to the larger personnel process can be substantial.[3]

Functional Separation

Many probation organizations have separated the investigative and supervision function, assigning probation officers exclusively to one or the other task. The expectation is that staff assigned to produce PSIRs will become familiar with resources and information sources and will become more efficient. Separation is not feasible in all agencies. There must be enough investigative workload to justify specialization, and smaller agencies may not be able to take advantage of the efficiencies produced by functionalization.

Specialized PSIR Writers

Carrying functional separation one step further, some probation agencies have begun to designate certain staff as PSIR specialists for certain types of cases. White collar crime, child abuse, drunk driving, and family violence are examples of cases where special expertise and training can result in a better, more sophisticated report completed more rapidly.[4] This can enhance the court's decisionmaking capability, and also lead to more efficient use of PSIR resources.

Advisory Committees

A recent federally funded project on the PSIR called for advisory committees for the PSIR process. The committees were composed of representatives from the judiciary, corrections, parole, prosecution, defense, police and academia. All members had a special interest in the preparation, use or management of the PSIR. These committees provided a unique opportunity for dialogue on a variety of issues, particularly access to information for the PSIR, and the format and content of the report. Evaluation of the advisory committees by the committee members was very positive.[5] The staff of the national project also endorsed the use of advisory committees, in particular when change is being contemplated.[6]

Information Sharing

As an offender is processed through the criminal justice system, information is collected and decisions are made at many different points. It is common for identical information to be collected repeatedly by investigators in different agencies. Rarely is the information shared across agency boundaries. If there are no compelling reasons not to share information, this is an inefficient use of resources. For example, as a result of law enforcement investigators' failure to share information about the Manson murders in California, the investigation dragged on much longer than was needed.[7]

There are three decision points where information can easily be shared. These are the pre-trial release decision (bail/release on recognizance), the pre-trial diversion decision (suspended prosecution) and the sentencing decision. At each stage, the same demographic information is collected, often addressing the same issues: offender risk and offense seriousness. If the information collected were passed along to the next investigator, significant savings could result from eliminating the duplication of effort. Coordinating such an information-sharing is made very difficult because of "turf" concerns of agencies; none of the presentencing agencies wishes to become reliant for information on the work of another.

Verticalized Case Management

The information sharing idea is one of the main objectives underlying the use of the Criminal Case Management Offices (CCMO) in the New Jersey courts. All of the predispositional case functions in the criminal area are consolidated under a single CCMO unit, including pretrial release, diversion, pretrial conferences, scheduling and PSIRs. In short, all of the activity on the criminal case before disposition is controlled by the CCMO. When a case enters the system, it is assigned to a team in the CCMO and they are responsible for moving it through to disposition in a timely fashion. All aspects of case processing are vested in that team. Initial results show that many of the old "turf" battles have been eliminated and information sharing has become the rule, not the exception.[8]

Workload Based Budgeting

The managment of probation services has traditionally been based on the idea of assigning individual cases to staff for their work. This approach does not take into account the amount of time a particular task requires to complete. In recent years, a new approach known as the "workload model", has gained popularity.[9] This approach calculates the average amount of time required to complete a given task, whether it be a PSIR or supervision of a probation case. Adjustments are made for special versions of the PSIR or for intensive supervision. Ultimately, each case is assigned a time value which is based on the estimated amount of time required to complete the tasks on the case.

The total time demand on staff, individually and as a group, can then be calculated, and the staffing and budget for the agency becomes reviewable and subject to evaluation.

An example of a workload budget for investigations and for a full department are shown in Figure 17-1.

Training for High Quality PSIRs

Training is generally accorded a higher status in private companies than in government agencies because it is one way to make a company more efficient and effective. Government agencies are not held to the same standards of financial accountability as the private sector, with the result that training (and retraining) of personnel is often viewed as a helpful, but not essential function.

In recent years, government agencies have come under increasing pressure to operate under stable or reduced levels of funding.[10] A public attitude that government services are too costly and too ineffective[11] has led to a widespread need for public administrators to cut services.

Figure 17-1
Agency Workload Budget

WORKLOAD CLASSIFICATIONS	AVERAGE TIME	POPULATION	FY '83 TOTAL HOURS PER MONTH	FIELD* POSITIONS REQUIRED	POPULATION	FY '84 TOTAL HOURS PER MONTH	FIELD* POSITIONS REQUIRED
Supervision							
High	2.5 hrs./mo.	2,000	5,000	40.0	2,140	5,350	42.8
Medium	1.2	3,500	4,200	33.6	3,745	4,494	36.0
Low	0.5	2,000	1,000	8.0	2,140	1,070	8.6
Administrative	0.15	900	135	1.1	960	144	1.2
TOTAL – Supervision		8,400	10,335	82.7	8,985	11,058	88.6
Investigation							
Presentence	8.0 hrs./mo.	3,300	2,200	17.6	3,531	2,354	18.8
Postsentence	6.0	4,000	2,000	16.0	4,280	2,140	17.1
TOTAL – Investigation		7,300	4,200	33.6	7,811	4,494	35.9
GRAND TOTAL			14,535	116.28		15,552	124.4

*Positions Required equals total hours divided by average hours available per month.

HOURS AVAILABLE

START 40 Hours/Week @ 52.2 Weeks — 2,088 hours/year (-)

LESS Vacation, Sick Leave, Holidays — 250 hours/year (-)

LESS Administrative, Personal, Professional Development — 338 hours/year (=)

EQUALS Hours available per year — 1,500 hours/year or 125 hours/month

In most instances, the question is what part or how much of the budget is cut, not whether cuts will be made. When this happens, agency administrators will look to cut costs in any way feasible, without hurting the core functions of the agency. Training is often a prime target for reduction, if not elimination. Training cut backs have a long-term impact on the personnel system of an agency. Qualified candidates meet only the minimum requirements for the job. If the training to perform the specific job tasks is not provided, where does this leave the employee, and the agency? Can the employee fairly be held accountable for job performance without the necessary training? How can the agency evaluate performance for retaining or promoting the employee without training? Clearly, training is essential to the well managed agency in both the short and long term. This is as true for the PSIR process as for any other aspect of probation.

The Timing of Training

Few would disagree that a newly appointed probation officer be given training before being assigned a PSIR by the court. Even someone with experience from elsewhere in the criminal or juvenile justice system should receive training in the purpose of the PSIR and how it differs from investigative reports used elsewhere. A new probation officer, fresh from college or otherwise lacking in experience, certainly needs training. The central role the PSIR plays in sentencing underscores the importance of training to enable the employee to prepare an adequate PSIR. Shoddy work may have a deleterious impact on the offender or the community.

So if there is an obvious need for training of the new employee, what about later on? Once mastered, the PSIR process can become a series of routine tasks; interviewing, investigating, verifying, analyzing and writing. Where then, is the need for training?

One obvious time is when important changes have occurred. Changes in the sentencing statutes are very common, and often far reaching. Recently, sentencing structures governed by the idea of rehabilitation have been redrafted to be based on punishment and desert. Information to guide new sentencing practices can be very different, and the PSIR writer needs to be aware of these changes.

Appellate courts are also a source of change, through appeals of sentences, making modifications in sentencing procedure. Three cases decided by the New Jersey Supreme Court in 1984 and 1985 substantially reshaped the sentencing process, five and six years after the enactment of a revised sentencing statute.[12]

There are also revisions in agency policy and procedure promulgated by the probation agency itself. Probation officers need to be kept abreast of improvements in the technology of preparing the PSIR.

Finally, a 35 to 40 hour annual requirement of training is a common standard of operation.[13] Regular training also helps to keep employees motivated, as it shows them that the agency values them enough to spend time to train them. Cross-training in other functions increases the agency's flexibility in staff assignments by ensuring that all staff have a basic knowledge of all the agency's functional assignments.

Therefore, programs to provide initial and ongoing training are important to a motivated and career oriented staff.

Content of Training

The PSIR process involves four generic skills: investigation (including interviewing), assessment, analysis and writing. These are the skill areas a probation officer will need to acquire to prepare an adequate PSIR.

Investigation Skills

The art of investigation lies in gathering information through a process of examination and inquiry. The PSIR writer must be able to identify sources of information, obtain the information either through interview, examination or observation, and organize the information in a useful manner.

Much of the information in the PSIR is gained through personal interviews. Contacting the person involved and arranging for the interview is not always a simple matter. Often, the PSIR writer has to do a good deal of investigation and legwork just to locate the proper people because of long delays from the time the crime occurred to the time the PSIR is ordered. Victims and witnesses move, become disillusioned or lose desire to be involved further. Yet, their information is crucial to the preparation of the PSIR. The burden falls to the PSIR writer to locate and secure the cooperation of the reluctant person. Interviewing skills are crucial when the interviewee is not readily cooperative.

There are many, varied sources of information for the probation officer preparing the PSIR: official government files, criminal justice and other, private agency records, personal documents of the defendant and others; the list is nearly inexhaustible. It is critical for the probation officer to be familiar with information sources that may be available, including methods of access and interpretation, restrictions as to use, and reliability. The training program should spend significant time on information sources.

Assessment Skills

Offenders appearing before the court for sentencing often suffer from one or more serious behavioral problems. These include drug and alcohol abuse, emotional and psychological disorders, aggressive or violent behavior and inappropriate sexual behavior, among many others. The PSIR writer needs to be able to recognize symptoms of these disorders, both in personal interviews and in the official records. In many jurisdictions, sentencing statutes provide for specialized treatment or enhanced penalties in these cases.

The PSIR writer must be familiar with the future implications of these disorders for the behavior of the offender when formulating a sentencing recommendation for the judge.

Analysis Skills

Because the probation officer preparing the PSIR will be confronted with great volumes of information, skills in analysis of information are crucial. Not all information is of equal value or importance for the PSIR. The probation officer should be able to differentiate information which is crucial to the report from that which is not really important.

To perform this task, the PSIR writer must know the information judges regard as crucial and what, to them, is irrelevant. In a national PSIR project, surveys were administered to judges, probation officers and others involved with the PSIR process. They were asked to rank the relative importance of the information items. There was a great deal of agreement between the rankings of judges and PSIR.[14]

Analytic skills are also important because the information gathered from the various sources is often contradictory. It is the PSIR writer's job to resolve the inconsistencies, if possible, or present them to the court in a useful manner because the judge is unable to follow up on the PSIR. The judge needs a report which is immediately useful for sentencing.

Writing Skills

Once information is collected and analyzed by the PSIR writer, it must be presented to the court in a readable report. It is assumed, sometimes erroneously, that everyone can write adequately. Training in the PSIRs must include an assessment of how well the PSIR writer can write. If there are writing deficiencies, training can be provided to upgrade skills, and close supervision and regular feedback can reinforce good writing habits. Some officers' deficiencies may be so irremediable that assignments other than the PSIR would be appropriate.

Writing a good PSIR is not easy. There is a great deal of information to be presented, much of it dry and relatively uninteresting. The bulk of the report, excluding the summary recommendation, should be objectively descriptive, not drawing conclusions. The information is sometimes repetitive from report to report, and it is hard to find new ways to present similiar facts and situations over and over again.

The volume of information available for the PSIR is often a problem for the writer. What to include and what to leave out is a tough decision. Too much information leads to information overload, making the report ineffective. Leaving information out can expose the writer to the criticism that the information was in fact important. It is helpful to the PSIR writer to learn to present information in as concise a form as possible.

Some agencies have forced PSIR writers to be concise by limiting the space available for each PSIR topic. The PSIR format is pre-printed pages with boxed-in segments for each topic. The writer must stay within the space allowed, unless compelling circumstances provide otherwise. This technique is effective at reducing the length of the PSIR, but it often results in awkward or unsightly documents, when the writer tries to "squeeze in" needed details. Usually, the PSIR format is a free-flowing narrative, leaving the PSIR writer and/or supervisor to keep the report's length reasonable. This sometimes results in overly lengthy reports containing information of questionable value.

In agencies with high volumes of PSIRs, the writers usually dictate their reports for later transcribing by secretarial staff. This is efficient, but training in dictation is needed. A novice confronting a dictating machine will be uncomfortable and give dictation that is difficult for the secretary to transcribe.

The Training Process

As part of the national PSIR project mentioned earlier, several states developed model PSIR training packages for their probation staff. The training packages from the states of Connecticut and Texas provide models of well integrated training programs.

Office of Adult Probation, Connecticut[15]

Training for PSIR writers in Connecticut is centralized, through the Office of Adult Probation and the Connecticut Justice Academy. Connecticut is a small state with a centralized administrative structure, so uniform training fits the state's needs well.

Each new probation officer receives one full week of training in every aspect of the investigation process.   After each segment of training (composed of lecture, demonstration and discussion) the trainee is required to complete a presentence investigation and the PSIR is critiqued in the classroom setting.

To accomplish this, the training staff have developed a series of video and audio tapes of simulated interviews with persons in a typical PSIR process. All of the sources of information needed to complete the investigation are available to the trainee, either through tapes or documents. Each trainee selects the people to be interviewed, and also decides whether to have a personal or telephone interview, both of which are available. The training staff build in realistic limitations on time by restricting the number of personal interviews a trainee can select. This is designed to make the trainee sensitive to the time constraints which exist in reality in the PSIR process. Each trainee takes notes during the taped interview, as though they were actually conducting the interview.

The taped interviews were conducted by current probation officers, exposing the trainees to a variety of interviewing styles and techniques. An opportunity is afforded to critique the interviews and interviewers, reinforcing the interviewing skills of the trainees. The trainer acts as an additional source of information, answering any questions which may not have been covered in the interviews or documents.

Once the trainee has finished gathering information, a PSIR is composed and dictated. The final product is then rated on its completeness, conciseness and the appropriateness of the assessment and recommendation. The feedback helps the trainee to improve basic skills in each area.

There are several key benefits to the Connecticut approach. It is based on generic skills and can be adapted to many different jurisdictions, simply by structuring the interviews to fit local policies and procedures. The curriculum also allows the trainer to evaluate the abilities of the PSIR trainees, in a setting where all of the external variables have been controlled. This has proven useful in assessing the abilities of new staff and identifying deficiencies for improvement before these staff are given field assignments.

Texas Adult Probation Commission[16]

In contrast to Connecticut, Texas presents a very different situation for PSIR training. Probation services are provided by local county probation departments, which vary dramatically in size, philosophy and structure. Moreover, the state of Texas is more than 20 times the size of Connecticut.

The training package developed by the Texas Adult Probation Commission reflects these differences in local services. Nevertheless, the Texas PSIR training package is an integrated approach, reponsive to the needs of other users of the PSIR beyond the local court.

The training package is divided into eight modules, each representing an aspect of the investigation process.

1. *Investigation Techniques.* The major emphases of this module are on the groundwork for the PSIR process: planning and conducting the investigation.

2. *Interview Techniques.* This module covers planning and conducting the interviews. The emphasis is on practical techniques to facilitate the gathering of reliable information.

3. *Choosing Relevant Information.* This module teaches how to determine what information is to be included in the PSIR, based on relevancy to judges and other users of the PSIR.

4. *Case Classification.* This module covers the classification process in probation supervision, helping to integrate the PSIR with the supervision function.

5. *Confidentiality.* The questions of access to reports, confidentiality and liability are dealt with in this module, drawing from Texas statutory and case law.

6. *Writing Skills.* The essential skill of converting known information into written text is covered.

7. *Management.* This module addresses the management concerns in the PSIR function: how to make the PSIR operation effective and efficient.

8. *Community Resources.* The final module provides information about dealing with outside agencies and resources in the community.

The Texas model is useful because it demonstrates how generic aspects of the PSIR process can be broken down into self-contained training modules. Even though local circumstances may vary, people who attend the modules will find the training useful for developing PSIR skills.

Summary

This chapter has presented considerations in managing the PSIR process. One of the most prominent considerations is efficiency. Ways of streamlining the PSIR process include use of paraprofessionals/volunteers, functional specialization, information sharing, advisory committees, verticalized case management and workload budgeting. Perhaps the most important aspect of managing the PSIR is training. Two illustrations of training for PSIR writers were provided.

Notes

[1] Joan Petersilia and others. *Granting Felons Probation* Santa Monica, CA: RAND Corporation, 1985.

[2] S. Christopher Baird. *Intensive Supervision Programs in Probation*, Madison, WI: National Council on Crime and Delinquency, 1983; James M. Byrne, *The Control Controversy: A Preliminary Examination of Intensive Probation Supervision Programs in the United States*. 1985, mimeo. Gettinger, Stephen. "Intensive Supervision: Can It Rehabilitate Probation?" *Corrections Magazine*, v.9, n.2, April, 1983. pp. 7-17.

[3] Eric W. Carlson and Evalyn C. Parks. *Critical Issues in Adult Probation: Issues in Probation Management*. Washington, DC: National Institute of Law Enforcement and Criminal Justice, 1979. Chapter 5, Use of Paraprofessionals in Probation, pp. 191-233. Chapter 6, Use of Volunteers in Probation, pp. 234-289.

[4] National Highway Traffic Safety Administration. *Court Intervention: Presentence Investigation Techniques for Drinking/Driving Offenses*. Washington, DC: U.S. Department of Transportation, 1980. Kirkpatrick, Kenneth. "Presentence Investigation and Report" in *Improved Probation Strategies*. Washington, DC: University Research Corporation, 1978.

[5] Loren A. Beckley and others. *Presentence Investigation Report Program Final Report*. Sacramento, CA: American Justice Institute, 1981. p. 174.

[6] *Ibid*. p. 175.

[7] Vincent Bugliosi. *Helter Skelter*. New York: Bantam Books, 1975, pp. 46-47, 217, 377, 399.

[8] *Final Report of the Management Structure Committee.* New Jersey Law Journal, August 4, 1983. *Criminal Court Management Structure Proposal* Trenton, NJ: Administrative Office of the Courts, 1983 (draft) pp.19-52.

[9] Brian J. Bemus and others. *Workload Measures for Probation and Parole.* Washington, DC: National Institute of Corrections, 1983.

[10] Jan M. Chaiken and others. *The Impact of Fiscal Limitation on California's Criminal Justice System*, Santa Monica, CA: RAND Corporation, 1981. For similiar experiences in New York City, consult *Lost Opportunities – A Study of the Promise and Practices of the Department of Probation's Family Court Services in New York City.* New York: Citizen's Committee for Children of New York, 1982. pp. 14-18, and *Organization Report on the New York City Department of Probation.* New York: Economic Development Council, 1977. p. 113.

[11] Remarks made by Charles M. Friel, Ph.D. at National Academy of Corrections, Boulder, CO. January 29, 1984.

[12] *State v. Hodge* (95 NJ 369 [1984]), *State v. Roth* (95 NJ 334 [1984]), *State v. Yarbough* (100 NJ 627 [1985]), Chapter 95, Laws of 1978 (Code of Criminal Justice, New Jersey Statutes Annotated).

[13] Commission on Accreditation for Corrections. *Standards for Adult Probation and Parole Field Services* 2nd. ed. College Park, MD: American Correctional Association, 1981. Standard 2-3060. id. *Standards for Juvenile Probation and Aftercare Services* 2nd. ed. College Park, MD: American Correctional Association, 1983. Standard 2-7055.

[14] Loren A. Beckley. *Presentence Investigation Report Program Final Report.* Sacramento, CA: American Justice Institute, 1981. pp. 162-163.

[15] Office of Adult Probation (Connecticut). *Pre-Sentence Investigation Training Program.* mimeo, 1980.

[16] Texas Adult Probation Commission. *PSIR Training Manual.* mimeo, 1980.

GROUP EXERCISE

A management team has been notified that the budget is to be cut by 15% next year. The team consists of 1 Director of Probation, 1 Juvenile Chief, 11 Juvenile Officers, 9 Adult Officers, 1 Field Investigator, 6 Secretaries and 1 Receptionist. In addition to customary office expenses, what possibilities does the team consider to cut the budget?

DISCUSSION QUESTIONS

1. As you reflect on the job assignment of writing a PSIR, it is natural that you feel some insecurity. What aspect of the function bothers you most? Why, and what would help you prepare better for the task?

2. If you are adequately prepared and have been writing PSIRs satisfactorily for a few years, of what value is cross-training? In what way would it justify the cost?

3. Do you feel comfortable when you read about behavioral disorders and that "the PSIR writer must be familiar with the future implications of these disorders for the behavior of the offender..."? How do you propose to handle such a PSIR assignment?

4. Training usually includes sections on investigative skills (including interviewing), assessment skills, analysis skills and writing skills. Where do you feel weakest, and how do you think you should reinforce your ability?

Chapter 18
The Future of the PSIR

The PSIR has been a prominent aspect of probation services since probation began in Massachusetts in the mid-1800s. It continues to play a key role, not only in probation, but in other aspects of the criminal justice system as well. There is no reason to think that this central role will be diminished in the future. If anything, the need for accurate information will increase as we move more deeply into the information age brought on by the advent of computers.

The PSIR will not remain stagnant, however. Trends appear on the horizon which will have an impact on the nature of the PSIR and its preparation. In this chapter, several of those trends are examined: computerization, standards and accreditation, and privatization.

Computerization and the PSIR

As computer technology becomes more powerful, more common and less costly, it will play a greater role in the PSIR process. Three areas of computerization have impact on the PSIR: access to criminal records, word processing and computer generated narrative reports.

Access to Criminal Records

A key element of any PSIR is a complete accounting of all prior criminal activity. This often includes records of any activity in the juvenile justice system, and, if applicable, the military justice system as well as the adult justice system.

Access to these records in a timely and inexpensive manner is crucial to the preparation of the PSIR. Courts wish to sentence without long delays, but need to have the complete record before them to sentence appropriately. When asked to rank items of information as to importance in sentencing, judges regard the prior record second only to the current offense.[1] Statistical analyses have revealed that the extent of the prior record accounts for a significant portion of the variation in sentences for offenders convicted of the same offense.[2] The importance of the information is clear, but problems exist making it difficult to compile the information. Records of arrests, convictions and sentences are created and maintained by local units of government, often of different jurisdictions (across geographic lines). These records may be unverified, incomplete or contradictory. Probation agencies do not have unlimited resources to ensure that prior record information will always be complete and accurate.

Within the last 20 years, most states and many of the larger counties and municipalities have computerized their criminal history records. Access is made much more easy and records are relatively more complete when they have been computerized. For the near future, there will be a need for follow-up to insure completeness of records, but computerization has reduced the follow-up considerably.

When the New Jersey State Police automated their State Bureau of Identification files, they developed a report format that was designed to address specifically the needs of PSIR investigators and sentencing courts. Known as the "Detail Record", this report treats each arrest as the beginning of a cycle which is followed through as a complete transaction to ultimate discharge from the system.[3] Each cycle provides for data on any criminal processing event, including arrest, arraignment, indictment, conviction, sentencing, probation, incarceration, parole and discharge from the system. An example of a detail record is shown in Figure 18-1.

The Federal Bureau of Investigation's files are also automated and can be accessed through the state criminal history system. One request can generate both state and federal records. Often a local or county records system will also have access to the state system, and thus ultimately to the FBI criminal histories, increasing total efficiency.

Computer technology is one of the most rapidly advancing forms of contemporary communication. Almost no idea is too far-fetched to be at least technically feasible. When government resources catch up to the potential of the computer age, accurate, detailed records of past criminality will be the norm.

Word Processing

Word processing is a computerized system wherein the text of the report is displayed on a computer screen before it is ever committed to paper. This allows any changes to be made quickly and efficiently, without the waste of paper or use of correction fluids or tapes. The expansion of automated word processing has already had an impact on probation agencies across the country. Where it has been adopted, word processing has resulted in marked productivity improvements in the PSIR process.

Figure 18-1
CRIMINAL HISTORY DETAIL RECORD

STATE OF NEW JERSEY
DEPARTMENT OF LAW AND PUBLIC SAFETY
DIVISION OF STATE POLICE
RECORDS AND IDENTIFICATION SECTION
BOX 7068 WEST TRENTON, N.J. 08625

COMPUTERIZED CRIMINAL HISTORY RECORD

THE DISSEMINATION OF THIS RECORD IS GOVERNED BY STATE AND FEDERAL
SECURITY/PRIVACY REGULATIONS. THIS RECORD SHALL NOT BE USED FOR
ANY PURPOSE OTHER THAN THAT REQUESTED. IT IS SUBJECT TO CHANGE AND
SHOULD NOT BE UTILIZED BEYOND THE USEFULNESS OF THE INFORMATION.

**** THIS RESPONSE NOT SUPPORTED BY FINGERPRINT COMPARISON ****

```
DATE OF RECORD      03/09/78              RECEIVING AGENCY      TEST

IDENT          SBI/    1111      FBI/544332244      FPC/POPOPOPIPIDIDIPMAATT
   NAM/TEST,RECORD                          SEX/M   RAC/W   POB/NC  DOB/050543
   HGT/510   WGT/160   EYE/BRO   HAI/BLK  SKN/      BLN/
   MNU/                 MRN/      MFN/
   SOC/123456789   HFC/15    O  13    R   OOM          16      3   5R2−
                            I  22    T   OI                    3   5T−

   ADDITIONAL IDENTIFIERS/HEART
   SMT/TAT LF ARM
   AKA/TEST, FICTITIOUS                    /

CYCLE  01      DOA/070776
               ANA/                                   DOB/050543

ARREST         AGCY/NJNSPOOOO SP HDQ TRENTON                   OCA/12345
               ACH/01   AON/3562−MARIJUANA−POSSESS−UND 25 GRM
                        CIT/NJ2421−20A.4         DOO/
                        ADN/    −
               ACH/02   AON/1313−SIMPLE ASSLT−
                        CIT/NJ2A170−26          DOO/
                        ADN/    −
               ACH/03   AON/2200−BURGL−
                        CIT/NJ2A94−1            DOO/
                        ADN/    −
                        ADD/    −

COURT          AGCY/NJ011013A MERCER CO PROS
               CCT/ 1    IDENTIFIER/W2345
                        CON/2200−BURGL−
                        CIT/NJ2A94−1          DISPO/        −RETURN LWR COURT
                        DISP−DATE/080176   CMT/            SSC/              CFN/

COURT          AGCY/NJ011051J MUNICIPAL COURT TRENTON
               CCT/ 1    IDENTIFIER/W1234
                        CON/3562−MARIJUANA−POSSESS−
                        CIT/NJ2421−20A.4        DISPO/316−CONDITIONAL DISCHARGE
                        DISP−DATE/070876   CMT/            SSC/              CFN/
                        SSF/      COS/        SSK/      CPR/      CDT/ 6M
```

continued

Figure 18-1 (*continued*)

```
COURT          AGCY/NJ011051J MUNICIPAL COURT TRENTON
               CCT/ 1        IDENTIFIER/W1235
                    CON/1313—SIMPLE ASSLT—
                    CIT/NJ2A170—26          DISPO/310—CONVICTED
                    DISP—DATE/070876    CMT/      364D    SSC/              CFN/

CONDITIONAL DISCHARGE FINAL DISPOSITION
               AGCY/NJ011051J MUNICIPAL COURT TRENTON
               CCT/ 1        IDENTIFIER/W1234
                    CON/3562—MARIJUANA—POSSESS—
                    CIT/NJ2421—20A.4          DISPO/305—DISMISSED
                    DISP—DATE/110876    CMT/             SSC/              CFN/

POST CONVICTION CHANGE DISPOSITION
               AGCY/NJ011043J MERCER COUNTY COURT
               CCT/ 1        IDENTIFIER/W1235
                    CON/1313—SIMPLE ASSLT—
                    CIT/NJ2A170—26          DISPO/305—DISMISSED
                    DISP—DATE/080176    CMT/             SSC/              CFN/

REMAND TO LOWER COURT DISPOSITION
               AGCY/NJ011051J MUNICIPAL COURT TRENTON
               CCT/ 1        IDENTIFIER/W2345
                    CON/2206—BURGL—TOOLS—POSSESS—
                    CIT/NJ2A170—3           DISPO/310—CONVICTED
                    DISP—DATE/090976    CMT/6M           SSC/          CFN/000150

CUSTODY        AGCY/NJ011013C MERCER CO JAIL TRENTON          CBN/1257
               DATE/090976    STATUS/421—RECEIVED
               SLE/                                    SW-IA/W2345

CUSTODY        AGCY/NJ011013C MERCER CO JAIL TRENTON          CBN/1257
               DATE/012177    STATUS/409—DISCHARGED
               SLE/                                    SW-IA/W2345

CYCLE  02      DOA/010177
               ANA/                            DOB/050543

ARREST         AGCY/NJ0031200  EDGEWATER PARK TWP PD          OCA/236-77
               ACH/01    AON/1300—ASSLT—
                         CIT/NJ2A90—1              DOO/
                         ADN/
                         ADD/

COURT          AGCY/NJ003013J  BURLINGTON COUNTY COURT
               CCT/ 1     IDENTIFIER/I12—77
                    CON/1300—ASSLT—AA&B
                    CIT/NJ2A90—1            DISPO/310—CONVICTED
                    DISP—DATE/032077    CMT/           SSC/          CFN/000500

CYCLE  03      DOA/070277
               ANA/                            DOB/050543

ARREST         AGCY/NJ0110200 EWING TOWNSHIP PD               OCA/3377
               ACH/01     AON/2804—POSSESS STOLEN PROP—
                          CIT/NJ2A139—1             DOO/
                          ADN/   —
                          ADD/
```

With word processing, the author of the PSIR can dictate and receive a draft copy for review. This can be modified as necessary and then resubmitted to the typist. Only the changes need be retyped; everything else is taken care of by the computer's "memory". Modifications to the text are simply made on the computer screen before the final copy is printed out. This represents a major time and energy savings over older methods of correction and modification.

In two instances in a national demonstration project on the PSIR, the potential productivity gains of word processing were astounding. The District of Columbia Superior Court's PSIR operation increased report output by 30% with no increase in staff after word processing was introduced.[4] In the Connecticut Office of Adult Probation, report output remained constant after a 30% cut in clerical staff.[5]

Computer Generated Narrative Reports

In 1984, a product was introduced that appears to represent the ultimate in marriage of the computer and the PSIR. The Automated Social History (ASH) (Anderson Publishing Co.) is a microcomputer-based software package that will produce a narrative report from the answers to a lengthy series of questions.[6]

The text is developed by the program, which bases the narrative on the answers given to multiple choice or forced choice questions. The questions in ASH deal with straightfoward factual concerns and are derived from validated and accepted psychological and social inventories.

Examples of some of the questions in ASH are shown in Figure 18-2.

The ASH can be administered in a number of ways. If the offender who is the subject of the investigation has the reading capability, the questionnaire and answer sheet can be completed independently and then submitted to staff. If the offender cannot read or refuses the questionnaire, the PSIR writer can administer it, reading the questions and recording the offender's answers. With offenders who possess more sophisticated skills, it may even be possible to have them complete the ASH at the computer.

Critics of the automated PSIR model say that it removes the human element from the PSIR process. As with any technique, if the automated approaches are misused, they can seriously dilute the quality of the PSIR. Use of unverified offender answers to questions, and sole reliance on unnecessarily restrictive multiple choice questions cannot provide the kind of accurate, qualitative information the court needs for sentencing.

Figure 18-2

PAGE 1 →

1. What is your present religion?

1 None
2 Protestant
3 Catholic
4 Other Christian
5 Jewish
6 Muslim
7 Buddhist
8 Other non-Christian

2. In your opinion are you a religious person? (Y = Yes   N = No   D = Don't know)

3. How often did you attend religious services during the past year?

1 not at all
2 on special days
3 occasionally
4 regularly

4. What sex are you? (F = Female   M = Male)

5. What is your ethnic background?

1 Caucasian (White)
2 Negro (Black)
3 American Indian
4 Asian/Pacific Island
5 Hispanic
6 East European
7 Southern European
8 Northern European
9 Other

6. Is your cultural heritage important in your life now?

7. How often have you been unfairly treated because of your cultural heritage?

1 every week
2 once a month
3 once or twice a year
4 once or twice in my life
5 never
6 don't know

8. What type of home do you live in?

1 room
2 apartment
3 condominium
4 house
5 other

9. How many years have you lived in this home?

1 one or less
2 two
3 three
4 four
5 five
6 six or more

10. How many other people live in this home with you?

0 no one
1 one other person
2 two other people
3 three other people
4 four other people
5 five other people
6 six other people
7 seven other people
8 eight or more people

11. How would you describe most of the people who live in your neighborhood?

1 mostly poor people (unemployed or on public assistance)
2 mostly factory workers or manual laborers
3 a mixed group of people with different occupations
4 business people (clerks, managers)
5 professionals (doctors, lawyers)

12. During most of your childhood with whom did you live?

1 both natural parents
2 parent & step-parent
3 single parent
4 adoptive or foster parents
5 relatives
6 other

13. How would you describe the home in which you grew up?

1 poverty level (not enough $)
2 working class (barely enough $)
3 middle class (a little extra $)
4 upper middle (some extra $)
5 upper class (a lot of extra $)

Source: *ASH Plus*, Joseph Waldron, Anderson Publishing Co., 1988.

Yet, properly used, the automated PSIR can actually *increase* the quality of human involvement in the case by releasing the PSIR writer from some of the more clerical aspects of the work. The following describes what might be commonplace in probation by the turn of this century.

> Offender Joe Smith, having been convicted in court of assault, is ordered to report to the probation department at 9 a.m. the next day for a PSIR. He arrives, is given a questionnaire and answer sheet, and escorted to an interview room to complete it. Probation Officer Alice Jones is advised that Smith is here, and she plans to see him at 10 a.m.. At 9:45, Smith gives the completed questionnaire to the secretary who enters the data in the computer. The narrative report quickly emerges and is given to P.O. Jones. She quickly scans the report and notes any items which will need follow up, clarification or expansion.
>
> Smith arrives in Jones's office shortly after 10 a.m. and the interview commences. Since most of the personal and social history information has been gathered, that part of the interview goes quickly. P.O. Jones is able to concentrate on listening and can focus on inconsistencies or gaps in information. With Smith, she is able to help him clarify his own confusion about dates of critical events in his family history. After completing the interview, P.O. Jones proceeds to verify critical information, set up interviews with other key persons and arrange for criminal history records to corroborate Smith's answers. Once she has all of this information at hand, P.O. Jones is ready to dictate the PSIR, which goes quickly because of word processing.

Standards and Accreditation

As emerging professions, corrections and probation have endeavored to establish and maintain high standards of practice through professional standards and accreditation.

Standards

A standard is an established measure or model which is used to guide practice. Several groups have addressed the PSIR through establishing standards. Since 1946, the American Correctional Association has included the PSIR in its Manual of Correctional Standards.[7] The American Bar Association issued its Standards Relating to Probation in 1970, which included the PSIR.[8]   In 1973, the National Advisory Commission on Criminal Justice Standards and Goals issued its report on Corrections, and it too targeted the PSIR.[9]   The National Council on Crime and Delinquency prepared recommendations about the PSIR in 1955 and 1972,[10] as did the President's Commission on Law Enforcement and the Administration of Justice in 1967.[11] From 1946 to 1973, no less than six sets of "national standards" addressed the PSIR.   This process of prescribing standards culminated in 1978 with the publication by the National Institute of Law Enforcement and Criminal Justice of the *Presentence Report Handbook*.[12]

This document reviewed all the available literature on the PSIR and conducted a national survey of probation agencies about their PSIR practices and procedures.   The handbook concluded with 64 prescriptions or recommendations related to all aspects of the PSIR, including format, content, organization of the process, and so forth.   The text of the prescriptions is contained in Appendix B.

Publication of the handbook was followed by the funding of a national demonstration project to field test the prescriptions.   Nine sites around the country participated in the project, and the results showed that the prescriptions formed a solid basis for organizing the PSIR process.[13]

Accreditation

Accreditation is a process certifying that a person or organization has achieved certain educational credentials or meets certain performance standards.   Accreditation is a natural outgrowth of the establishment of professional standards.   Standards serve as guides for practice, but accreditation is the formal recognition of compliance with those accepted standards.

The field of corrections undertook accreditation with the establishment of the Commission on Accreditation for Corrections (CAC) in 1977.   An outgrowth of the Committee on Standards of the American Correctional Association (ACA), the CAC developed standards for all areas of correctional practice, adult and juvenile, pre- and post-conviction, institutional and community based.[14]   Agencies which apply for accreditation are carefully reviewed and audited to ascertain whether they are in compliance with the CAC standards.   This process includes on-site visits to the agency or facility and evaluation of written documents.

Investigative reports such as the PSIR are addressed in both the Standards for Adult Probation and Parole Agencies and the Standards for Juvenile Probation and Aftercare Agencies.   Selected standards are shown in Appendix F.

Establishing standards and developing an accreditation mechanism represent a consistent and active effort on the part of probation professionals to upgrade the quality of professional practice. The future of the PSIR process lies partly in an increased emphasis on standards as part of the larger trend toward professionalism in probation. This will have two aspects. First, the field will become more consistent in the content and style of the PSIRs. Second, the standards themselves will change to reflect the need to adapt to new technologies.

Privatization

Privatization of publicly delivered services has become a popular concept in recent years. Private contractors have sometimes been able to provide services less expensively, faster or better than governmental agencies.

Corrections has not escaped this trend. Private corporations are running institutions for profit, and there have been some experiments with privately prepared PSIRs. There are three main trends that have led to the private PSIR experiments.

Prison Crowding. Jails and prisons all across the country are over capacity and under great pressure to reduce populations. Sentencing courts are looking at every possible alternative that could avoid incarceration without excessively risking public safety. One role of the PSIR is to explore alternatives.

Fiscal Constraint. Probation departments are experiencing cutbacks, and the result is often fewer resources for the PSIR function.

Changing Sentencing Laws. Sentencing laws have become more punitive and deserts oriented, requiring less offender oriented information from the PSIR.

The private PSIR responds to these trends by concentrating on the offender in detail, presenting to the sentencing judge a thorough and well developed plan for keeping the offender in the community. For those who fall into the "gray area" of sentencing, a comprehensive plan for tight supervision in the community could well tip the balance in favor of a probation sentence.

The reactions to the private PSIR range from encouragement[15] to vehement opposition.[16] Opponents of the private PSIR argue that the private sector has no appropriate role in the sentencing process; the private PSIR ignores the need for consistency in sentencing; and its cost effectiveness is questionable.

Although it doesn't seem likely that the private PSIR will replace the probation PSIR, there is a clear role for it as a supplemental part of the sentencing process. The preparation of a plan in which the offender agrees to adhere to certain requirements increases the offender's responsibility to the community and the chances of successfully completing supervision.

If the private PSIR, as an adjunct to the sentencing process, can contribute to keeping more offenders out of prison without unduly jeopardizing community safety, their use will probably continue to grow in the future.

Summary

This chapter has investigated the future of the PSIR. Likely trends include greater computerization, greater professionalization through the use of standards and accreditation, and the advent of the privately prepared PSIR.

Notes

[1] Loren A.Beckley and others. *The Presentence Investigation Report Program, Final Report*. Sacramento, CA: American Justice Institute, 1981, p. 162.

[2] John P. McCarthy, Jr. *Report of the Sentencing Guidelines Project to the Administrative Director of the Courts*. Trenton, NJ: Administrative Office of the Courts. n.d. pp.26-29.

[3] New Jersey State Police. *Automated Master Name Index and Criminal History Records*. Trenton, NJ: Division of State Police, 1978.

[4] "An Evaluation of the Impact of the LEAA Supported Report Production Equipment," Washington, DC: District of Columbia Superior Court, Social Services Division. 1981, mimeo.

[5] Office of Adult Probation (Connecticut). Unpublished report on word processing experiment. 1980, mimeo.

[6] Joseph Waldron. *Automated Social History*. Cincinnati: Anderson Publishing Co., 1986.

[7] American Correctional Association, *Manual of Correctional Standards* rev. ed. College Park, MD: 1966.

[8] American Bar Association, *Standards Relating to Probation*. Chicago,IL: 1970.

[9] National Advisory Commission on Criminal Justice Standards and Goals, *Corrections*. Washington, DC: 1973.

[10] National Council on Crime and Delinquency, *Model Sentencing Act* Paramus, NJ: 1972. id. *Standard Probation and Parole Act*. New York: author, 1955.

[11] President's Commission on Law Enforcement and the Administration of Justice, *Task Force Report: Corrections*, 1967.

[12] Robert M. Carter *Presentence Report Handbook.* Washington, DC: National Institute of Law Enforcement and Criminal Justice, 1978.

[13] Beckley, *Final Report*, iii.

[14] Commission on Accreditation for Corrections. *1982 Annual Report*. Rockville, MD: Author, 1982.

[15] Judy Barrasso. "Rehabilitative Planning Services in a Public Defender's Office" in *Offender Rehabilitation*, v.2, n.2, Winter, 1977. pp. 153-158. Richard J. Medalie "The Offender Rehablitation Project: A New Role for Defense Counsel at Pretrial and Sentencing". *Georgetown Law Journal*. v.56, n.1, 1967. pp. 2-16. Sheldon Portman. "The Defense Lawyer's New Role in the Sentencing Process" in *Federal Probation*, v.43, n.1, 1982, pp.3-8. David Wald. *The Use of Social Workers in a Public Defender's Office*. San Jose, CA: Public Defender's Office of Santa Clara County, 1972.

[16] Kulis, Chester J. "Profit in the Private Presentence Report" in *Federal Probation* v.47, n.4., December, 1983. pp.11-15.

244 The Future of the PSIR

GROUP EXERCISE

Any group is likely to contain some who respond favorably to anything electronic, seeing it as the "Great Answer," and some who long for the good old days of the personal touch in human relations. Let a couple of persons from each orientation re-read the section on Automated Social History (ASH), then discuss pros and cons of this now-functioning system in which the offender writes his own PSIR by punching selected computer buttons.

DISCUSSION QUESTIONS

1. Standardization of PSIRs has moved ahead rather consistently since the movement started more than 40 years ago, but it has been received differently in different settings. How would you expect a rural Mississippi county probation department to respond to a standard acceptable to the probation department in Chicago and vice-versa? What are problem areas?

2. In principle, how do you feel about the privatization of PSIR writing and other probation functions? What is the role of a for-profit professional PSIR writer or probation supervisor?

3. Comment: The privately written PSIR is just another example of "the best justice a man can afford" and will result in the rich man getting another unfair break.

4. Nearly everyone concedes that the computer provides masses of readily accessible information for the PSIR writer. What dangers do you see in the trend toward the computer world? Can it become a threat to professional excellence? Likely?

Appendix A

PSIR for John Franklin

Face Sheet

In the Paine County Circuit Court
Paine County, Alabama

Before the Hon. Thurman Thurston
Mack Ray, Probation Officer

IDENTIFICATION

Court Name: <u>Franklin, John R.</u>
True Name: <u>John Ryford Franklin</u>
Alias/Nickname: <u>"Slim"</u>
Date of Birth: <u>June 15, 1967</u>
Soc. Sec. No.: <u>602-57-82xx</u>

Sex: <u>M</u> Ht.: <u>6'1"</u> Wt. <u>150</u>
Race: <u>W</u> Eyes: <u>Hazel</u> Hair: <u>Brown</u>
Complexion: <u>Light</u>
Build: <u>Slender</u>
Marks: <u>Tattoo on left bicep;</u>
<u>scar on right thumb</u>

Present Address: <u>Paine County Detention Center</u>

PERSONAL DATA

Yrs. in Co.: <u>16</u> State: <u>20</u> U.S.: <u>20</u>
Birthplace: <u>Sylacauga, AL</u>
Nationality: <u>USA</u>
Citizenship: <u>USA</u>

School Attainment: <u>11th grade</u>
Occupation: <u>Unemployed</u>
Marital Status: <u>Divorced</u>

FAMILY

Father: <u>Jerry Franklin</u>
Birthplace: <u>Alabama</u>
Mother: <u>Nora Brown Franklin</u>
Birthplace: <u>Alabama</u>

Closest Living Relative: <u>Parents</u>
Relative's Name:
Address: <u>1412 S.E. 9th St.</u>
<u>High Plateau, NM 32375</u>

INSTANT OFFENSE

Offense: Ct. I - Burglary, Class B Felony
            Ct. II - Theft, Class D Felony
            Ct. III - Resisting Law Enforcement, Class A Misdemeanor
Docket No.: CR 80-86   Co-Defendants: Mark Jones
Prosecutor: William Jarvis
Defense Atty: Arthur Wohlford
Address: Anderson, IN   Previous Record: See
Convicted by: Plea Agreement   "Previous Trouble"
Jail Time: 309 days on 4/3/87

PRE-SENTENCE INVESTIGATION REPORT

In the Paine County Circuit Court   Cause No.: CF-80-439
Before the Honorable Thurman Thurston   Sentencing Date: April 3, 1987

              RE: John R. Franklin
                    Paine County Detention Center
                    Paine, AL
                    Age: 20
                    Marital Status: Divorced

Offense: CT. I - Burglary, Class B Felony
            CT. II - Theft, Class D Felony
            CT. III - Resisting Law Enforcement, Class A Misdemeanor

OFFICIAL VERSION: See Information Sheet attached.

DEFENDANT'S VERSION

I was drinking with three friends in the State Park on Labor Day. We saw the caretaker's home, and it looked like it was empty. We broke out a glass in the rear door and went in and took a .410 shotgun, some shells, and food from the refrigerator, and a bowl of change, and a diamond ring, and a VISA card. When we were leaving the park, a police car stopped us and frisked us, and roughed us up, and cussed us out, and told us they were going to throw the book at us.

VICTIM IMPACT

Mr. Gary Ronheim, the victim, reported the following losses. Receipts were shown for all but the three items designated as estimated.

Repair to door		$ 18.87
Shotgun		110.95
Food (est.)		5.00
Change (est.)		20.00
Ring (est.)		300.00
VISA charges:		
Deductible		50.00
VISA		319.68
	Total	$924.50

If restitution is ordered, $ 319.68 should be paid to VISA, via the Louisville National Bank, 101 Main St., Louisville, KY, 40290, and the balance should be paid to Mr. Gary Ronheim, Superintendent, Oak Hill State Park, State Road 104, Paine, Alabama, 69738.

JAIL TIME

The defendant was detained on a warrantless arrest on June 30, 1986, and has remained in custody. On April 3, 1987, he will have accumulated a total of 309 days in jail.

PREVIOUS FELONY

On April 19, 1985, Franklin was sentenced to two years, suspended, in Paine County Court, Div. 2, for Theft, a Class D Felony, in Cause Number PCC 2-85-43. A copy of the Minutes of the Court is attached to this report.

PREVIOUS TROUBLE

The combined files of the Paine County Police Department, the Paine, Alabama, Police Department, and the Alabama State Police Department contain the following entries:

Date	Offense	Disposition
10/10/81	Curfew	Office adjustment
6/16/82	JD Public Intoxication	Informal prob., 6 mos.
4/19/83	Vandalism	10 days, Detention Center
6/11/83	JD Burglary	State Boys' School, 1 yr.
8/18/84	JD Criminal Conversion	State Boys' School, 180 days
3/3/85	Public Intoxication	Probation, 90 days
----------------------(6/15/85 Eighteenth Birthday)----------------		
7/5/85	Public Intoxication	$100; 10 days
	Resisting Arrest	
7/30/85	Stop Sign	Warning
8/4/85	Burglary, Class B Felony	Pending
	Burglary, Class B Felony	Pending
8/14/85	Escape	

1/13/86	Theft	Nolle Pros.
3/7/86	Public Intoxication	5 days; $25
5/1/86	Public Intoxication	5 days; $25
5/5/86	Speeding	$25; $31 costs
6/30/86	Burglary	Instant case: CR-86-439
	Theft	
	Resisting Law Enforcement	

SOCIAL HISTORY

PARENTS

The defendant's parents were separated for two years when the defendant was about 7 years old, during which time he lived with his mother and siblings. He recalls that his parents got along reasonably well after their reconciliation. Father was a good provider, and the son reports that he got along well with both parents. Both parents are seen as strict disciplinarians, the father at times becoming physically brutal, although the defendant is not willing to characterize the treatment as child abuse. Both parents drank to excess on occassion, and the father had several arrests for Public Intoxication and Driving Under the Influence. Both remain in good health. The father completed the 9th grade, the mother the 11th. In a previous marriage, the father had two children, and in a previous marriage, the mother had one. When asked which was his favorite parent, the defendant replied, "Neither; I hate them both!" The family apparently moved frequently, and never developed a feeling of interdependence. The mother worked outside the home most of the years while the defendant was growing up, usually as a bar maid or a waitress. When he was 15 years old, the defendant left home for the first time, entering Boys' School. When he was 17, he left to move in with a girlfriend. The home life during the growing-up years is described as turbulent and destructive, with little consideration from the parents.

SIBLINGS

There is a brother one year older than the defendant, a sister one year younger, and another brother five years younger, the defendant being the second in birth order. He reports that they never did have a very harmonious relationship, which he attributes to the attitude which the parents had toward the children, who were seen as nuisances for which they accepted little responsibility. The older brother also was sent to State Boys' School for Vandalism and Incorrigibility. None of the four was graduated from high school.

DEFENDANT

Franklin sees himself as a loner, with very few friends. When he is with friends, however, he thinks he characteristically performs the role of follower. The person who has been most influential in his life is a boyfriend who constantly suggested mischief to him and who remained in trouble with the school authorities throughout the years they were in school. He presently is serving a ten-year sentence in State Prison for Battery. When Franklin was asked what he thought his friend would say about him if he were present, he said, "He would say I've got a lot of good qualities, but never did have a chance to show them much." When he was discussing the unusual problems he had as a child, the defendant recalled that the succession of boyfriends that his mother had was a constant embarrassment to him, and that while the father was living at home, he was placed on probation for Child Molesting and Resisting Arrest, all of which made it difficult for the defendant to relate to peers. When he was in the 4th through 7th grades, he was in special education classes because of poor reading ability, and has never recovered from the handicap.

EDUCATIONAL HISTORY

Formal education was received at Edwarton Elementary, MacArthur Junior High, and Parkview Senior High Schools. When he was in the 11th grade, he was expelled because of smoking in the restroom, followed by striking the assistant principal who reprimanded him. Prior to that, attendance had been poor and grades were failing. His best subject was Shop and his poorest was English. He went out for cross-country briefly, but had to drop out when the next grading period revealed his academic incompetence. Parents were not active in PTA. In a simple office reading test, he performed on the 4.7 grade level, failing to read "collapse." Franklin has an interest in auto mechanics and hopes that he will be able to follow that vocational track while he is serving sentence.

MARITAL HISTORY

In 1985 Franklin married Mona Johnson, and she divorced him in 1986. They have one child, a girl now 2 1/2 years old. Franklin explains the break-up of the marriage as the result of her "running around, hanging out in bars." He has been ordered by the Court to pay $40 per month in support payments.

EMPLOYMENT HISTORY

At the time of his arrest, the defendant was employed in maintenance at Griswold's Chrysler Service. He had been there about two years, and previously had worked in similar work in the public schools.

ECONOMIC SITUATION

The defendant has been in detention for about ten months, during which time he has had virtually no income. He reports that he still owns a 1977 Chevrolet worth about $300 and a 1977 Kawaski motorcycle worth $400, both of which are free of debt. He has no savings or investments. During the time he was working, his weekly take-home pay was about $120.

RELIGIOUS ASSOCIATION

Franklin infrequently attends the Beulah Bible Church on East 9th Street, Paine AL, but he is unable to name the pastor.

OUTSIDE INTERESTS

Free time is spent mainly in hunting, fishing, and working on old cars. He reports that he does not do any recreational reading.

HEALTH

When he was about 13 years old, Franklin fell from a horse and broke his arm, but there is no residual problem. Two years later, a spark from a campfire struck him in the eye and left him with a scar on the eyelid, but no permanent damage to his eyesight was done. At the age of 17 there was a suicide attempt which came about when he broke up with a girlfriend. Franklin reports that he frequently uses alcohol to excess, occassionally uses marijuana, and never uses hard drugs. He thinks that he has no physical or mental problem, although when he entered the State Boys' School, he had several sessions with the psychiatrist. He reports that alcohol became a problem to him when he was about 15 years old. His father supplied the alcohol, amused when he saw the son drunk. Franklin was referred to a drug-treatment program by the school counselor, but dropped out in the middle of the six-week program. He denies drinking and driving, asserting that whenever he has been drinking he knows enough not to get behind a wheel. There is some indication that he has been mixing alcohol with hard drugs, but this has never been brought to the attention of the authorities.

PRESENT ATTITUDES OF THE DEFENDANT

Franklin believes that the police have been unfair and unprofessional with him. "They hate my guts and nail me whenever they see me. I never done anything against them, but they watch for me all the time." His perception of the Prosecutor is that he is just doing his job. Franklin has no opinion about the Court. The Defense Attorney "has done everything anybody could do," and he says of the victims, "hell, I don't know those people, but I'm sorry I took that stuff. I was drunk." Does he see himself as a criminal? "No, I'm just a guy who's got a problem." When he was asked what he thought the sentence ought to be, Franklin indicated that he thought it should be probation because he would not be coming back before the Judge again, for any reason.

PLEA AGREEMENT

A signed plea agreement in the file provides that the defendant will plead guilty to all charges, that he will receive one year executed, and the balance suspended.

FISCAL IMPACT

Mr. Gary Ronheim, the victim, lost $604.82 and VISA lost $319.68. Should the court accept the plea agreement, the sentence of one year executed will cost the state approximately $100,000 (assuming good time, reducing the period of incarceration to six months). An unofficial estimate by the Department of Human Services is that payments under Aid to Families with Dependant Children will increase by about $240 while he is institutionalized, then about $40 per month until he finds employment and resumes child support payments. The defendant's employer will not hold the job for him, so Franklin probably will return to the streets without employment.

PSYCHIATRIC INSIGHTS

Because the psychiatric examinations were focused upon competency to stand trial, there is not the full-orbed analysis that the Court might prefer for an understanding of the inner workings of the defendant. Both Dr. Jeffries and Dr. Weinberg find him competent to stand trial, with no evidence of psychosis.

Dr. Jeffries does go a bit further when he summarizes evaluations made at St. Joseph's Medical Center in 1974, 1976, and 1981. On the basis of these reports, Dr. Jeffries says that Franklin functions at a low average level of intelligence and has the following personality characteristics: impulsivity, deficiency of behavioral control, tendency to act out frustrations, deficiency of self-confidence, and hostility and depression related to repeated frustrations.

Any one of this catalogue of personality characteristics could be found in most normally functioning persons, but Franklin possesses more than his share of the assortment and he posseses the traits in more profound and intense form. This fact is reflected in some of the crisis incidents: attempted suicide in State Boys' School, arson of a neighbor's house after a confrontation, and setting himself afire while alone in the police interrogation room.

STATEMENT BY THE PROBATION OFFICER

It is obvious that Franklin was badly scarred long before he cut his arms with a blade. His mother had been before the Court in Paine County on numerous occassions, and has been committed to mental institutions on several occassions. She was in prison when he was an infant, and she is in prison today. His upbringing was anything but salutary, and it is not surprising that he is standing before the Court at this time. It is to be noted that there is pending against him a charge of Robbery in Hamilton Circuit Court. In addition, the arrest sheet shows an escape incident on August 4, 1985, and warrants for two counts of Burglary, (B/C Felonies) on August 14, 1985. Clearly, the defendant is a chronic problem as an adult, the natural outgrowth of his abundant juvenile record.

Although it is not necessary to look very far to find the root of his antisocial behavior, given the kind of parental home in which he was reared, he is now 20 years old and must be held accountable for his actions as an adult. It would be possible to suspend the sentence on both of these felonies, but in view of the defendant's history, that seems not advisable. For whatever deterrent value there may be in it, it is recommended that the Court seek to shock him into compliance with an insider's view of the correctional system. If he is to avoid his mother's history, perhaps a firm hand at this point might be helpful.

The State Correctional System has tried to meet the needs of the defendant and has not achieved very good results. Perhaps no institution could. It is apparent that his current adjustment to society is not acceptable and that something else must be tried. Perhaps "big time" incarceration would have a salutary deterring impact. It is worth trying, since it seems to be about the only option remaining open to the Court.

It is suggested that Franklin be sent through the Reception and Diagnostic Center, then enter the general population of the Department of Correction. Traumatic treatment sometimes achieves a cure, as in the case of schizophrenia with electrical shock. Upon completion of a year (actually six months), it is recommended that he be given three years of probation in order to keep him under the supervision of the Court for a good period of time. Since the gestation period of his problem has continued for nineteen years, the convalescent period, if there is one, should be stretched to the limit available to the Court.

RECOMMENDATION

1. For Ct. I, Burglary, a Class B Felony, sentence to the Department of Correction for six years, one year to be executed and the balance suspended;

   For Ct. II, Theft, a Class D Felony, sentence to the Department of Correction for two years, one year to be executed and the balance suspended, to run concurrently with Count I;

   For Ct. III, Resisting Law Enforcement, a Class A Misdemeanor, sentence to the Department of Correction for one year, to run concurrently with Count I;

2. Credit for 309 days of jail time, with no good time allowed;

3. Probation for three years upon release from incarceration, with special conditions as indicated under the Probation Plan prepared by the Department of Probation;

4. Restitution to Gary Ronheim in the amount of $604.82, and $319.68 to VISA for charges made on the credit card;

5. Probation User's Fees (initial fee of $50; monthly fee of $24 for 36 months);

6. Court costs of $75 payable within sixty days of release from incarceration.

PROBATION PLAN

1. Formal probation for three years;

2. Semi-monthly reporting for three months; thereafter, monthly, unless modified by Probation Officer;

3. Enrollment in a job placement program at the Vocational School;

4. After employed, enrollment in a G.E.D. course;

5. Community service of 60 hours, preferrably in Oak Hill State Park, if available.

March 25, 1987   Respectfully submitted,

_____   _____
Orville Cornwell   Mack Ray
Chief Probation Officer   Adult Probation Officer

Attachments:
    Information Sheets
    Arrest Record
    Plea Agreement

Appendix B

Suggested Interview Schedule

Face Sheet

Full Name:_____

Alias/Nickname:_____

Address:_____ Phone:_____

Date of Birth:_____ Age:_____ SS#:_____ Sex:_____

Height:_____ Weight:_____ Race:_____ Eyes:_____ Hair:_____

Complexion:_____ Build:_____ Marks:_____

Marital Status:_____ Education:_____

Birthplace:_____

Father:_____ Address:_____

Mother:_____ Address:_____

Closest Relative:_____ Relationship:_____

Address:_____

Employer:_____ Job:_____

Address:_____ Phone:_____

Weekly Income:_____ % time employed last year:_____

Prosecutor:_____ Defense Attorney:_____

Convicted by: _____Plea _____Plea Agreement _____ Court _____Jury

Jail Time:_____ # addresses last year:_____ Co-defendant:_____

PARENTS

Still married_____ Age when parents   separated_____
                                                 divorced_____
                        Age when step-parent appeared_____

Father's occupation:_____ Good provider? Yes_____ No_____
Get along with father? Yes_____ No_____   Mother? Yes_____ No_____
Parents get along? Yes_____ No_____ Still married_____ Divorced_____ Deceased_____
Father: Strict_____ Easy_____   Mother: Strict_____ Easy_____
Mode of punishment_____   Child abuse?_____
Father drink? Yes_____ No_____   Mother? Yes_____ No_____
Record: Father: Yes_____ No_____   Mother? Yes_____ No_____
Health: Father: Good_____ Poor_____   Mother? Good_____ Poor____
School: Father: _____grade   Mother: _____grade
Previous marriage
    Father: Yes_____ No_____   Mother Yes_____ No_____
    # children_____   # children_____
    Remarried? Yes_____ No_____   Remarried? Yes_____ No_____
Favorite parent: Father_____   Mother_____   Neither_____
Family move often? Yes_____ No_____   Close knit unit? Yes_____ No_____
Mother work outside home? Yes_____ No_____ At what?_____
Age when left home:_____ Why?_____
Brief description of home life:_____

SIBLINGS

Present age(s) of brother(s)_____ sister(s)_____
Birth order of defendant:_____ Siblings get along? Yes_____ No_____
Sibling juvenile record?_____ Adult?_____
Number graduated high school:_____ Attended college_____

DEFENDANT'S SELF-PERCEPTION

Friends: Many_____ Few_____ Loner? Yes_____ No_____   Neither_____
When with friends: Leader_____ Follower_____ Neither_____ Both_____
Who most influential (good/bad)?
    What would say to you now?

Other unusual problems as child:

MARITAL HISTORY

Never_____
Spouse name_____
Date_____
Lived without marriage_____
Reasons for break-up_____
Children/ages_____
Get along with present spouse?_____
Effect on marriage?_____
Paying support?_____ $_____/month

MILITARY HISTORY

Never_____
Month/year in:_____ Discharged date:_____ Kind:_____
Branch:_____ Final rank:_____
Job:_____ Where:_____
Disciplinary:_____ Commendation:_____
How do you feel about your military experience?

EDUCATIONAL HISTORY

Elementary:_____ Junior High:_____
Senior High:_____ College:_____
Why?Graduated_____ Quit_____ Expelled_____
        Age quit_____ Reason
School attendance: Good_____ Poor_____
Grades: Good_____ Average_____ Poor_____
Best subject_____ Poorest_____
Sports_____ Letter?_____
PTA, etc.?_____
Reading test? _____Grade   Failed on_____
Plans

RELIGIOUS ASSOCIATION

Attend church at:_____ Frequency/month:_____
Pastor:_____ Member? Yes_____ No_____

OUTSIDE INTERESTS

Free time:
Reading: Much_____   Little_____   None_____
          Newspaper_____   Magazines_____   Fiction__   Non-fiction_____   Bible_____

EMPLOYMENT HISTORY

Current job:_____
Recent jobs:_____
Other jobs you can do:_____

ECONOMIC SITUATION

Unemployed for how long?_____
Own property: $_____ owe $_____
Vehicle   #1: Model_____ Worth $_____ Owe $_____
          #2: Model_____ Worth $_____ Owe $_____
Savings/investments $_____
Take-home pay $_____week/mo.   Spouse $_____week/mo.

HEALTH

Serious injury: Age_____: _____ Residual: Yes_____ No_____
Serious injury: Age_____: _____ Residual: Yes_____ No_____
Blackouts?_____
Use of:
       Tobacco: Never_____ Used to_____ Occassional_____ Lot_____
       Alcohol: Never_____ Used to_____ Occassional_____ Lot_____
       Marijuana: Never_____ Used to_____ Occassional_____ Lot_____
       Hard drugs: Never_____ Used to_____ Occassional_____ Lot_____
When/how alcohol/drugs first became problem:

Alcohol/drug therapy: Never_____ When/where_____
Are you alcoholic/addict? Yes_____ No_____
Have mental problem? Yes_____ No_____ Ever see psychiatrist? Yes_____ No_____
Other health problem?

Ever seen psychologist/psychiatrist? Yes_____ No_____
       When:_____
       Occassion:_____
       Name/agency:_____
       Findings:_____

Mind if I consult? Yes_____ No_____
What is "real you," down deep inside?

Why commit crime?
Hidden reasons?

PREVIOUS TROUBLE

Juvenile: Never   _____

Adult: Never_____

Previous felony? Yes_____ No_____ Out-of-state offense? Yes_____ No_____
License suspended? Yes_____ No_____
Jail time:_____ to _____
Charges pending? No_____ Where?_____

PRESENT ATTITUDES OF DEFENDANT

Police
Court
Prosecutor
Defense Attorney
Victim
See self as criminal?
Goals/aspirations in life

DEFENDANT'S VERSION OF CRIME

What happened?

Is there plea agreement? Yes_____ No_____
Content
    Restitution?
What do you think sentence ought to be?

WORKSHEET

Fiscal impact
    Cost to victim
    Cost of incarceration
    Family maintenance
    Other costs
Mitigating factors:

Aggravating factors:

Sentence perimeters: Maximum_____   Minimum_____
                                Maximum fine: $_____
Probation plan: Level: Low_____ Medium_____ High_____
              Period
                         Special conditions:
                              G.E.D.
                              Job training
                              Community service
                              Alcohol/drug evaluation/treatment
                              Abstain alcohol/drug
                              In-house detention
                              Split sentence
                              Transfer to other jurisdiction
                              Probation user's fees
                              Other considerations

Sources:

Appendix C

Sample Release Form

AUTHORIZATION FOR RELEASE OF INFORMATION

I authorize _____ to release to:

NAME: _____

ADDRESS: _____

information from records including identity, diagnosis, prognosis and treatment of:

NAME: _____

ADDRESS: _____

DATE OF BIRTH: _____

SOCIAL SECURITY NUMBER: _____

Unless otherwise indicated, this authorization extends to such psychiatric, alcohol or drug abuse information, if any, as may be contained in records.

PURPOSE OF DISCLOSURE: _____

I understand that this consent will remain in force for a reasonable time in order to effectuate the purposes for which it is given. I also understand that I may revoke this consent at any time except to the extent that action has been taken in reliance upon it. This consent will automatically expire sixty (60) days after the date of this consent or on the following earlier date, event or condition unless earlier expressly revoked by me:

_____   _____
Client's Signature   Court Case Number

_____   _____
Date   Signature of witness and date

Appendix D

Sentencing Worksheet

Defendant_____

Ct.   I_____ Executed_____ Suspended_____ DOC_____ Jail_____
          (charge)

      II_____ Executed_____ Suspended_____ DOC_____ Jail_____

      III_____ Executed_____ Suspended_____ DOC_____ Jail_____

      IV_____ Executed_____ Suspended_____ DOC_____ Jail_____

Probation _____years (Split sentence, start _____)

    Special terms

    _____G.E.D.

    _____Work empowerment

    _____Hours community service restitution

    _____Evaluation and treatment (including in-patient)

    _____Totally abstain alcohol and illicit drugs

    _____Donation of $_____ to _____ by _____
                                                                    (date)

Fine $_____ within _____days

Restitution $_____ to _____
                              within _____days/months

                           Work Release   _____
Alternative sentence: In-house detention _____
                           Other   _____

Jail time: _____days credit

Costs and probation user's fees ($50 + $10 or $_____)

Appendix E

Short Form PSIR on John Franklin

Presentence Investigation Report
Short Form PSIR

RE: CF-80-439

John R. Franklin
Paine County Detention Center, Paine, AL

OFFENSE: Ct.I - Burglary, Class B Felony
Ct. II - Theft, Class D Felony
Ct. III - Resisting Law Enforcement, Class A Misdemeanor

OFFICIAL VERSION: See attached Information

DEFENDANT'S VERSION: "I was drinking with three friends in the State Park on Labor Day. We saw the Caretaker's home and it looked like it was empty. We broke out a glass in the rear door and went in and took a .410 shotgun, some shells, and food from the refrigerator, and a bowl of change, and a diamond ring, and a VISA card. When we were leaving the park, a police car stopped us and frisked us, and roughed us up, and cussed us out, and told us they were going to throw the book at us."

VICTIM IMPACT: Mr. Gary Ronheim lost $604.82 and VISA lost $319.68.

JAIL TIME: 309 days.

PREVIOUS TROUBLE:

Date	Offense	Disposition
10/10/81	Curfew	Office adjustment
6/16/82	JD Public Intoxication	Informal prob., 6 mos.
4/19/83	Vandalism	10 days, Detention Center
6/11/83	JD Burglary	State Boys' School, 1 yr.
8/18/84	JD Criminal Conversion	State Boys' School, 180 days
3/3/85	Public Intoxication	Probation, 90 days

——————————(6/15/85 Eighteenth Birthday)——————————

7/5/85	Public Intoxication	$100; 10 days
	Resisting Arrest	
7/30/85	Stop Sign	Warning
8/4/85	Burglary, Class B Felony	Pending
	Burglary, Class B Felony	Pending
8/14/85	Escape	
1/13/86	Theft	Nolle Pros.
3/7/86	Public Intoxication	5 days; $25
5/1/86	Public Intoxication	5 days; $25
5/5/86	Speeding	$25; $31 costs
6/30/86	Burglary	Instant case: CR-86-439
	Theft	
	Resisting Law Enforcement	

SOCIAL SETTING: Home life was turbulent. Both parents were problem drinkers, separating for two years when the defendant was seven years old. The defendant was sent to Boys' School when he was fifteen, repeating the performance of his older brother. Franklin cultivated friends on the edge of criminal culture; his closest associate is currently serving a ten-year sentence for Battery. The father was convicted of Child Molesting and Resisting Arrest. For four years Franklin was in special education classes and still has difficulty reading.

ATTITUDES OF DEFENDANT: Franklin evades responsibility for his own actions, laying the blame on his problem with alcohol. The only time he gets into trouble, he rationalizes, is when he is drunk. He is convinced that the police have a vendetta against him. Psychiatric reports indicate that he has more than his share of emotional problems.

STATEMENT BY PROBATION OFFICER: Franklin is correct when he lays blame for his problems on alcohol, but this is only a small part of the story. He has serious psychiatirc problems stemming from his defective parental home environment, exacerbated by an unsatisfactory experience in school. He rarely has a success experience of any kind and nearly all interpersonal relationships are flawed. Incarceration would not improve any of these handicaps, but there is some hope that the relationship he recently established with a therapist at the Comprehensive Mental Health Center, Dr. James Forstead, might turn things around somewhat. Good rapport has been established, and for the first time in his life Franklin has someone whom he accepts and admires. It is suggested that continuation of counseling be a condition of probation and that the supervising Probation Officer work closely with Dr. Forstead.

PLEA AGREEMENT: A signed plea agreement in the file provides that the defendant will plead guilty to all charges and that he will receive six years, suspended, and two years of probation, with special conditions to be set by the court.

RECOMMENDATION:

1. Count I, Burglary, a Class B Felony, sentence to the Department of Correction for six years, 309 days executed and the balance suspended;

   Count II, Theft, a Class D Felony, sentence to the Department of Correction for two years, suspended and concurrent with Count I;

   Count III, Resisting Law Enforcement, a Class A Misdemeanor, sentence to the Department of Correction for one year, suspended and concurrent with Count I;

2. Credit for 309 days in jail, with no good time allowed;

3. Probation for two years, with special conditions as listed in the Probation Plan;

4. Restitution to Gary Ronheim in the amount of $604.82 and to VISA in the amount of $319.68;

5. Probation User's Fees (initial fee of $50: monthly fee of $25 for 24 hours);

6. Court costs of $75 payable within 30 days.

PROBATION PLAN

1. Formal probation for two years;

2. Semi-monthly reporting for three months; thereafter, monthly unless modified by the Probation Officer;

3. Enrollment in a job placement program approved by the Probation Department;

4. Continuation in counseling with Dr. James Forstead or another therapist approved by the Probation Department;

5. Community service of 60 hours, preferably in Oak Hills Park if available.

Appendix F

STANDARDS
for
Adult Probation
and Parole Field Services

Second Edition
March 1981

AMERICAN CORRECTIONAL ASSOCIATION

In cooperation with the
COMMISSION ON ACCREDITATION
FOR CORRECTIONS

This project was supported by Grant #79-ED-AX-0007 and #79-ED-AX-0007 S-1 awarded by the Law Enforcement Assistance Administration, United States Department of Justice. Points of view or opinions stated in this publication are those of the American Correctional Association and do not necessarily represent the official position of the United States Department of Justice.

PRESENTENCE INVESTIGATION AND REPORT

2-3185 Written policy specifies that the primary purpose of the presentence report is to provide the sentencing court with timely, relevant and accurate data so that it may select the most appropriate sentencing alternative and correctional disposition; subject to this primary purpose, the report is prepared in a manner to serve the needs of any correctional institution or field agency which may receive the offender. (Essential)

> DISCUSSION: The needs of the sentencing court must have first priority in preparing the format and content of the presentence report. But if and when the offender goes to an institution, the staff there, and later the police authority, may have little or no background information on the offender except as found in the presentence report. Accordingly, it is vital to the interest of both the institution and the sentencing court for the presentence report to serve the institution and parole authority if they in turn are to handle the offender appropriately and with due respect to the intent of the court.

2-3186 The agency assigns the resources required to ensure the submission of investigation reports within three weeks for confined offenders and four weeks for offenders who are not confined. (Essential)

> DISCUSSION: Sufficient staff, time, space and equipment should be assigned to all presentence functions. However, the resources assigned to the presentence investigation and report function should not adversely affect the delivery of other probation services. A presentence investigation and preparation of a report should not exceed four weeks in general, or three weeks for offenders in custody. These time frames, however, will vary depending on the nature of the offense, complexity of the offender's circumstances, possible dispositions, availability of prior reports, and necessity of delivering the report to the court in time for review and analysis.

2-3187 Written policy and procedure govern the conduct of presentence investigations, preparation of reports, and provision of sentencing alternatives for the court. (Essential)

> DISCUSSION: Written guidelines help ensure high quality investigations and reports, and minimal disparities in the provision of sentencing alternatives. The guidelines should be developed in collaboration with the court and reviewed regularly.

2-3188 Policy and procedure provide for interviewing the victim when appropriate or possible. The information obtained is contained in the presentence report. (Important)

DISCUSSION: Interviewing the victim for the presentence investigation (victim impact statement) allows the victim to not only tell his story in his own words but also offers an opportunity for him to express his feelings about the disposition. At the same time the probation officer is given the opportunity to explain to the victim the offender's situation. For example, in some jurisdictions the victim and offender are brought together in face to face confrontation with the probation officer acting as a mediator. At this time the amount of payment is determined and agreed upon by both parties.

2-3189 The administrator of field services supervises and reviews, on a continuing basis, the conduct of presentence investigations, the preparation of reports, and the provision of sentencing alternatives for the court. (Essential)

DISCUSSION: None.

2-3190 Written policy specifies that a presentence investigation is not conducted nor a presentence report prepared until the defendant has been adjudicated guilty of an offense, unless the defendant, on advice of counsel, has consented to allow the investigation to proceed before adjudication, and adequate precautions are taken to ensure that information disclosed during the presentence investigation does not come to the attention of the prosecution, the court or the jury prior to adjudication. (Essential)

DISCUSSION: While there are occassional and exceptional situations in which a short cut may be taken in the interest of both the court and the defendant, the basic rights of the defendant are ordinarily jeopardized if the investigative process is conducted before adjudication. Also, since a full account of the offense is an important element in a competent report, it is difficult for the probation officer to get the needed information in a case for which guilt has not been finally determined. If it does become necessary to conduct a preadjudication investigation, it is essential that the defendant's informed consent be given and that inadvertent premature disclosure of the report be conscientiously avoided.

2-3191 Written policy and procedure permit the use of staff other than probation officers to collect information during the presentence investigation. (Essential)

DISCUSSION: Some of the data required for an investigation and the presentence report may be collected by nonprofessional staff (i.e., paraprofessionals, volunteers, students, clerical), thus freeing probation officers to use their skills for interpreting the data and developing a probation plan.

2-3192 When probation is not prohibited by statute, a potential supervision plan is developed during the presentence investigation and included as part of the presentence report. (Essential)

DISCUSSION: It is necessary to ensure that, if probation is granted, a plan will be available on the first day of supervision. The plan should include such consideration as employment, residence, education, etc., and should be developed with the offender. To the degree possible, the probation officer who will supervise the probationer should participate in the development plan. The plan should be realistic in that both the goals set and the resources required are attainable.

2-3193 Written policy and procedure provide that probation officers are to consider innovative sentencing alternatives in all cases in which incarceration is not clearly imperative for reasons of immediate public safety. (Essential)

DISCUSSION: The traditional dispositions in adult courts are probation, confinement in a local facility, or confinement in a state correctional institution. It is important to seek other alternatives that may permit a better balance between the dual needs of protecting the community and providing for the welfare of the defendant. The appropriate time to search for alternatives is during the presentence investigation, and any feasible alternatives should be set forth in the presentence report. The use of alternatives such as halfway houses, detoxification centers, civil addict commitment programs, and self-help groups may be appropriate. Attention also should be given to finding resources that would permit use of individualized probation supervision programs if probation is ordered.

2-3194 The probation agency can document efforts to promote the resources necessary to process a presentence report in every case in which there is a potential sentencing disposition involving incarceration for one year or longer, and in every case involving first offenders and minors. (Important)

DISCUSSION: As correctional institutions become more expensive and more crowded, it becomes especially important to ensure that incarceration is not resorted to in any case in which viable alternatives are available and appropriate. Minors and first offenders should be diverted from an institutional career whenever possible. The presentence report in such cases may have particular utility in outlining, when justified, feasible alternative plans.

2-3195 Written policy and procedure govern the use of different presentence report formats to meet the specific needs of the courts and correctional agencies. (Important)

DISCUSSION: The establishement of standard formats to be used without devia-
tion is an important contribution to quality control and efficiency in presentence
report production. However, there may be proper reason to have more than one
standard format to adapt efficiently to different types of cases while still avoiding
uncontrolled variations from case to case. To this end the agency should collabo-
rate with the courts to design a standard report format to be used for particular
types of cases. As a basic principle, enough data should be collected and analyzed
so that the most appropriate sentencing alternative may be selected to protect the
community and serve the needs of the offender.

**2-3196 If probation is one of the sentencing alternatives, the probation offi-
cer identifies the need for special conditions of probation, if any, and recommends that these special conditions be appended to the general conditions of probation. (Essential)**

DISCUSSION: In addition to those general conditions of probation which are applicable to all probationers, possible special conditions should be identified during
the presentence investigation, recommended to the court, and appended to the
general conditions by the court if it appears that these additional conditions will
enhance public safety or increase the probability of a successful community adjustment. Special conditions should be few in number, realistic, and phrased in positive
rather than negative terms.

**2-3197 When statutes permit, confinement, full- or part-time, is part of a
probation grant only in selected cases when circumstances clearly indicate
the need for confinement as part of a prescribed program plan.
(Important)**

DISCUSSION: Confinement disrupts many aspects of life. As a condition of probation it should be discouraged unless it clearly will contribute to public safety or
the likelihood of better community adjustment.

**2-3198 The presentence report is submitted to the court for review and
evaluation a minimum of two working days in advance of the date set for
sentencing. (Essential)**

DISCUSSION: The court requires sufficient time to read and assess the document
and perhaps discuss it with probation staff. A minimum of two full days is seen as
essential for the court's review, but this generalized time frame must be adjusted to
judicial schedules and workloads.

**2-3199 All presentence reports and recommendations are subject to review
by a supervisor prior to submission to the court. (Essential)**

DISCUSSION: Supervisory review of presentence reports and recommendations serves several purposes including the following: ensures that functions are being properly implemented in accordance with policy, objectives and procedures; helps to determine that the court will get the needed information in the correct format; ensures that each recommendation is reasonable and supported by the information provided; and, contributes to the training of personnel and the development of skills and knowledge.

2-3200 Written policy and procedure protect the confidentiality of presentence reports and case records. (Essential)

DISCUSSION: The issue of confidentiality extends beyond the courtroom and should premeate the entire investigation and report process from receipt of the case for investigation through final destruction of documents. Information about cases should not be discussed openly, and files and records should not be left unattended or given to persons who do not have a proper and legitimate interest in the case. This principle is not to interfere with the sharing of the report with the defendant and his counsel wherever "disclosure" is recognized in law or court policy.

2-3201 Written procedure provides for the prompt transmittal by the probation agency of presentence report data to institutional personnel when confinement of the adjudicated offender is ordered. (Essential)

DISCUSSION: In those instances in which the offender is ordered confined, presentence materials should be provided to the receiving institution to assist in its classification process. Written guidelines, developed in collaboration with agencies receiving committed offenders, should be available and cover such matters as method and timing of transmittal of documents. In consideration of vital institutional need, the agency should make every effort to deliver the presentence report to the institution at the same time that the offender is transferred there.

Index